REMAKING DIXIE

REMAKING DIXIE

THE IMPACT OF WORLD WAR II
ON THE AMERICAN SOUTH

Edited by Neil R. McMillen

University Press of Mississippi/Jackson

Library of Congress Cataloging-in-Publication Data
Remaking Dixie : the impact of World War II on the American South /
    edited by Neil R. McMillen.
        p.   cm.
    Includes bibliographical references and index.
    ISBN 0-87805-927-X (alk. paper).—ISBN 0-87805-928-8 (pbk. : alk. paper)
    1. World War, 1939–1945—Social aspects—Southern States—
Congresses.   2. Southern States—Social conditions—1865–1945—
Congresses.   3. World War, 1939–1945—Influence—Congresses.
I. McMillen, Neil R., 1939–   .
D744.7.U6R46   1997
975.8'042—dc20   96-33266
                                                                  CIP
British Library Cataloging-in-Publication data available

In Memory of
Charles W. Moorman

. . . then Warsaw and Dunquerque . . . and now the planter's not-yet-drafted son drove the tractor: and then Pearl Harbor and Tobruk and Utah Beach displaced that son, leaving the planter himself on the seat of the tractor, for a little while that is—or so he thought, forgetting that victory or defeat both are bought at the same exorbitant price of change and alteration; one nation, one world: young men who had never been further from Yoknapatawpha County than Memphis or New Orleans (and that not often), now talked glibly of street intersections in Asiatic and European capitals, returning no more to inherit the long monotonous endless unendable furrows of Mississippi cotton fields, living now (with now a wife and next year a wife and child and the year after that a wife and children) in automobile trailers or G.I. barracks on the outskirts of liberal arts colleges, and the father and now grandfather himself still driving the tractor across the gradually diminishing fields between the long looping skeins of electric lines bringing electric power from the Appalachian mountains, and the subterrene steel veins bringing the natural gas from the western plains, to the little lost lonely farmhouses glittering and gleaming with automatic stoves and washing machines and television antennae;

One nation: no longer anywhere, not even in Yoknapatawpha County, one last irreconciliable fastness of stronghold from which to enter the United States. . . . one world: the tank gun: captured from a regiment of Germans in an African desert by a regiment of Japanese in American uniforms, whose mothers and fathers at the time were in a California detention camp for enemy aliens, and carried (the gun) seven thousand miles back to be set halfway between, as a sort of secondary flying buttress to a memento of Shiloh and The Wilderness; one universe, one cosmos: contained in one America: one towering frantic edifice poised like a card-house over the abyss of the mortgaged generations. . . .

William Faulkner, *Requiem for a Nun*

CONTENTS

PREFACE

For a century and more conventional wisdom has argued that the Civil War was the one great turning point in the history of the American South. Even today, when tradition-minded Southerners speak of "The War" they mean, of course, the "War Between the States"—or as some white southerners would still have it, "the War of Northern Agression." University courses and college textbooks typically divide the region's history at Appomattox Court House—the "Old South" expiring as General Lee surrendered his sword to General Grant; the "New South" rising with Emancipation and Reconstruction.

In recent years scholars have challenged this convention. Many have argued that complex patterns of regional persistence and transformation defy easy, convenient categorizations of "Old" and "New." Some have concluded that the region's very identity is to be found in its improbable mix of tradition and progress. An emerging consensus emphasizes the impact of World War II on a modernizing region. *Remaking Dixie* examines the ever-changing, ever-abiding South in the context of World War II.

Early versions of these essays (save for that by Morton Sosna) were presented at the second Charles W. Moorman Symposium held on the fiftieth anniversary of Allied victory in Europe and Asia at the University of Southern Mississippi in October, 1995. Entitled "World War II and the American South: The War that Drove Old Dixie Down?" this conference was funded primarily by the National Endowment for the Humanities, through the Mississippi Humanities Council. Other contributors to the conference included the Phil Hardin Foundation, the USM Foundation, and the University of Southern Mississippi. We are all grateful for this support. The editor also deeply appreciates the assistance and encouragement of President Aubrey K. Lucas, Dean of Liberal Arts Terry

Harper, and History Chair Orazio Ciccarelli of the University of Southern Mississippi. Noel Polk deserves particular commendation for his usual mix of warm friendship and intelligent advice: he contributed importantly at every stage of this enterprise. The students of the Theta Kappa chapter of Phi Alpha Theta supplied their enthusiasm and their time; much of the symposium's success should be credited to them. Finally, the editor wishes to acknowledge a personal debt to the late Charles W. Moorman, an inspiring teacher, a scholarly model, a complicated man.

INTRODUCTION

Morton Sosna

This is a collection of essays about the other war that greatly affected the American South. As the Civil War gave the South a regional identity unique within the United States, producing a distinctive politics, economy, culture, and literature and creating at once an "Old South" and a "New South," World War II provided another important if less well recognized watershed in the region's history. The contributors to this volume look at the South's economy, its politics, its racial and gender relations, its literary and cultural traditions, even its system of higher education, and assess the degree to which the Second World War affected them and Southern regionalism more generally.

The impact of war on any given society—be it a nation, region, state, province, or city—is most often understood in terms of the war's social, economic, and political consequences for that society. Obviously, it matters greatly whether a conflict ends in victory or defeat, or is inconclusive. But wars also have social consequences regardless of their military outcomes. Among the most notable are demographic changes resulting from persons engaged in military service, civilian and/or military casualties, refugees, or other population shifts, such as the movement of people into areas of defense production or military staging and training. Historically, wars have represented the most significant economic undertakings of nation states, bankrupting some and enriching others, but in any case profoundly effecting the availability and distribution of goods and services within a society as well as the nature of employment and the constitution of the workforce in that society. Modern wars, especially, have uprooted and separated families, mobilized women and minority groups, altered the practices and concerns of educational, religious, scientific and other institutions, and provided more impetus for the expansion of government into everyday life than almost any other single factor. The greater the scale of the conflict, the greater its social and economic effects. Of all the wars engaged in by the United States, none was conducted on a larger, more encompassing scale than World War II and none, including the Civil War, carried more social and economic consequences for the nation. All America felt the impact of the war, but in the South, more than elsewhere, this impact must be judged against the South's long history as America's most distinctive region.

As a regional watershed, World War II appears deepest when examined within the South's economic and social frameworks. Such scholars as James C. Cobb, Pete Daniel, David R. Goldfield, Jack Temple Kirby, Bruce J. Schulman, and Gavin Wright have recently considered the war against the larger background of the South's twentieth-century transformation from a provincial backwater characterized chiefly by ruralism, agrarianism, poverty, and racial apartheid to a more recognizably modern society with patterns of urbanization, industrialization, and race relations similar to other parts of the United States. In Schulman's words, the South has mutated "from cotton belt to Sunbelt." However much these scholars disagree over whether this change has benefited or only further damaged the South, or whether it has produced the liberalization of Southern society that many proponents of economic modernization predicted, they all judge World War II to have been an important catalyst in the region's economic and political restructuring—a restructuring that has propelled the South into greater convergence with the rest of the United States and, for better or worse, identified it with the Sunbelt.[1]

In the decade before World War II, there was no perceived Sunbelt of urban and suburban prosperity and, if there were, the South surely would not have been part of it. In 1940, agricultural employment in the South was 73 percent above the national average, and the region was 63 percent rural, nearly twice the national average. The South's per capita income was about 40 percent lower than the rest of the nation's. Approximately 77 percent of America's black population lived in the South, of which nearly 50 percent lived in the rural South. By almost any measure, the South was considerably poorer, blacker, and more rural than any other part of the United States.[2]

By virtue of these differences, the South was widely considered the most "regional" of all American regions. In 1934, a New York writer, Carl Carmer, stated the case hyperbolically. Writing of Alabama, Carmer claimed that the "Congo is not more different from Massachusetts or Kansas or California."[3] By any objective (or even common sensible) criteria, surely this was not true unless the mere presence of a sizable though still minority black population qualified "the heart of Dixie" for comparison with "the heart of darkness" more, say, than with New England, the Midwest, or the West Coast. Embedded in Carmer's statement is less an appreciation for Southern distinctiveness than a sense that the South's characteristics and historical experiences were fundamentally at odds with those of the rest of the United States.[4]

Although World War II did not diminish the South's mythological status—indeed it enhanced it—the social changes it brought to the region were vast and far reaching. The accelerated urbanization and industrialization wrought by a massive modern war, which greatly affected the entire United States, would have a particularly dramatic impact on the South. In effect, the South after World War II would be different from what it had been in 1940. During the war, approximately 1.6 million civilians left the South for other parts of the country. More significantly, the region's disproportionately large rural population declined by nearly 3.5 million persons, a drop of more than 20 percent. The movement of black Southerners was especially momentous. In out-migration, blacks accounted for approximately two-thirds of those leaving the South, and in rural-to-urban intra-regional migration, they made up nearly half the number of those moving to Southern cities. As a result, the South's historically most distinguishing feature, its large black rural population, dropped by 30 percent while its total share of the nation's black population also fell, from 77 percent to 68 percent.

Demographically, the traditionally large gap between farmworkers and production workers in the South lowered dramatically. In 1939, farmworkers outnumbered production workers 3 million to 1.4 million. By the end of the war, Southern farmworkers declined to 2.6 million while production workers in the region rose to over 2.2 million. These changes, occurring within five years, narrowed by a full 10 percent the discrepancy in per capita income between the South and the rest of the nation.[5] James C. Cobb's essay reflects upon the social and cultural implications of these shifts and contends that World War II led to a much less homogeneous Southern mindset than the one W. J. Cash analyzed in his 1941 classic, *The Mind of the South*.

One reason for the Second World War's great impact on the South was its timing. By 1939, when the war began in Europe, the economic and demographic restructuring of the South was well underway. The decline of sharecropping and dissolution of the cotton belt, the migration of rural Southern whites and blacks to the cities of the North and West as well as to those of the South, the growing urban and industrial sectors within the region—along with the determination of the Roosevelt administration to devise federal policies toward the South worthy of its oft-proclaimed status as the nation's leading economic problem—all began before World War II. However, so greatly did the war accelerate these trends that rare was the wartime article about the South in the national press that failed to report one regional "revolution" or another, all pointing to the South's convergence with the nation.

Despite this regional convergence, World War II proved a critical moment in what the historian C. Vann Woodward has called "the North-South dialogue." A time of intense American nationalism, the World War II period witnessed efforts within both popular and intellectual culture to define a certifiably "American" identity and "way of life." The degree to which the South was seen deviating from this supposed "American way of life" became an increasingly significant preoccupation during the war years and would continue into the postwar period. Nowhere was this discrepancy between the South and the nation more apparent than in the congressional politics of the 1940s during which, as Dewey W. Grantham observes in his contribution, the South's political sectionalism dramatically increased.

In one sense, the South, long isolated from the main streams of immigration that so greatly affected other parts of the United States, itself became something of a melting pot during World War II. As the nation mobilized an ethnically diverse population of 130 million into a military force of nearly 13 million persons, men and women from different parts of the country were suddenly brought together on a scale that remains unprecedented. The total number of Americans who served in the armed forces during World War II, roughly 16 million, was greater than the *combined figure* for all other U.S. wars up to that time, including both the Union and Confederate forces during the Civil War (about 2.6 million) and the American forces during World War I (about 4.8 million), and is roughly equivalent to the total number of Americans who served in the military during the Korean and Vietnam Wars, *again combined*. Moreover, many of these Americans were first brought together in the South, which beginning with World War II became the principal site of America's military training bases. Indeed, of the nine largest Army training camps during World War II—those with capacities for 50,000 or more military personnel—only one, Fort Lewis, Washington, was located outside the South. The others were Fort Benning near Columbus, Georgia; Camp Shelby, outside Hattiesburg, Mississippi; Fort Bragg next to Fayetteville, North Carolina; Camp Hood on the outskirts of Killeen, Texas; Fort Jackson, adjacent to Columbia, South Carolina; Camp Claiborne near Alexandria, Louisiana; Camp Blanding near Starke, Florida, and Fort Knox south of Louisville, Kentucky. Most had been only recently carved out of farmland or wilderness as part of the nation's crash defense program begun in 1940, and they instantly turned their surrounding communities into war boom towns. This was especially true in the case of Camp Shelby, whose impact on neighboring Hattiesburg is vividly recollected by Arvarh E. Strickland in his essay on growing up black in that wartime Southern city.

The massive inter-regional encounters that places like Camp Shelby came to symbolize during World War II brought new participants as well as an old subject—the status of African Americans—into the North-South dialogue. Many Northern GIs were either themselves immigrants to the United States or the children of immigrants, people not only without personal linkages to the Civil War but Americans for whom the term "Yankee" was itself problematical. The observations of millions of outlander GIs mustering through the South played into traditional regional stereotypes, with direct contact often serving to confirm negative or exotic images of the South and Southerners previously encountered principally through books, movies, and the press. Further, given the historic connection in Western Culture between military service and the perquisites of citizenship, the approximately one million black Americans in the U.S. Armed Forces, itself a racially segregated institution during World War II, assured that African American voices would also have a greater say in the North-South dialogue than in the past. The symbolism of a Southern restaurant serving German war prisoners while denying similar service to a group of black GIs, as actually happened, greatly highlighted the discrepancy between national ideals and regional realities. In his essay on black veterans from Mississippi, Neil R. McMillen explores the tension between the heightened wartime expectations on the part of blacks and the determination of whites—both in the military and at home—to maintain a Jim Crow South.

The ideological dimensions of World War II amplified prevalent attitudes about the South among Northerners and Southerners, whites and blacks. That the war was primarily directed against an enemy, Nazi Germany, whose master-race ideology made it the archetypical enemy of liberal democracy, was pregnant with implications for a part of the United States where white supremacy and Jim Crow were still articles of faith as well as established facts. Comparisons between the South and Nazi Germany lay just beneath the surface of the wartime regional dialogue and would play an important role in shaping the civil rights movement's formative years. Yet, as Harvard Sitkoff points out in his comparison of wartime black militancy with the black activism that inaugurated the Civil Rights Movement of the 1950s and 1960s, the war constrained black protest even as it drew attention to the inconsistencies between democratic war aims and Southern racial practices.

As the Civil War has produced (and continues to produce) a fictional literature emphasizing the South's qualities as a distinctive society in the nineteenth century, World War II has also yielded a surprisingly large and still growing fictional literature about Southern distinctiveness during the 1940s. This, too, is a subject that has hitherto not received nearly the attention it warrants. A regionally, ethnically, and racially diverse group of writers including William Faulkner, Flannery O'Connor, Norman Mailer, William Styron, Peter Taylor, John Oliver Killens, Harriette Arnow, Charles Fuller, Neil Simon, Karl Shapiro, and Louis Simpson, to name but a few, have produced numerous novels, short stories, plays, and poems about World War II that are also part of the North-South dialogue. In "Faulkner and World War II," Noel Polk raises the question of why, with the exception of Faulkner, this task proved far more difficult for white Southern writers and literary critics than for their black and Northern counterparts.

Two essays in this volume deal with the impact of World War II on Southern women. Drawing upon the wartime correspondence of both white and black Southern women, Judy Barrett Litoff shows how these women were profoundly affected by their wartime experiences either in the military or as civilians, even as the society around them refused to countenance wartime changes in women's roles as more than temporary aberrations. A very different perspective is offered by Anne Goodwyn Jones. In "Every Woman Loves a Fascist: Writing World War II on the Southern Home Front," Jones argues that World War II not only failed to confront the gender inequalities that arguably were more pronounced in the South than elsewhere in America but that all wars, including World War II, generally serve to reinforce patriarchal authority. Unlike Southern race relations, Southern gender relations, regardless of their changed wartime circumstances, confronted no ideological challenge attributable to the war. Gender was not yet part of the "American dilemma."[6]

If the democratic ideology associated with the war only partially affected race relations and virtually ignored larger questions of gender relations, the war's impact on Southern higher education was more immediately apparent. In "World War II and the Transformation of Southern Higher Education," Clarence L. Mohr discusses how the war greatly democratized access to Southern colleges and universities—at least for whites—while ending the supposed incompatibility between war and "the higher learning."

To the extent that large pockets of poverty, religious intolerance, and racial inequalities still bedevil the South, they do so as national and not as inherently regional problems. If the contemporary equivalent of Faulkner's Quentin Compson were now asked by an outlander to "tell about the South," that person would undoubtedly offer a far different story from the one revealed by the troubled narrator of *Absalom, Absalom!* As slavery and the Civil War were essential to Faulkner's tragic saga, World War II and the Civil Rights Movement would surely occupy central roles in explaining the South today.

Remaking Dixie

1 WORLD WAR II AND THE MIND OF THE MODERN SOUTH

James C. Cobb

As he brought his classic *Mind of the South* to a close, Wilbur J. Cash surveyed "the forces sweeping over the world in the fateful year of 1940" and warned that "in the coming days, and probably soon," the South was "likely to have to prove its capacity for adjustment far beyond what has been true in the past." As its "loyal son," Cash could only hope that in the coming confrontation the South's virtues would "tower over and conquer its faults." Yet, there was next to nothing in his decidedly pessimistic treatise to suggest that the South's "capacity for adjustment" would see it through or, for that matter, that it even possessed such a capacity. As the conflict with the Yankees escalated from words to war, a pervasive and enduring conformity had descended on the region, stifling creativity and intellectual curiosity by stigmatizing them, in Cash's words, as "anemic and despicable," not just alien and unsouthern but unmanly to boot. (The southern mind as Cash saw it was not only all white but, despite its showy and largely symbolic celebrations of white womanhood which were closely related to its very real racial and sexual paranoia, it was all male as well.) Crippled by racism, an exaggerated sense of individualism, a tragic proclivity for violence and the "savage ideal" of hostility to criticism or innovation, what Cash presented as a deeply flawed mind was actually more like a regional temperament, a remarkably consistent behavioral pattern forged in the crucible of Civil War and Reconstruction and still dominant and unyielding more than sixty years later.[1]

Unfortunately, the uncertain prospect of a second global conflict had driven an already neurotic Cash even closer to the edge. Hoping for the best, but expecting the worst, Cash knew that something big was about to happen to the South. He could hardly have dreamed, however, that had he not taken his own life in 1941, five months after his book was published and two months after his forty-first birthday, he might actually have lived to hear southern historians begin to attach a significance to World War II once reserved exclusively for the Civil War.[2]

Indeed, to paraphrase Gerald R. Ford, had Cash been alive, he would have been spinning in his grave when he learned that at the November 1982 meeting of the Southern Historical Association in Memphis, Morton Sosna, then of Stanford University, planned to read a paper whose title suggested that in its impact on the South, World War II had actually been "More Important than the Civil War." As a commentator on this session and a friend of Mort's, I felt obliged to warn him that while such radical notions might be tolerated or even encouraged at Stanford, it was quite another thing to stand at the northern terminus of the Mississippi Delta and dare to suggest that any event in human history, save perhaps for the birth and resurrection of Jesus Christ, was more important than the Civil War. To my dismay, Sosna ignored my warnings, and to my surprise, he not only delivered his paper but lived to see it published.[3]

In reality, Sosna's paper was not quite as audacious as his title implied. Several years earlier, for example, historian John R. Skates, Jr., had insisted that "the Second World War was a watershed for Mississippi, a convenient and readily identifiable era, before which there was basic historical continuity for more than a century, but after which nothing ever again was quite the same."[4]

By the 1980s, after three decades of relatively unproductive historical wrangling about the genealogy and ideology of the post-Reconstruction South's political leadership, historians were beginning to realize that it was not the misdeeds of Redeemer Era politicians but fundamental economic and demographic factors that had been the primary influences in making the South of 1930 look so much like the South of 1877. Writing in 1980, economist William N. Parker implied that it was time to move on, arguing that the South's socioeconomic and political development between the end of Reconstruction and the beginning of the Great Depression could have been altered only by a national economic and social policy which would have "redistributed labor and capital within the nation. . . . without regard to race, locality or previous social structure." The first attempt to enact such a policy came with the New Deal, and Parker believed that it was not until the New Deal/World War II era that "southern institutional peculiarity" began to break down and the region's "energies and resources" were freed "to be merged with the national society."[5]

In 1983 Numan V. Bartley observed that "while it would not be entirely appropriate to insist that nothing very important happened in the 1860s and the 1890s, those decades no longer seem . . . to be the great watersheds" that historians once assumed they were. Instead, Bartley believed, contemporary scholarship increasingly suggested that "far more fundamental changes came out of the middle years of the twentieth century, with perhaps 1935 to 1945 best qualifying as the latest crucial decade of New South historiography."[6]

The changes that occurred during this decade were dramatic indeed. One of the most significant and relatively immediate ones was the transformation of southern agriculture. The New Deal's acreage-reduction incentives and the resultant consolidation and mechanization of agriculture were reinforced by the pull of military service and the opportunity for relatively lucrative employment in the defense industries. Between 1940 and 1945 alone, more than 20 percent of the South's farm population abandoned the land. The modernization of southern farming all but mandated a much more intensive emphasis on industrialization, forcing the region's commercial and professional classes who were once primarily dependent on agriculture to seek a broadened industrial base that would in turn expand both regional and local consuming potential. Efforts to recruit new industry had already accelerated significantly in response to the Depression, and the industrial stimulus of the war both intensified and institutionalized this trend. Launched in 1936, Mississippi's Balance Agriculture with Industry program of municipal subsidies to new industrial facilities had produced just twelve plants employing only 2,700 workers by 1940. As a result, disenchanted legislators allowed the BAWI law to lapse. Spurred by the wartime economy, however, the twelve plants were operating at full capacity by 1944, with the Ingalls Shipyard at Pascagoula providing more jobs than all the other subsidized plants combined. The Mississippi legislature speedily reinstated the BAWI program, and the other southern states quickly followed suit with subsidy plans of their own. By the early 1950s, a southern governor's obligation to recruit new industry was second only to his obligation to defend segregation.[7]

In time, economic development would even supersede the defense of Jim Crow as, however unevenly, in state after state, the post-World War II era saw the reins of power pass to more dynamic, metropolitan-oriented elites who sought fuller integration of both local and state economies into the national and global economy. "More young men came home from World War II with a sense of purpose than from any other American venture," former Mississippi congressman Frank Smith insisted. He was one of them, and so was Greenville's Hodding Carter. The war against Nazism inspired Carter's postwar crusading for improved race relations as did his service as editor of the Middle East edition of *Stars and Stripes,* which allowed him to see firsthand the resentment harbored by native peoples against British racial and colonial policies. In the wake of the war, Carter was soon clashing with Greenville whites who objected to an honor roll for World War II veterans that would include the names of both black and white servicemen.[8]

Another veteran who came home with a sense of purpose was Doyle Combs, who became an NAACP leader in Northeast Georgia and vowed to vote even if he "had to kill somebody" because "I went into combat and lost a portion of my body for this country." The growth of black dissatisfaction during the war was more than obvious to contemporary observers, and the widespread participation of black veterans in postwar civil rights activities is well documented. In Mississippi the list included Medgar Evers, Amzie Moore, and Aaron Henry, while veteran Harry Briggs was the plaintiff in the legal assault on segregation in Clarendon County, South Carolina, that paved the way for the 1954 Brown decision. Many black former G.I.'s showed a surprising level of militance. In Monroe, North Carolina, Robert F. Williams armed himself and other black veterans, and his "Monroe Rifle Club" became the only organization ever identified with both the NAACP and the National Rifle Association.[9]

At the same time, some white veterans admitted, more of them privately rather than publicly, that their wartime experiences had changed their racial views. One of the most startling public statements to this effect came from Lt. Van T. Barfoot of Carthage, Mississippi, who was awarded multiple decorations for his heroism in combat. In June 1945, Mississippi senator James O. Eastland had insisted that "numerous high ranking generals" had told him that "nigra soldiers" had proven an "utter and abysmal failure" and had "disgraced the flag of their country." Not surprisingly, Eastland's remarks were seconded by the state's other senator, Theodore G. Bilbo. When Bilbo and Eastland and the rest of the Mississippi congressional delegation sought a photo session and the opportunity to bask in the glow of the heroic Barfoot, Bilbo asked him eagerly, "Did you have much trouble with nigras over there?"[10]

Bilbo was soon red-faced and squirming as Lt. Barfoot announced, "I found out after I did some fighting in this war that the colored boys fight just as good as the white boys. . . . I've changed my ideas a lot about colored people since I got into this war and so have a lot of other boys from the South."[11]

Barfoot's case was by no means an isolated one, but it was hardly a representative one either. If it was true, as Frank Smith insisted, that many Americans returned from World War II with a sense of purpose, it did not follow that they all returned with the same sense of purpose or that many of them did not return at cross purposes. Smith discovered this himself when he encountered a young Mississippi farmer who told him, "Fight integration? Why, I've just begun to fight. When I was on a beach in the South Pacific I was fighting and I didn't know why. Now we know what we are fighting for, and nothing is going to hold us back."[12]

As a racial moderate, Smith often clashed with the Citizens' Council founded at Indianola by World War II paratrooper Robert Patterson. Another thorn in Smith's side was a former Marine wounded in the Pacific, Byron de la Beckwith of Greenwood, who would eventually be convicted of the murder of fellow veteran Medgar Evers. Finally, Smith admitted that as many as half of his former student colleagues who had served in World War II and survived wound up as active members of the Citizens' Council or "their political satellites."[13]

The Ku Klux Klan, the Columbians, and several other hate groups also drew a number of recruits from the ranks of former soldiers. Deploring veteran participation in the revival of the KKK, the editor of the *Montgomery Advertiser* found it difficult to understand "how a veteran who risked his life to stop the terror of Hitlerism can come home to play Hitler himself."[14]

During the war, racial tensions had exploded during six civilian riots, over twenty military riots and mutinies, and from forty to seventy-five lynchings. The resurgence of Ku Klux Klan activity paralleled a horrifying explosion of post-war violence, much of it directed against returning black veterans. Georgia and Alabama were the most homicidal states in the nation in 1946, with murder rates nearly seven times that of New York. Walton County, Georgia, was the scene of one of the most shocking racial murders involving two black men, one of them a veteran, and two black women, one of them pregnant. Clinton Adams, a frightened white youngster, watched from hiding as a group of white men executed the four. In 1981 Adams finally confronted one of the killers who explained that black veteran George Dorsey had been killed because "Up until George went into the army he was a good nigger. But when he came out, they thought they were as good as any white people."[15]

Violence also crept into postwar southern politics, especially the so-called "G.I. Revolts" that erupted at the state and local level in the first few elections after the war as militant former soldiers sought to overturn entrenched political machines. In Hot Springs, Arkansas, future governor Sid McMath spearheaded a victory over the McCloughlin machine that involved armed partisans on both sides, as well as the sabotage of phone lines by the veterans in order to frustrate opponents' efforts to steal the election with fraudulent ballots.[16]

Expanded economic opportunity was often a goal of politically active veterans, but as Jennifer Brooks has shown, they sometimes disagreed as to how this worthy goal might be best achieved. In the spring of 1947, veterans took over the picket lines when tobacco workers struck against the R. J. Reynolds Tobacco Company, carrying signs reading "From the Firing Line to the Picket Line" and vowing that "R. J. Reynolds can't beat us when the Nazis couldn't." Other veterans organizations, however, warned that labor unions were a serious threat to the economic aspirations of returning G.I.'s. The Veterans Industrial Association recruited veterans as strike breakers, insisting, "We have as hard a war to win freeing ourselves from the so-called labor leaders here as we had with Germany, Japan, and Italy."[17]

For all the disparity and contradictory sense of purpose manifested in the activities of World War II veterans, it was nonetheless possible to discern among them a widespread inclination toward a more "modern" or "progressive" approach to government and politics, one that stressed economic development and favored moderation over demagoguery on the race issue. Georgia's demagogue for all seasons was Eugene Talmadge, whose red-suspendered rusticity and cagy manipulation of the state's outrageously antiurban county-unit electoral system had made him the dominant force in Georgia politics for the better part of two decades. In 1946, "Old Gene" faced a formidable challenge from James V. Carmichael, a former legislator who had managed the Bell Bomber plant in Marietta during the war. While not all of Georgia's veterans supported Carmichael, a large number did, many of them echoing the sentiments of a Navy veteran who noted that "Hitler, Mussolini, and Tojo are gone" and expressed his hope that "Eugene Talmadge is joining them." Veteran after veteran linked Carmichael with "good government," and organizations such as the "B-29ers-for-Carmichael Club" appeared all over the state.[18]

Although Carmichael won the popular vote, the county-unit system gave the election to Talmadge, who proceeded to die of cirrhosis of the liver before he could take office. Foreseeing this possibility, Talmadge supporters had engineered a general election write-in effort for Talmadge's son Herman, who was in fact a veteran himself. In the end, the younger Talmadge's flimsy claim to the governorship rested on the last-minute discovery of additional write-in ballots from voters in Talmadge's home county who, in a remarkable display of loyalty, had risen from the grave to mark their sheets for Herman and, in an equally inspiring display of unity, had marked them all in the same handwriting. During the ensuing controversy, Georgia had not one but three governors, but when a special election finally put Herman in office, he surprised a great many Georgians. Though he went on to author a pamphlet which insisted that

"God Advocates Segregation," Talmadge also pursued an impressive agenda of educational reform and industrial recruitment, explaining, "When I came along it was after World War II, and I think the people of Georgia had made up their mind that they wanted to see more progress in state government."[19]

Though no admirer of Talmadge, another Georgian, Katharine Dupre Lumpkin expressed similar sentiments. As she surveyed the South in 1946, Lumpkin noted that the cumulative impact of depression, war, agricultural mechanization, and industrial development was weakening the region's resistance to change: "I know the old life continues, but not serenely, not without a struggle to maintain its existence. . . . The Southern people are pressing against the enclosing walls." In the same year that Lumpkin offered this observation, Helen Douglas Mankin drew heavily on the support of newly enfranchised blacks to become the first woman elected to Congress from Georgia.[20]

While it was difficult at the end of the 1940s to look back much beyond the War itself, the perspective of the 1990s both affords us the luxury of the longer view and requires that we take it. When we do, we can see that, to some extent, the changes in southern agriculture, the outmigration of blacks, and the move to industrialize were actually rooted in conditions and trends visible as early as or even before World War I. In fact, the years from the boll weevil invasion of the early twentieth century through the beginnings of the Great Migration of blacks to the North and the descent into the Great Depression might be seen as the harbingers of a great turning period, a protracted drama for which the New Deal and World War II constituted the final acts.[21]

Most scholars have argued that of the two acts, World War II clearly deserves top billing, but it is virtually impossible to assess the impact of the New Deal and World War II separately. Both the New Deal and the war contributed heavily to the modernization of southern agriculture and the South's subsequent efforts to industrialize. While the New Deal's acreage-reduction programs rendered much of the old farm labor force marginal, if not superfluous, however, the war offered alternative employment opportunities and threatened to create a labor scarcity sufficient to boost farm wages above levels that southern landlords were willing to pay. Meanwhile, although the war seemed ultimately to undermine southern liberalism and strengthen anti-New Deal conservatism, the conflict did not cancel the Roosevelt administration's stated commitment to improving economic conditions in the South and arguably even facilitated it by removing the restrictions on spending that had hampered New Deal recovery efforts.[22]

The $52 billion paid out on just the ten largest government defense contracts between 1940 and 1944 was roughly equivalent to total government expenditures between 1932 and 1939. Not surprisingly, southern manufacturing employment grew by 50 percent during the war, and annual wages climbed by 40 percent between 1939 and 1942 alone as war-induced competition for labor quickly rendered the New Deal's Fair Labor Standards minimums obsolete in some southern industries. For all the undue influence still wielded by reactionary southern politicians, the Roosevelt administration also seized numerous wartime opportunities to exempt the South from its official "hold the line" policy on wages while affording significant support to organized labor as well. Although the South remained a decidedly low-wage region, it emerged from the conflict with an expanded industrial labor force and a markedly more affluent consumer pool which became a crucial part of the region's postwar attraction for market-oriented industries. If it is correct to credit the war with finishing what the New Deal started, it seems reasonable as well to think of World War II functioning, at least in part, as a sort of unarticulated Third New Deal, one freed from some of the most severe economic constraints that hampered the first two.[23]

Wartime spending created many new job opportunities for southerners, although not all enjoyed equal access to them. On any construction site, as one black southerner who spoke from experience explained, "If a white man and a black man both walk up for an opening and it ain't no shovel in that job, they'd give the job to a white man." This generalization applied to black veterans as well. Promiseland, South Carolina, veteran Isaac Moragne angrily rejected a Veterans Administration staffer's recommendation that he apply for a common laborer's position, explaining later, "I was a staff sergeant in the Army, . . . traveled all over England . . . sat fourteen days in the English Channel . . . I wasn't going to push a wheel barrow." A Southern Regional Council field agent reported that "Hattiesburg, Mississippi, is the most progressive city in Mississippi, yet the Negro veteran who struggles away from the battlefields of the world can expect to move back to the same old pattern of living, if he moves back to the 'progressive' city of Hattiesburg."[24]

During the war, men and women left the South's farms for its factories in almost equal numbers, and in many cases, employers preferred to hire the women. This was especially true when the choice lay between a white woman and a black man. In some instances, defense employers simply drew on the existing textile labor pool where white women were heavily represented and blacks hardly at all. Although many of these white women withdrew or were pushed out of the industrial workforce when the war ended, postwar economic expansion soon afforded them new opportunities to return to the factories while the concomitant shrinkage of the South's agricultural sector often made such a move a matter of absolute necessity. In Mississippi, the number of women employed in manufacturing increased by nearly 60 percent between 1940 and 1950, a rate nearly twice as high as that for their male counterparts. At the same time, continuing discrimination forced blacks of both sexes to pursue wartime opportunities in the North.[25]

In both the short and long terms, the war's impact on worker mobility was crucial in a number of ways. At the national level, while 12 million Americans were being shipped overseas, another 15 million moved to cities elsewhere in the nation, with half of these moving to different states. Meanwhile, between 1940 and 1945, three times as many people left the South each year as had departed during the preceding decade. A total of 1.6 million civilians moved out of the South during the war, and almost as importantly, three times that many moved elsewhere within the region. Prior to the war, southern workers had been far less mobile, sticking close to home either because they could not afford to move, had no incentive to move, or simply could not bring themselves to move. This labor market inflexibility was far less pronounced in the postwar South as outmigration, inmigration, and intraregional migration continually responded to and shaped economic, racial, political, and cultural trends.[26]

Among the cultural trends most affected by this newfound mobility and other war-induced changes was the evolution of southern music. As Bill C. Malone wrote, "while promoting major transformations in the habits, employment, and residence of rural southerners, the war effectively nationalized their music." Country music went both national and international thanks not only to the proliferation of country radio programming in response to the outmigration of southern whites but to the Armed Forces Radio Network, which carried what had once been seen as strictly regional "hillbilly" music all over the world. The major beneficiary of this was Grand Ole Opry star Roy Acuff, whose distinctive voice became so well known in the steamy jungles of the South Pacific that some Japanese troops reportedly spurned "banzai" in favor of "To Hell with Roy Acuff." Although this hateful rallying cry proved ineffectual in the short run, the Japanese finally won a measure of revenge in the 1990s as their karaoke machines subjected thousands of southerners to the drunken wailings of would-be country boys trying to sing "The Wabash Cannonball." A second beneficiary of wartime developments was the Texas Troubadour, Ernest Tubb, who pioneered in a musical style known as "honky tonk," which drew its name from establishments known for drinking and dancing and not infrequently fighting and shooting as well. The repeal of prohibition, the sense of rootlessness and transiency and the loosening of morals and family constraints occasioned by economic expansion and population redistribution shaped both the thematic and stylistic contours of honky tonk. The loud, twangy pedal steel guitar was a perfect accompaniment for tunes such as "What Made Milwaukee Famous Made a Loser Out of Me," and it also allowed the song to be heard over the clamor of the laughing, cursing, and fighting that filled the bars and beer joints where it was most often played.[27]

It was symbolically prophetic that the Japanese attack on Pearl Harbor bumped country music's pioneering Carter Family from the cover of *Life* magazine in December 1941 because the wartime changes in country music seemed to spell nothing but trouble for many traditional artists. Bill and Earl Bolick, the Blue Sky Boys, had been phenomenally popular performers on Atlanta's WGST before the war but soon fell by the wayside when they refused to add amplified instruments to back up their close and plaintive mountain harmonies. Fittingly enough, when the Blue Sky Boys broke up, Bill Bolick returned to his native North Carolina, but Earl remained in Atlanta and went to work for Lockheed in the postwar South's largest industrial plant. Elsewhere, however, Bill Monroe, another successful pre-war traditional musician, began his ascent to legendary status in 1945 when he incorporated the new three-finger banjo-picking style of Earl Scruggs into his music to create bluegrass, a musical style now viewed by self-appointed purists as "traditional" but described correctly by Alan Lomax as a sort of modernized "folk music with overdrive." Meanwhile, the commingling of country and black styles helped to insure the postwar appeal of Hank Williams, underscoring Charles Gillett's observation that during the 1940s "country music probably absorbed more elements of black music than were accepted into the mainstream pop of the time." This coming together or at least coming closer together of country music and black music was another striking development of the early postwar years. Southern black musicians who remained economically successful after the war did so primarily by electrifying their music, following the lead of Muddy Waters, who abandoned his tractor on the Stovall plantation near Clarksdale and headed north to Chicago in 1943, finally making good on his threat that "If I feel tomorrow, the way I feel today, I'm gonna. . . . pack my bags and make my getaway."[28]

During the war and after, younger and more urbane black audiences readily demonstrated their preference for the amplified dance-oriented stylings that became known as "rhythm and blues." Researchers who studied black life during the war had discovered a marked trend toward secularization as rural blacks acquired radios, automobiles, and telephones and generally transcended the barriers that had once insulated them from mass-society influences. Disgusted by the changes she observed, lifelong Mississippi Delta churchgoer Matilda Mae Jones complained, "Songs they sing in church now feel like fire burning. . . . all fast and jumpy and leapy like. . . . that's just the way these swing church songs are now." Jones's complaint foreshadowed a trend that would see performers like Clarksdale-born gospel singer Sam Cooke, who began his career singing songs such as "Jesus Gave Me Water," go on to fame as a rhythm and blues superstar with hits like "Chain Gang" and "Everybody Loves to Cha Cha Cha." Cooke's career paralleled those of countless others, such as James Brown and Otis Redding and Ray Charles, who, in succeeding years, not so much left gospel music as took it with them when they entered the secular, sensual world of rhythm and blues.[29]

For many black as well as white performers, their musical odyssey led to Memphis, where a war-inspired economic boom had played the key role in bringing both Firestone Tire and International Harvester plants to the city. Opportunities were by no means equal for both races, but the city offered the proverbial "day jobs" that would allow aspiring artists to play their music at night. It was here at Memphis's Sun Studios that rhythm and blues met country-derived rockabilly to produce the revolutionary musical hybrid known as rock and roll. As Pete Daniel observed, "The leisurely pace of rural life collided with urban haste, and the city allowed all genres of contemporary music to mix. The rhythm of the land collided with the beat of the city, and the energy generated by this chain reaction redefined American music."[30]

Writing in 1935, Greenville writer David L. Cohn described the Mississippi Delta as a land of "complete detachment," explaining that "change shatters itself on the breast of this society as Pacific breakers upon a South Sea reef." "Disturbing ideas" might "crawl like flies around the screen of the Delta," wrote Cohn, but "they rarely penetrate." In the wake of World War II, Cohn painted a decidedly different portrait, however, noting that "many changes have occurred in the life of the Mississippi Delta as elsewhere. We had scarcely emerged from a shattering economic depression before we were plunged into man's most catastrophic war. The foundations of our faith are severely shaken. We no longer believe, as we once did, in the inevitability of progress. Our compass is aberrant, our course erratic. We are more than a little fearful that we shall not make our landfall."[31]

Cohn's observation seemed to bear out George Orwell's contention that "if the war didn't kill you, it was bound to start you thinking," but in reality, southerners were already thinking, particularly about the South, well before World War II. The region once dubbed "The Sahara of the Bozart" by H. L. Mencken could by 1941 boast of having the nation's most dynamic literary community. The pivotal member of that community, William Faulkner, sought vainly to enlist in the military during World War II but wound up sitting out the war as a screenwriter in Hollywood, working on *Battle Cry, God Is My Co-Pilot,* and a number of other patriotic films. Still, Faulkner revealed his emotional involvement in the conflict in a letter to his stepson who was then serving in the military: "A change will come out of this war. If it doesn't, if the politicians and people who run this country are not forced to make good the shibboleth they glibly talk about freedom, liberty, human rights, then you young men who have lived through it will have wasted your precious time, and those who don't live through it will have died in vain." Looking beyond the war, Faulkner could only hope that there "will be a part for me, who can't do anything but use words, in the rearranging of the house so that all mankind can live in it."[32]

Ironically, some literary scholars now quote these eloquent lines as they mark World War II as the beginning of the end for Faulkner as a great writer, arguing, with *Intruder in the Dust* as a case in point, that his subsequent fiction became more didactic and mechanical and less open ended and artistically valid. Whether Faulkner was a less gifted writer is of less significance for our purposes than the fact that after the war he was far more widely read and appreciated. The contradictions raised by World War II and subsequently magnified by the tensions of the Cold War focused national and international attention on the South's deficiencies. World War II brought more than twice as many Yankee soldiers to the South as the Civil War and their wartime experiences often yielded specific and personal testimony to the South's backwardness. By 1948, then, Faulkner's Charles Mallison could perceive among nonsoutherners "a volitionless, almost helpless capacity to believe almost anything about the South not even provided it be derogatory but merely bizarre enough and strange enough." In a larger sense, the war had not only highlighted the South's abnormalities but helped to transform the nation into one where these abnormalities could no longer be tolerated. The result was the creation of what Sosna called "a bull market . . . for regional exposure, explanation, and analysis."[33]

Certainly, the war years inspired and nurtured a host of writers of both fiction and nonfiction who wrote with the clear purpose of focusing attention on the South's problems and stressing the urgency of finding solutions. Serving as a Naval officer in India, young historian C. Vann Woodward was struck by his visit with the leader of India's untouchables who "plied me with questions about the black 'untouchables' of America and how their plight compared with that of his own people." Already the author of a revisionist biography of Populist Tom Watson, Woodward returned from the war to write a sweeping reinterpretation of the Redeemer Era South and then to pen *The Strange Career of Jim Crow,* an enormously influential volume that struck at both the legal and emotional underpinnings of segregation.[34]

Meanwhile, Woodward contemporary John Hope Franklin, who had just received his Ph.D. from Harvard, offered his services as a historian to the War Department. Because he was black, he was rebuffed without receiving serious consideration. Then, responding to Naval recruiters' appeals for clerical personnel, Franklin was again rejected solely on the basis of his race. Finally, ordered to report for a draft physical, Franklin was subjected to further indignities, leading him to conclude that "the United States did not need me and did not deserve me." Consequently, he spent the rest of the war outwitting the draft board and "feeling nothing but shame for my country—not merely for what it did to me, but for what it did to the millions of black men and women who served in the armed forces under conditions of segregation and discrimination." Franklin went on to revise the traditional historical view of Reconstruction and of the role of blacks in southern history and to serve (as did Woodward, in a lesser capacity) as an adviser to the NAACP Legal Defense Team representing the plaintiffs in the *Brown* v. *Board of Education* case.[35]

Franklin's wartime experience reflected the ambivalence and frustration with which many black intellectuals approached the conflict. Determined to link the fighting abroad to the struggle for racial justice at home, poet Langston Hughes exulted in "Jim Crow's Last Stand" that "Pearl Harbor put Jim Crow on the run/That Crow can't fight for Democracy/And be the same old Crow he used to be." Hughes also urged black soldiers to get those "so bad, evil and most mad, GO AND GET THE ENEMY BLUES." As segregation continued to flourish throughout the war effort, however, a disappointed Hughes also mocked, "Jim Crow Army and Navy, Too/Is Jim Crow freedom the *best* I can expect from you?"[36]

By the time the war began, Richard Wright's angry fiction had already established him as the nation's preeminent black writer. As an increasingly disenchanted member of the Communist Party, however, Wright found himself zigging and zagging in response to a party line that was zigging and zagging as well. In the wake of the Nazi-Soviet Pact, he insisted that the conflict was "Not My People's War," pointing out that "the Negro's experience with past wars, his attitude towards the present one, his attitude of chronic distrust, constitute the most incisive and graphic refutation of every idealistic statement made by the war leaders as to the alleged democratic goal and aim of this war." After Hitler's invasion of Russia, however, the party suddenly had no more use for Comrade Wright's pacifism, and slightly more than a week after Pearl Harbor, a frustrated Wright pledged his "loyalty and allegiance" to the American cause, promising that "I shall through my writing seek to rally the Negro people to stand shoulder to shoulder with the administration in a solid national front to wage war until victory is won."[37]

Meanwhile, irreverent novelist and folklorist Zora Neale Hurston had drawn consistent criticism from Richard Wright and other black intellectuals for her failure to use her writings as a weapon in the struggle against racism and Jim Crow. Yet for all her apparent reluctance to devote her energies to solving the race problem, in the original manuscript for her autobiographical *Dust Tracks on a Road*, she pointed out that "President Roosevelt could extend his four freedoms to some people right here in America. . . . I am not bitter, but I see what I see. . . . I will fight for my country, but I will not lie for her." Like several others, this passage was subsequently excised after Hurston's white editor deemed it "irrelevant." After the war, however, writing in *Negro Digest*, Hurston cited Roosevelt's reference to the United States as "the arsenal of democracy" and wondered if she had heard him correctly. Perhaps he meant "arse-and-all" of democracy, she thought, since the United States was supporting the French in their effort to resubjugate the Indo-Chinese, suggesting that "the ass-and-all of democracy has shouldered the load of subjugating the dark world completely." Hurston also announced that she was "crazy for this democracy" and would "pitch headlong into the thing" if it were not for the numerous Jim Crow laws that confronted her at every turn.[38]

World War II also stiffened white crusader Lillian Smith's resolve to fight against segregation. She insisted in 1943 that fighting for freedom while acquiescing to Jim Crow amounted to "trying to buy a new world with Confederate bills." Condemned by Georgia governor Eugene Talmadge as "a literary corn cob," Smith's 1944 novel *Strange Fruit* was a searing story of miscegenation and murder that concluded with the lynching of an innocent young black man. It lay bare the pain and suffering caused by white racism and the hypocrisy and sexual repression that festered just beneath the surface of the southern way of life.[39]

The uncompromising Smith was hardly more contemptuous of those who defended Jim Crow than those who urged moderation in the fight against it. Yet, with external pressures mounting as the Supreme Court struck down the white primary in 1944, many white southerners who had once seemed most dedicated to racial justice found themselves urging the proponents of desegregation to slow down. Ardent and courageous spokesmen like Hodding Carter and Ralph McGill insisted that ending segregation would take time, and when they bristled at northern critics—members of the "hit-and-run school of southern writing," as Carter called them—they sounded a great deal like

Faulkner's Gavin Stevens in *Intruder in the Dust* and Faulkner himself a few years thereafter. As Numan V. Bartley observed, in the wake of the war "the very word 'liberal' gradually disappeared from the southern political lexicon, except as a term of opprobrum." Meanwhile, although the contradictions raised by Jim Crow were inconsistent with the United States's rise to free-world leadership, the anti-Communist hysteria of the early Cold War years made even northern liberals initially reluctant to encourage antisegregation litigation and protests.[40]

Alabaman Virginia Durr claimed that when she introduced him to a group of Mississippi Methodist women lobbying for repeal of the poll tax, Senator James Eastland had spluttered that they apparently wanted "black men laying on you." The anti-poll-tax movement weathered such opposition from Eastland and other southern politicians but fell apart after losing crucial support when the National Committee to Abolish the Poll Tax refused to purge itself of members belonging to groups targeted by the attorney general's list of "subversive organizations."[41]

Even before World War II, some southern intellectuals were beginning to behave according to a pattern that now seems fairly typical of emerging or developing nations around the world, agonizing about their region's backwardness but also expressing their fears about the loss of cultural identity and virtue that might accompany the accelerating effort to modernize their society. No writer struggled more painfully or brilliantly with the persistence of the South's deficiencies or the decay of its virtues than William Faulkner. In the wake of World War II, Faulkner's fictional Jefferson was already experiencing what Walker Percy later called "Los Angelization," its "old big decaying wooden houses" giving way to antiseptic one-story models crammed into subdivisions "with their neat plots of clipped grass and tedious flowerbeds" and its housewives "in sandals and pants and painted toe nails," puffing "lipstick-stained cigarettes over shopping bags in the chain groceries and drugstores." Meanwhile, mechanization of agriculture brought a dramatic change in the rhythm of southern rural life as machines came between men and women and the land and further separated them from the product of their labors. "I'd druther have a mule fartin' in my face all day long walkin' de turnrow than dem durned tractors," a Delta farmhand told David Cohn. "There ain't nothing about a tractor that makes a man want to sing," complained another worker. "The thing keeps so much noise and you so far away from the other folks."[42]

In "The Displaced Person," Flannery O'Connor told the story of a Polish immigrant, Mr. Guizac, who finds work as a hired hand on a run-down farm in early postwar Georgia and revitalizes it through his energy and mechanical expertise. Yet, for all the economic benefits he brings, Guizac is also infected with alien values. His employer, Mrs. McIntyre, is impressed by Guizac's accomplishments and happy with the potential profits his efforts might reap for her, but she also worries that Guizac is a stranger to the society and culture in which he lives. Her fears are confirmed when she learns that he plans to get a female cousin into the United States by betrothing her to a local black man, and in the story's startling conclusion, she looks on silently, offering no warning, as the unsuspecting Guizac is flattened by a runaway tractor.[43]

In his semi-autobiographical novel *The Year the Lights Came On*, Terry Kay described the postwar scene in Royston, Georgia: "The cotton mill placed an advertisement in *The (Royston, Ga.) Record*, seeking employees. A sewing plant was officially opened by His Honor the Mayor. Farmers began to listen to what county agents had to say about subsoiling, land testing, seed treating, or about planting kudzu and lespedeza to stop topsoil from washing away in the ugly scars of erosion. The sound of John Deere tractors stuttered even at night." In Royston, no less than elsewhere, Kay believed "everyone seemed aware of being embraced by a new history of the world, and everyone knew it would be a history never forgotten."[44]

Like Kay and O'Connor, Walker Percy was also witness to the destabilizing effects of urbanization, industrialization, and agricultural mechanization in the postwar South. Even as O'Connor worried that the changes sweeping across her region might purge the South "not only of our many sins but our few virtues," Percy was noting the "growing depersonalization" of southern social relations and suggesting that northernization of southern life would mean a society "in which there is no sense of the past, or of real community, or even of one's own identity." Percy would ultimately emerge as one of the dominant literary figures in the post–World War II South, and a new generation of writers such as Richard Ford and Josephine Humphreys now explore in their own work the validity of Percy's insistence that modern life subjects southerners, like all other Americans, to "deep dislocation in their lives that has nothing to do with poverty, ignorance, and discrimination."[45]

Expressing similar concerns, John Egerton worried in 1974 that the "Americanization of Dixie" simply meant that the South and the nation were "not exchanging strengths as much as they are exchanging sins." In his 1995 study of the pre–Civil Rights generation in the South, however, Egerton was more upbeat, crediting World War II with bringing the South into "the modern age" by turning "hard times into hopeful times," moving "people up and out," and changing "our ways of thinking and working and living. Practically everything about this war," Egerton believed, "from the way we got into it to the way we got out of it, suggested transformation."[46]

Confirming Egerton's assessment of the war as a watershed, Bertram Wyatt-Brown insisted in 1991 that "the South Cash knew has largely disappeared. In matters of economic prosperity, racial demography, urbanization, and politics, the fact is that the region has altered much more since the early 1940s than it did between 1865 and 1941."[47]

Few contemporary observers seem inclined to dispute Egerton or Wyatt-Brown, but if we are to understand the full impact of World War II on our region, we must take into account not only the magnitude but the limitations of the changes induced by the war. Upon close examination, we can also see that although the War is responsible for many of the differences between the South that Cash saw in 1940 and the South we see today, it also contributed to some of the similarities as well. For example, if the war made the South more attractive to industrial investors, its failure to destroy the region's heavy concentration in low-wage industries helped to explain why the postwar South retained a cheap-labor appeal that those investors still find significant. In addition, the war's stimulus to industrial mobility and to southern efforts to attract new and better industries meant that the South ultimately went from offering thousands of dollars in subsidies to underwear plants to offering hundreds of millions of dollars in subsidies to automobile plants.[48]

On another front, the war's acceleration of black migration from states where blacks could not vote to states where they could played a key role in spurring the Democratic Party's advocacy of civil rights, but in doing so, it also fed the nationwide white backlash that all but derailed the civil rights movement. Similarly, if the war-inspired Civil Rights revolution allowed southern blacks to claim the political rights and influence so long denied them, it also triggered the massive exodus of racially conservative southern whites from the Democratic Party, the cumulative result being a South that quickly amassed the nation's largest concentration of black officeholders while becoming its most predictably Republican region in presidential elections and a growing number of lesser contests as well.

While Cash would have found officeholding by Republicans or blacks almost equally startling, he would probably have been even more amazed to see that the changes set in motion or intensified by the war had rendered his version of the southern mind essentially obsolete, replacing it with a more heterogeneous and less exclusionary model, one open to anyone who saw themselves as southerners regardless of race or gender or even regional or national origin. Not only were blacks just as likely as whites to identify themselves as southerners by the 1990s, but in many cases, they actually seemed more confident of what that meant. Enduring taunts and threats and all manner of abuse from those who sought to preserve Cash's South, Charlayne Hunter-Gault had broken the color barrier at the University of Georgia in 1961. In 1988 she returned to Athens to deliver the commencement address, embracing the South as "my place" and paying tribute to southerners of both races whose "tumultuous" but shared history had melded them into the nation's only "definable people." Numerous such examples along with contemporary polls identifying Robert E. Lee and Martin Luther King as the South's most revered historical figures seem to point to a southern mind dramatically different though hardly less paradoxical or contradictory than the one that tormented Cash.[49]

Confirming the anxiety Cash had felt in 1940, Morton Sosna concluded that the South had emerged from World War II as "an arena where the forces of good and evil, progress and reaction, rapid change and seemingly timeless continuity were about to engage in a battle of near mythological proportions." As Sosna indicated, for the South, the end of the war meant not peace but another quarter century of struggle. More than any single preceding event, World War II helped to shape not only the contours of this struggle but its outcome, an outcome that finally allowed us to contemplate a South whose virtues, if they did not tower over its faults, were at least no longer totally obscured by them. All of this seems to have come out far better than Cash dared to hope. Yet, before we credit World War II with unloosing forces that destroyed Cash's South, we should first take note of the racism, violence, anti-intellectualism, and social indifference that now permeate American society at large and ask how the postwar historical context so clearly conducive to mitigating these characteristic vices of the southern mind in 1940 could have also set the stage for their ominous emergence as defining features of the national mind in 1996.[50]

11 THE SOUTH AND CONGRESSIONAL POLITICS

Dewey W. Grantham

In national politics, V. O. Key observed in 1949, the Democratic party in the southern states had long been "the instrument for the conduct of the 'foreign relations' of the South with the rest of the nation."[1] In the pursuit of their diplomatic objectives, southerners concentrated on Congress, an assembly in which they possessed singular advantages and exerted great influence. This was never more clearly demonstrated than during the Second World War. Despite the vast shift of power and discretion to the chief executive, the legislative branch remained a vitally important institution in a democracy engaged in all-out war. Writing near the end of the war, the journalist Thomas L. Stokes called attention to the way in which all of the "gripes and resistances" of the American people "reacted in Congress to provoke constant controversy and ferment, with a clash of interests among businessmen and farmers and labor and plain citizens belonging to no particular group, and with clashes among groups within these groups."[2]

Southern leadership was a dominant feature of Congress between 1941 and 1945. During the war years, southern Democrats constituted the largest regional representation of their party in Congress, and they tended to display greater coherence in their votes than any other group in the two houses. The congressional elections of 1942, which increased Republican strength and brought the defeat of many northern and western Democrats, enhanced the southern position in Congress.[3] In the Seventy-eighth Congress (1943–1944),

21

southern Democrats outnumbered nonsouthern Democrats in the House and held just under 44 percent of the party's seats in the Senate. More importantly, the seniority rule had enabled the southerners to assume the chairmanships and ranking positions of the most powerful committees in the two chambers.[4] The southerners' mastery of parliamentary procedure and legislative detail gave them a decided advantage and frequently made it possible for them to provide "the know-how" in disposing of congressional issues. They had grown accustomed to the role of congressional leadership, almost as if it was theirs by divine right. They met the test of leadership with skill and resourcefulness, while savoring the attention and recognition that came with national responsibility.

Yet there was a negative aspect to the southerners' role. Their performance as wartime leaders revealed, in addition to the influence they wielded, increasing ambiguity toward President Franklin D. Roosevelt, mounting opposition to his domestic policies, and growing distrust of the national Democratic party. Most of the southern congressmen viewed the federal government as an indispensable instrument in the economic development of the South, but they wanted such assistance without any strings attached. They opposed extensive changes in the southern social order or the region's power structure or its politics. Their dissatisfaction with the course of the national Democratic party, and their willingness to cooperate with congressional Republicans, as well as their deepening alarm over changes taking place in race relations, new national labor standards, and increasing federal intrusion, contributed to the rise of conservatism and greater resistance to Roosevelt's programs in Congress while preparing the way for later developments in regional and national politics.

In a seminal article published several years ago, Richard L. Watson evaluated southern congressional leaders during the First World War in terms of their responsibilities to "constituency, party, and principle."[5] Watson's analysis provides a useful approach to the role of southern congressmen during World War II. Beyond the immediate needs of their constituents and protecting the South's special interests—preeminently the inviolability of white supremacy and the autonomy of the one-party system—the southerners were dedicated to the task of fostering the economic improvement of their region. Eager to overcome decades of economic colonialism, they looked to Washington during the Roosevelt era for federal dollars to support agriculture and to build everything from dams and roads to military bases and industrial plants. Their traditional attachment to the Democratic party predisposed them to support Franklin Roosevelt and his administration in a time of national crisis, although many of them were suspicious of the president's urban liberalism and not altogether mollified by his emphasis on rearmament and international leadership. Most of the southerners were provincials, residents of small towns and advocates of state rights and agrarian values. They were also nationalists. Though inclined to champion the ordinary white man, they habitually served the interests of their community and state elites. Like their counterparts from other regions, these southern lawmakers endeavored to balance their responsibilities to "constituency, party, and principle." They were not always successful in that effort.

Once again, as in 1898 and 1917–1918, war brought a dramatic demonstration of the South's patriotism and nationalist sentiment, and after the United States entered the conflict no other region was more zealous in its support of the war effort. Southern enthusiasm for international involvement was to some extent a reflection of Democratic party loyalty and Wilsonian internationalism, but it was also related to the section's long military tradition and to economic and psychological factors. In any case, as his emphasis shifted from domestic reform to foreign affairs, Roosevelt was able to rely on the help of southern congressional leaders. Southern congressmen were part of an administration coalition that also included nonsouthern Democrats and a number of moderate and internationalist Republicans.[6] The southerners gave the president overwhelming and at times indispensable support during the difficult transition years of 1940 and 1941, and they provided a bulwark of strength in backing the administration's foreign and defense policies throughout the war. Senate majority leader Alben W. Barkley, Speaker Sam Rayburn, presidential assistant James F. Byrnes, and other southerners encouraged a fairly high level of party unity on many vital issues. The South also became conspicuously identified—through Secretary of State Cordell Hull, southern congressional leaders, and the force of public opinion—with Roosevelt's internationalism and his plans for a postwar system of collective security. Southern advocates of a Wilsonian organization, one scholar has written, "seemed to rejoice in the possibility that their benighted region had, after all, produced an idea that would rescue the world from itself and establish a new order under a progressive American leadership."[7]

Protecting agriculture was a major priority of southern congressmen, and in contrast to labor policy, the wartime handling of agricultural issues was strongly influenced by Congress. Increased demand for farm commodities eventually brought a sharp rise in the price of agricultural products, but farm leaders and their political representatives in Washington did not wait for market forces to bring this about. Pressured by the American Farm Bureau Federation and led by determined congressmen such as Senator John H. Bankhead and Representative Henry B. Steagall of Alabama, the farm bloc worked unrelentingly to raise government support prices on basic commodities, to revise the parity formula, and to defer farm laborers from the draft. At one point early in the war, agricultural representatives succeeded in raising ceilings on farm prices to 110 percent of parity. By 1944 Congress had increased the government loan rate to 95 percent of parity, and the Stabilization Act of that year directed the president to take all lawful action to assure that producers of basic farm crops received prices no lower than 100 percent of parity.[8] Despite its sectional dimensions, southern advocacy of special benefits for farmers was not inconsistent with New Deal agricultural policy. Although debate over farm policy tended to divide the core industrial Northeast and Midwest from the agrarian periphery in other parts of the country, the conflict was ameliorated by negotiations between farm bloc and industrial labor representatives within the Democratic coalition and by the committee system in the two houses of Congress.

The farm bloc was less successful in the long battle it waged against the Office of Price Administration's regulations and the related issue of food subsidies. The subsidy program, administered by the Commodity Credit Corporation, bought crops to bolster farm prices and sold them at a loss to keep the cost of living down. Farm leaders feared that subsidies would place a ceiling on agricultural prices and provide an undeserved bonus for urban consumers. Agricultural spokesmen, with business support, were pitted against the representatives of consumer interests, including organized labor, in a struggle over OPA's efforts to stabilize prices and hold down inflation. The farm alliance tried again and again to weaken the price control structure, winning some concessions but never managing to overturn the system. Congress voted on two occasions to terminate the food subsidy program, only to be blocked by presidential vetoes.[9]

One reason southern congressmen were strong backers of Roosevelt's defense program was their realization that it would open up new business and industrial opportunities for the South and contribute to the region's economic development. "It is essential for small Texas manufacturing plants to have a share in defense production," Representative Lyndon B. Johnson told the newspaper editors of that state on one occasion, for " . . . Texas not only wants to do everything it can for defense, but it foresees the need for preserving and expanding its manufacturing plants for normal demands of the future."[10] Military installations, defense plants, and other industrial enterprises were eagerly sought by southern business and political leaders. Southern congressmen played a central role in this endeavor, as did mounting state-level pressure for the South's "fair share" of military spending.[11]

If southern congressmen supplied the Roosevelt administration with essential support in the conduct of its military and international programs, the president and the war agencies went out of their way to promote the economic growth and diversification of the South. The administration decided to take advantage of the war emergency to develop and modernize the South—to move forward in the spirit of the *Report on Economic Conditions of the South* and the wages and hours law of 1938. This was evident in the military buildup of 1940–1941. In 1940, for example, Congress amended the Maritime-Naval Expansion Act of 1938 to make it possible for southern and West Coast shipbuilders to obtain contracts without necessarily presenting the lowest bids. The War Production Board, the National War Labor Board (NWLB), and other agencies adopted policies that facilitated the decentralization of war plants, improving wages for southern and western workers and stimulating the economies of the peripheral regions. The growth of government entitlement programs and the principle of equality in the disbursement of federal funds also promoted the southern economy. The Tennessee Valley Authority, with a mandate to expand its production of electrical power and to operate as a defense agency, became a champion of industrial growth in the valley.[12] Commenting on Roosevelt's contribution in this respect, Virginius Dabney, editor of the Richmond *Times-Dispatch*, declared that "no other President of modern times devoted an even remotely comparable amount of thought and effort to southern problems, and he alone among them had the vision and the courage to initiate a broad program addressed to the economic and social ills of the region."[13]

Nevertheless, southern congressmen were beginning to realize that federal programs and policies designed to diversify and modernize southern economic institutions were almost certain to entail more controls and regulations from Washington. They were, moreover, suspicious of Roosevelt's political motives, unhappy about his relationship with urban and labor elements in the party, and jealous of their own political independence. Some of their constituents were also opposed to certain policies of the Roosevelt administration. Industrialists and other influential business interests regarded the introduction of federal wage standards—minimum wages, maximum hours, and abolition of regional wage differentials—as an assault on an important southern advantage in the struggle for economic growth. The heightening of the southerners' conservatism tended to put them at odds with liberal currents in the Democratic party. In his study of congressional politics during World War II, Roland Young classified all members of the two houses, on the basis of party-votes, into three groups of roughly equal size.[14] Group I contained strong party loyalists, Group II moderate party supporters, and Group III mild or weak party members. The largest number of southern Democrats in both the House and Senate was located in Group III, and the combined percentage of southerners in Groups II and III came to 80 in the Senate and an astonishing 83 in the House. The southerners found common ground with conservative Republicans on such principles as state rights, fiscal conservatism, limited government, and the abolition of agencies that might disrupt social relations in their states.[15] A contemporary observer noted that, in addition to GOP gains in the two houses, the elections of 1942 had "placed the balance of power in the hands of the anti-New Deal Democrats."[16]

In the Seventy-eighth Congress conservative southerners and their Republican allies carried out a concerted attack on a number of New Deal agencies, reduced the progressively oriented National Resources Planning Board to a skeleton, defeated a federal aid to education bill, and turned back a proposal by northern Democrats for a massive public housing program. The southerners, reflecting the conservative views of the Farm Bureau and its allies in the South, took the lead in cutting the budget of the Farm Security Administration (FSA) and restricting its efforts to assist tenant farmers and small owners, used a joint committee on unnecessary expenditures under the chairmanship of Senator Harry Flood Byrd of Virginia to harass several of the war agencies and carry out a retrenchment campaign, helped secure Senate (but not House) passage of a measure introduced by Senator Kenneth D. McKellar of Tennessee to require Senate confirmation of all appointments to positions with salaries of $4,500 or more a year, and through the House Un-American Activities Committee, chaired by Representative Martin Dies of Texas, identified some forty agency administrators with alleged radical affiliations.[17] The voting alliance between southern Democrats and Republicans reached its peak in 1944, when the conservative coalition manifested itself on about 40 percent of significant votes in the Senate. The index of likeness between southern Democrats and Republicans in the upper chamber that year, according to one study, reached 63.4 percent, as compared with a likeness score for southern Democrats and nonsouthern Democrats of only 57 percent. James MacGregor Burns once described the southerners and other old barons who dominated Capitol Hill as "masters of procedure, evokers of memories, voices of ideology—and contrivers of deadlock." Roosevelt was quoted by an administration official as saying that "for all practical purposes we have a Republican Congress now."[18]

In three other areas, southern Democrats in Congress reacted defensively to wartime developments: the growing influence of organized labor, changing developments and new policies in race relations, and the nomination of the Democratic ticket in 1944. The expansion of organized labor in the South, especially the growth of the Congress of Industrial Organizations (CIO), provoked stubborn resistance in the region and the enactment of several state laws to hamstring labor unions. In Congress many southerners were vehemently opposed to the liberal demands and political activities of organized labor, particularly those involving the Democratic party. Most of the southern lawmakers were outspoken in their criticism of labor strikes in war industries. Although virtually all important labor controls emanated from the executive branch, Congress made full use of its investigative power.

Representative Howard W. Smith of Virginia and an antilabor bloc in the House of Representatives sponsored an antistrike bill as early as 1941 and were instrumental in the passage of the War Labor Disputes Act, a measure introduced by Smith and Senator Thomas T. Connally of Texas and passed over Roosevelt's veto in 1943. Only five southern Democrats voted against the bill in the House, and not a single southerner voted to sustain FDR's veto in the Senate. The Smith-Connally Act authorized the president to seize plants useful during the war and made it a crime to encourage strikes in such plants. It sought in other ways to limit the freedom of labor unions and to prevent the use of union funds in political campaigns. Southern congressional leaders were concerned by the threat trade unions posed to their region's existing labor system, as well as their political influence. Organized labor's wartime gains in the South, fostered by federal protection and the rulings of the NWLB, set the stage for Operation Dixie, the CIO's postwar campaign to unionize southern workers.[19]

Congress provided an important center for wartime decisions affecting African Americans, and southern congressmen spent a great deal of time on such issues. Southern support of the move to abolish the National Youth Administration, for example, resulted in part from disapproval of the agency's efforts to recruit and train black workers for war industries. The southerners fiercely resisted an anti-poll tax bill, which twice passed the House during the war only to be defeated by a southern filibuster in the Senate. The 1944 filibuster, in David Brinkley's pungent language, was "a charade, a political carnival: a contrived, tedious, often odious discussion of a bill that every member realized would ultimately be defeated."[20] Southerners were quick, following the Detroit race riot of 1943 and other racial disturbances in northern cities, to instruct northerners on their failures in race relations. They were leaders in the emasculation of an administration proposal to authorize a federal ballot for soldiers in the election of 1944, charging that it represented an assault on state rights, including the right of southern states to determine their own voting requirements, and they loudly protested the Supreme Court's invalidation of the Democratic white primary in *Smith* v. *Allwright* (1944).[21] Their most impassioned denunciation was reserved for the Fair Employment Practice Committee, the target of a sectional crusade during the war. Early in 1944, for instance, Representative Smith turned an investigation of the agency into "a public forum for segregationists," and in 1945 the committee's opponents, led by Senator Richard B. Russell of Georgia, managed to cut its budget in half and to provide for its early dissolution.[22]

Few white southerners had anything good to say about the FEPC, and Dixie congressmen attacked it throughout the war. Inadequately funded and unable to force compliance with its decisions, the agency enjoyed only limited success. Even so, it was able to settle about two-fifths of more than twelve thousand cases it processed, 20 percent of which originated in the South. President Roosevelt's own support of the FEPC was vacillating and halfhearted. He seemed intent above all else on winning the war and, if possible, holding the Democratic party together through the election of 1944. He was reluctant to offend southern political leaders. Roosevelt apparently encouraged Attorney General Francis Biddle to abandon a move to prosecute Alabama officials for denying blacks the right to vote in the Democratic primary of 1944, and he failed to act promptly in backing the FEPC's ongoing effort to force southern railroads to stop discriminating against African Americans.[23] Southern leaders wanted to promote economic progress in the region but not at the cost of disrupting its traditional social order. As Gilbert C. Fite has said of Richard Russell, the senator found himself "in the grasp of a great contradiction from which he was unable to escape. His very success in helping to expand old federal facilities and to bring new ones into Georgia during the war worked against the status quo in race relations."[24] Finally, the southern outcry against racial change contributed to the sectional division within the Democratic party and to the northern image of an undemocratic and reactionary South fundamentally opposed to the national struggle against totalitarianism and intolerance abroad.

As the presidential election of 1944 approached, sectionalism assumed a more prominent place in Democratic party affairs than at any time since 1928. The Democrats were divided along ideological and regional lines, divided into what commentators referred to as a northern liberal wing and a southern conservative wing. Conservative Democrats in the South had become increasingly belligerent and outspoken during the past year and a half. They made much of the changing character of the national party—of the activities of the CIO's Political Action Committee, urban bosses, and black organizations—and of the South's declining influence in the party. They began to talk ominously about leaving the party of their fathers and acting independently. Roosevelt had advocated social welfare legislation, a federal ballot for soldiers, and the rights of organized labor, and he had indicated his intention of reviving the New Deal following the war. In the meantime, southern conservatives found their own hero in Senator Harry Byrd. A Byrd-for-President Committee was established, and conservative revolts were planned in several southern states.[25]

Pro-Roosevelt or loyalist factions managed to overcome the insurgent Democrats in these states, Roosevelt was nominated for a fourth term, and the
Democratic ticket swept the South as usual in the November election. A group
of conservative rebels known as the Texas Regulars did succeed in placing an
independent slate of electors on the ballot in the Lone Star State, but they
received only 11.7 percent of the vote.[26] Franklin Roosevelt was too widely
admired and too strong a wartime leader to lose in the South in 1944. Most of the
congressional Democrats from the South gave him their support. The president
was the commander in chief, he was the leader of their party, and he was the
central figure in the Allies' march toward victory. Southern lawmakers were
conscious of the fact that, with their backing, the South had fared exceedingly
well in the allocation of agricultural benefits, military bases, war contracts, and
federal assistance generally. The Dixie congressmen realized, of course, that
Roosevelt remained popular with their constituents. A Gallup poll taken in
the summer of 1943 had shown that 80 percent of the southern respondents
favored FDR's renomination.[27] Southern leaders could take some satisfaction
in their efforts to hobble the FEPC, preserve state rights, and curb an aggressive
labor movement. They had been instrumental in preventing the renomination
of Vice President Henry A. Wallace, the symbol of northern liberalism in the
national Democratic party. Indeed, southerners were inclined to give themselves
credit for the nomination of Senator Harry S. Truman of Missouri as Wallace's
replacement on the national ticket. When Roosevelt died in April 1945, many
southern politicians turned to the new president with a sense of relief, hoping
for an end to federal intervention and national reform.

If southerners had reason to be cautiously optimistic, many of them were
troubled. Allen Drury, a young southerner who covered the Senate for the
United Press, pictured the South in 1944 as "unhappy, restless, confused,
embittered, torn by pressures steadily mounting."[28] What especially bothered
the region's political leaders was the evolving shape of the national Democratic
party and their own uncertain future in it. In December 1942, Senator Josiah W.
Bailey of North Carolina expressed what soon became a familiar lament: "It is
a great pity that our Party has fallen into the hands of a faction of extremists
most of whom never were Democrats, and it is a great pity also that it is the
Democratic Party which has destroyed States' Rights and it is the Democratic
Party which has erected certain labor leaders into the position of tyrants."[29]
White southerners were beginning to change the image of their traditional
party. As one scholar has remarked, "Whatever courses southerners subsequently
took, the Democratic party was never again upheld as the embodiment of race,
country, God, and southern womanhood."[30]

Meanwhile, Americans in other parts of the country were becoming more aware of the South, both because of its pronounced conservatism and the fact that it was increasingly identified as a national problem. Outside observers began to ask, "What can be done about the South?" Federal intervention in creating the FEPC, invalidating the white primary, attempting to outlaw the poll tax, and nationalizing labor standards touched on the problem. White southerners tended to regard these measures as intrusive and threatening. In a period of intense nationalism and general approval of democratic practices, many Americans formed negative impressions of the South. This seems to have occurred, more often than not, in the case of the millions of soldiers who were stationed at training camps and military bases in the South. Morton Sosna has suggested that mobilizing a huge military force had "the unintended effect of mobilizing an army of critics against the South."[31]

In a sense the South, led by its congressional delegations, carried out a kind of dress rehearsal during World War II in preparing for a greater challenge in the future. The southerners made an effort, in and out of Congress, to unify their constituents in support of the region's special interests. They tried to increase their influence in the Democratic party's national conventions and to present "a united front" in such conclaves. They discussed pursuing an independent course in the national party, experimented with uninstructed delegates and uncommitted electors, and when provoked threatened to bolt the party. They spoke of resisting assaults from the outside and of their determination to preserve southern institutions. Thus Senator Burnet R. Maybank of South Carolina declared, in the wake of the *Smith* v. *Allwright* decision, that the South would deal with the problem as it saw fit, "regardless of what decisions the Supreme Court may make and regardless of what laws Congress may pass."[32] The pressure to conform was doubtless a factor in the growing conservatism of the southern states. Even Lyndon B. Johnson, an ardent advocate of Roosevelt and the New Deal, found it expedient to temper his liberalism in the face of Texas conservatism. In 1945 and 1946 he voted against an anti-lynching bill and repeal of the poll tax, against the FEPC, and with opponents of organized labor in the House.[33]

The South's most important means of protecting its interests in national politics was its powerful voice in Congress. The southerners' entrenched positions and skillful maneuvering enabled them to play an essential part in revising, passing, or defeating important legislation. During the war years, their voting alliances with Republicans appeared more frequently and became more potent than in the prewar period. An example of the South's influence in defeating an administration appointment occurred early in 1945 during the heated controversy over the Senate's consideration of Aubrey W. Williams to be head of the Rural Electrification Administration. Williams, an Alabamian who had served as director of the National Youth Administration, was too much a New Dealer, too liberal on the race question, and too blunt in expressing his views to suit congressional conservatives. Despite Roosevelt's support, Williams was rejected by the Senate, and seventeen of the nineteen Democrats who voted against his confirmation were southerners.[34] "All in all," V. O. Key wrote of the southerners' role in Congress and in national politics, "their strategy of obstruction provides an instructive illustration of the great power—at least negative power—of cohesive and determined minorities."[35]

Southern congressional leaders, through their support of Roosevelt's defense and international policies, assumed a progressive role in the war effort and encouraged the more complete integration of the South into the Union. Yet, as George B. Tindall has observed, in domestic affairs the region's political leaders "retreated back within the parapets of the embattled South, where they stood fast against the incursions of social change."[36] That retreat had important consequences, both for congressional action during the war and for the southern experience after 1945. Thus southern congressmen reinforced the dominance of the agricultural establishment in the South and facilitated the restructuring of southern agriculture; laid the groundwork for the Dixiecrat revolt of 1948, "massive resistance" to school desegregation, and the conditions that led to the civil rights movement and the Second Reconstruction; and demonstrated the possibilities of the conservative coalition in Congress and of broader agreement on issues and principles that eventually brought a flowering of Republicanism and a remarkable realignment of political parties in the southern states.

At the end of the war, the future remained, as always, inscrutable and problematic. The southern congressmen could not know that Harry Truman would soon commit himself to a list of reforms that went beyond Roosevelt's New Deal, including a comprehensive civil rights program; that the disturbing racial changes of the war years were only the premonitory rumblings of a far-reaching civil rights movement in which black southerners would play a leading part; that within four years southern Democrats would launch an open rebellion against their national party; and that the Democratic party would never be restored to the party they had known before the great realignment of the 1930s. But the southerners knew they had done their part to win the war and to usher in a period of American internationalism. Those with a taste for irony might have reflected on the twists and turns in their long association with Franklin D. Roosevelt, and on the way in which recent social and economic changes had encouraged the convergence of North and South, while simultaneously enhancing the South's cultural and political distinctiveness.[37] Many of the congressional leaders no doubt understood that they had resorted to guerrilla warfare in the politics of sectionalism. One thing was apparent: The southern congressmen, so accustomed to leadership and power—to the independence and privileges of their fiefdoms—were confident that they would continue to conduct the foreign relations of the South with the rest of the nation.

III WORLD WAR II AND THE TRANSFORMATION OF SOUTHERN HIGHER EDUCATION

Clarence L. Mohr

A generation ago, when Americans marked the centennial of the Civil War, the black freedom struggle provided the moral and intellectual context for scholarly participation in events commemorating the conflict between North and South. Just as the Civil War centennial spoke to the concerns of a rising generation faced with the unfinished agenda of emancipation, the 50th anniversary of World War II speaks—or should have spoken—to a different aspect of that same generation's historical experience, one symbolized in part by the influx of veterans to American college campuses during the late 1940s and the subsequent arrival of their children at the gates of academe during a decade which began with the collapse of institutional segregation and ended with the protest rallies, the mass marches, and the impassioned intellectual debates over war, racism, and poverty which shattered the tranquillity of picturesque Southern campuses.

If the historical landmarks suggest that baby boomers were both the beneficiaries and the moral burden-bearers of allied victory over the Axis powers, they also point to the key importance of higher education in determining the social meaning of the war and its aftermath. So far as I am aware no historian during the period of the Civil War centennial devoted more than passing attention to the subject of higher education.[1] The omission, if that is what it was, underscored the marginal significance of higher learning in a preindustrial slave society and pointed up the basic irrelevance of colleges and universities to the Southern war effort. A scholarly paper on the subject might almost have begun and ended with the observation that the war brought higher education to a standstill in the Confederacy as students and faculty abandoned their studies to join a conflict in which the activities of educational institutions would play no part.

As late as the time of the first World War, an event which helped propel the South into the modern world, institutions of formal learning remained peripheral to the nation's overall military success. This was true despite an unprecedented military reliance on the specialized skills and knowledge which university graduates possessed. The army of 1917 had need of physicians, chemists, engineers and even Ph.D.s in psychology to devise and administer the standardized group tests used to classify recruits and select potential officers— the same tests which would later be used to argue that human inequality was a function of heredity rather than environment.[2] Indirectly, of course, universities provided the Army's trained professionals and academic experts. But their services were usually rendered in uniform after enlistment had removed them from an academic setting. In the end production and logistics rather than research or technological innovation were what mattered on the killing fields of France. Despite the launching of a short lived Student Army Training Corps during the closing months of the bloody conflict, an enterprise that anticipated the shape of things to come, colleges and universities, *as institutions*, had little chance to participate directly in America's first global conflict. As had been true in the 1860s, academic mobilization manifested itself primarily through the depopulation of campuses when male faculty and students heeded the patriotic summons of America's Ph.D.-holding Commander-in-Chief.[3]

The historic pattern of incompatibility between war and higher learning in America ended abruptly in the aftermath of Pearl Harbor. Its demise reflected the burgeoning power and complexity of science during the interwar decades as well as the recognition that advanced training and specialized skills had become central to the functioning of a bureaucratic and technological society. In ways that were not always immediately clear World War II constituted a turning point both for American higher education and for Southern colleges and universities, bringing the latter into a new relationship with the national government and setting in motion forces that would permanently reorder their priorities, remake their institutional culture, and alter their relationship with society at large.

In assessing the Second World War's meaning for Southern schools it is useful, at the outset, to differentiate between higher education's short term response to the conditions of national emergency between 1942 and 1945 and the long term changes that were often implicit in wartime events. Strictly speaking all but a few wartime educational programs were "temporary" measures important less for their direct accomplishments than for the precedents they established. In the areas of research and graduate training, social access to higher education, gender relations, and even intercollegiate athletics conventional practices were altered during the war and future educational patterns were established or anticipated by wartime events. It is at this level, as a harbinger of the Cold War's far reaching impact upon education and other phases of American domestic life, that the campus militarization of the 1940s assumes historical significance. With the preceding considerations in mind one may begin to explore the admittedly fascinating subject of how Southern colleges and universities experienced World War II and how they were transformed by the forces it unleashed.

Perhaps the central message conveyed to educators by developments of the 1940s was that the welfare, the fate, and often the very survival of individual schools would hinge directly upon their ability to serve the needs of the federal government—to become what University of California Chancellor Clark Kerr would later describe as "instruments of national purpose," a phrase pregnant with meaning for Southern schools. Any thought that institutions of higher education would be less than active participants in the war against fascism was dispelled at a meeting in Baltimore, Maryland, on January 3–4, 1942, attended by officials of the Office of Education, the Army, the Navy, and 1000 college and university executive officers from forty-six states. The meeting resulted, among other things, in unambiguous declarations concerning the importance attached to higher education by the armed services, together with a general understanding that colleges would adopt "accelerated" year round schedules allowing graduation in three years, while placing increased emphasis upon physical conditioning of male college students, and allowing academic credit for various types of war-related instruction.[4]

Even before this time, under the stimulus of President Roosevelt's 1939 preparedness initiatives, ROTC programs had been established or expanded at a number of Southern schools, ranging in size from small junior college units to the mammoth enterprise at Texas A & M University which, directly or indirectly, claimed credit for training some 14,000 officers who served in World War II.[5] With the age for conscription set at 21 in the 1940 Selective Service Act—the nation's first peacetime draft—most college men were initially able to continue their studies by joining one of the Navy's V-1, V-5, V-7, or comparable Army and Army Air Corps Enlisted Reserve programs which proliferated on college campuses during 1942.[6] These arrangements together with an increased enrollment of female students on many campuses kept undergraduate attendance at or near normal levels during the war's first year as college and university administrators waited uneasily for the government's announcement of specific educational plans. By 1943, however, the lowering of the draft age to 18 together with the actual or impending mobilization of many reserve units, presented Southern schools with a potential crisis. It was at this juncture that the previous year's discussions bore fruit in the form of three large scale military initiatives that would replace the dwindling supply of civilian students on college campuses with what often seemed like an invasion of blue or khaki uniforms.

Beginning in the summer of 1943 and continuing for the next twelve to eighteen months the great majority of white colleges and universities in the South, plus a smaller number of black schools, took part in some phase of the Army Specialized Training Program (ASTP), the Navy College Training Program, better known as the "V-12" Program, or the Army Air Forces College Training Program. Each of the plans brought students into higher education as active duty, uniformed soldiers or sailors whose room, board, medical, and instructional costs were paid by the military. The Army program was the most rigid of the three, segregating its student-soldiers into separate classes with a basic curriculum that was heavily weighted toward engineering and mathematics and prohibiting the trainees from joining regular campus organizations or participating in intercollegiate athletics. Presumably the weekly schedule of 24 hours of course work and an equal amount of "required study" plus five hours of military drill and six hours of physical training left little time for extracurricular pursuits.[7] Because of its curricular requirements in engineering the ASTP functioned in the South primarily at leading technological schools and Land Grant universities such as Virginia Polytechnic Institute, Georgia Tech, Texas A & M, and Auburn, together with public 'flagship' institutions such as the University of Alabama, Louisiana State University, and the University of Virginia which hosted a school for military government of occupied territories.[8] On occasion leading private universities such as Vanderbilt or smaller institutions like Washington and Lee also received ASTP contracts.[9]

Forced on a reluctant Army high command which saw the college program as an obstacle to rapid mobilization, the ASTP lacked clear goals and was often at odds with the basic norms of academic life. Most students joined the program expecting to become officers but relatively few outside the professional specialties of medicine and dentistry were able to achieve even NCO status, much less go on to Officer Candidate School. When most campus programs were abruptly terminated in March, 1944 many ASTP students found themselves headed for duty as combat riflemen during and after the Normandy invasion.[10] A fairly typical experience was that of young Leon Standifer, a white Mississippian who graduated from high school in 1942 and signed up for ASTP while spending his freshman year at Mississippi College, a small Baptist institution. Assured that he would be sent to study engineering at the University of Arkansas, Standifer instead found himself wading ashore on D-Day at Utah Beach after preliminary stops at Fort Benning, Georgia, and Camps Shelby and McCain in Mississippi. Standifer's experience, which was replicated for perhaps 100,000 ASTP trainees, gave both students and college administrators ample grounds for dissatisfaction with the Army's approach to higher education.[11]

Far more compatible with the normal academic agenda of most colleges was the Navy's V-12 program which functioned at a total of thirty-two Southern schools. Host institutions included a number of the South's leading private universities including Duke, Rice, Emory, and Tulane as well as major public schools such as Georgia Tech and the state universities of Virginia, Texas, North Carolina, and South Carolina. Programs at these institutions typically enrolled 900–1300 students per term although V-12 contracts were also extended to smaller second tier schools including the University of Miami, the University of Louisville, Louisiana Tech, Arkansas A & M, Southwestern University, and Texas Christian University. Smaller scale V-12 programs enrolling 200–400 students operated at a number of church-related liberal arts colleges including four Baptist schools (Mississippi College in Clinton, Mississippi, Howard College in Birmingham, Alabama, Mercer University in Macon, Georgia, and Carson-Newman College in Tennessee), and two Methodist colleges (Millsaps College in Mississippi and Emory and Henry in Virginia). The Episcopalian University of the South in Sewanee, Tennessee, Mount St. Mary's College in Maryland, a Catholic school, the Presbyterian Hampton-Sidney College in Virginia, and Kentucky's Berea College, a non-denominational Christian school supported by northern missionary groups, also had V-12 units.[12] Unlike the ASTP, the V-12 program was primarily a mechanism for recruiting college educated Naval officers and from the outset the Navy sought to cooperate with academic administrators in designing curricular requirements and regulations that would be nonintrusive and infringe as little as possible upon institutional prerogatives. "They do not expect to run the place," Duke University's President noted with obvious relief after an initial meeting in which Navy officials sought to contract for the housing and instruction of some 1600 student reservists in medicine, advanced engineering and the basic V-12 curriculum.[13] Inevitably, of course, the Navy program, like its Army counterpart, produced changes in the academic emphasis and campus environment of the schools involved, a point that will receive further discussion. But unlike ASTP trainees the V-12 students attended normal civilian classes, joined a full range of campus organizations, and were allowed to participate in intercollegiate athletics. The basic V-12 curriculum emphasized math, physics, and engineering but also included five hours of history and English, or foreign languages, in the first and second semester, thereby staying reasonably close to a normal liberal arts pattern. Naval ROTC which already existed at Tulane, Rice, Texas, and other schools was absorbed by the V-12 program and student reservists were allowed to continue studying at their home institutions whenever V-12 programs existed at the schools.[14]

Less well known than the Navy and Army programs, but probably having a direct effect on more Southern schools, was the Army Air Forces College Training Program. Nominally intended to give future aviation cadets academic preparation for future preflight training, the program kept each trainee on a college campus for only 21 weeks and offered a rather muddled curriculum that eventually included many remedial courses aimed at poorly prepared students including some enlisted men who had not attended high school. Although the program accommodated groups of 1000–1200 students at the University of Tennessee, Texas Tech, the University of Arkansas, and Texas A & M, and somewhat smaller groups at North Carolina State University, Mississippi State, the University of Alabama, the University of Florida, the University of West Virginia, and the University of Tampa, it was of particular financial benefit to small liberal arts colleges which faced critical shortages of students and could not qualify for other military training programs. The Air Force contracted with many of the South's best known church related and secular colleges including Birmingham-Southern, Centenary College in Louisiana, Southwestern in Memphis, Maryville College in Tennessee, Transylvania in Kentucky, Elon College in North Carolina, and Furman University in South Carolina, as well as a number of public normal schools such as Southwest Texas State Teachers College and Western Kentucky State Teachers College. Detachments of from 200–500 students were common at small colleges where they often outnumbered civilian students and kept enrollment at near normal levels.[15]

The preceding summaries inevitably oversimplify an exceedingly complex picture of Southern higher education's involvement in wartime student training. Tabulating all types of war-related educational programs the historian of Texas A & M University concluded that the school trained 23,604 personnel in the Engineering, Science, and Management War Training Program administered by the U. S. Office of Education under nominal military supervision, while giving instruction to an additional 13,364 students in radar and radio operation and maintenance. These short courses were in addition to the main work of educating 4000 Air Corps preflight cadets and 4105 ASTP students.[16] Large universities often contracted to provide educational services for two or even all three of the armed services and small schools occasionally shared facilities in order to accommodate a single program. In Louisiana, for example, Shreveport's Centenary College, a Methodist institution located near the huge Barksdale Air Force base, arranged with nearby Dodd College, a Baptist School, to provide housing for the 750 Air Force cadets assigned to Centenary's program. Another type of sharing took place in the tiny hamlet of Statesboro, Georgia, where, in 1943, Georgia Teachers College became a Specialized Training and Reassignment (STAR) center, absorbing the overflow of 500 officer training recruits and staff personnel from a larger STAR unit at the University of Alabama.[17] Schools of all sizes, whether or not they were parties to the major college training programs, provided more limited kinds of vocational and technical instruction for military personnel or civilians employed in defense industries. The University of Houston, for example, conducted courses in internal combustion engines and welding, and also trained machinists, electricians, and radio technicians for the Navy. Morehead State College in Kentucky carried on a similar range of programs while Mississippi Southern College—the present day University of Southern Mississippi—ran a series of eight week courses in military administration with a staggered schedule that kept two 165 member classes continually on campus.[18]

If small colleges were generally at a disadvantage in securing federal programs, the South's Negro institutions, as they were then called, labored under a double handicap. On many black campuses the contradiction inherent in battling Nazi racism while maintaining racial segregation at home gave rise to considerable ambivalence over the place of African-Americans in the war effort. At Fisk University in Nashville the president was a Quaker pacifist who took a leave of absence to organize conscientious objectors for the American Friends Service Committee. The President of Alabama's Talladega College refused to involve his school in war programs after his proposals to use the campus for interracial officer training were rebuffed.[19] More common than overt gestures of protest were efforts on the part of adroit but politically vulnerable black educators to link patriotism with the cause of racial progress. In Georgia the president of Albany State College cultivated a positive public image by serving as co-chair of the local war finance committee. In this capacity he invited black marching bands and prominent speakers to promote the Red Cross and the sale of war bonds while simultaneously supporting drives for black voter registration and inviting the NAACP Youth Council to establish a chapter on his campus. Many black colleges participated in war-related educational programs by offering special courses for various agencies within the military along with noncredit civilian courses sponsored by the Engineering, Science, and Management War Training Program. In 1943 Atlanta University conducted an Army Air Forces Administration School for black enlisted men and also offered a variety of courses under the auspices of the ESMWT program. Other black schools offering courses through ESMWT included Dillard University in New Orleans, Delaware State College, Howard University, West Virginia State College, North Carolina Agricultural and Technical College, Virginia State College, and Hampton Institute where a wide variety of vocational classes were available for black enlisted personnel in the Navy and Marines.[20]

Aviation provides a good example of the range of college programs connected with a single military activity. The Navy established a total of five college-based preflight schools, two of which were located in the South—one at the University of North Carolina, the other at the University of Georgia. The Georgia school was a massive undertaking which made use of eighteen existing buildings, enlarged two others, and paid for construction of three new dormitories, a garage, a field house, a new track and four new athletic fields used to train over 6000 cadets. The University also conducted a small Navy Officers Flying School and had additional training contracts with the ASTP, and the Army Signal Corps.[21] North Carolina's efforts were also ambitious. The University of South Carolina played a more restricted role when it inaugurated a V-5 Naval Flight Preparatory School in 1943 as well as a separate course for 100 men assigned to the Civil Aeronautics Administration's War Training Service Program. Furman University, another South Carolina school, combined preflight instruction for some 300 Air Force cadets with a special program to train 85 glider pilots during a six month period in 1942–43.[22] In 1941 Alabama's Tuskegee Institute, which had operated a civilian program for black pilots since 1939, became the training center for fighter pilots in the all black 99th Pursuit Squadron commanded by Colonel Benjamin O. Davis. Controversial from its inception, the Tuskegee program inspired pride among many blacks even as it drew criticism for perpetuating segregation within the military.[23]

A third aspect of Southern college involvement in wartime aviation training could be seen at Louisiana State Normal College in Natchitoches, renamed Northwestern State College of Louisiana in 1944. Before the war the State Normal had offered a pilot training course sanctioned by the Civil Aeronautics Authority and from January, 1943 until December, 1944 Northwestern conducted a Navy Flight Preparatory School for classes of 600 trainees, the majority of whom were active duty Navy, Marine, or Coast Guard personnel transferred from the enlisted ranks. Unlike V-12 trainees the Flight Preparatory students were not officer candidates. Few, if any, were high school graduates and many had only eight years of formal education. Although their courses in mathematics, physics, navigation, communications, principles of flight, aircraft engines and similar matters did not carry academic credit they were taught by regular college faculty using books and syllabi furnished by the Navy.[24]

By the war's end, when Northwestern Louisiana's Flight Preparatory School had been replaced by a Navy V-5 Refresher Unit offering college courses to active duty personnel seeking officer's commissions, the once sleepy normal school campus had played host to more than 2000 Navy men representing "Every state, every economic level, [and] education[al backgrounds] ranging from 8 grades to three years of college. . . ."[25] Although the range of educational backgrounds was unusual similar patterns of socioeconomic and geographic diversity prevailed among Army and Navy students at other Southern schools where religious homogeneity and localism had previously held sway. Naval authorities sent hundreds of Texans to Georgia and dispatched large California contingents to Texas schools. Nearly half of the first group of V-12 trainees at South Carolina's Newberry College came from Illinois or Iowa while the future University of Southwestern Louisiana counted Navy students from 43 states, the District of Columbia, Puerto Rico, and Mexico.[26] Northern Catholic students cracked the hard shell of Baptist institutions such as Alabama's Howard College and Georgia's Mercer University where an active sectional rivalry developed between students from Texas and Illinois. A fascinating glimpse of the "culture shock" experienced by an urban "Yankee" thrust unceremoniously into the educational milieu of the rural South is provided in the memoirs of Clarice Fortgang Pollard, a Jewish WAAC from Brooklyn, New York, who studied Army Administration at Stephen F. Austin State Teachers College in Nacogdoches, Texas. Repelled by the emphasis on fried foods and lard in the local diet, and amused by the sound of Hebrew passages read with a "warm Texas drawl" during Passover services in a private home, Pollard found classes conducted during 100 degree heat to be "an experience to melt the mind." Her most lasting impressions of the teaching staff centered around an assortment of colorful figures whose "habits of expression were highly individual." The pedagogical approach of one instructor made a particularly strong impression.

> Lieutenant Harrington read all his lessons to us from a notebook, which kept him one page ahead of us. With the delivery of a Boy Scout leader giving instructions to an eager troop, he shouted his lessons phrase by phrase from his notes. When he misread, he called out "Hold the Phone!" or "Wait a Minute!" and recounted the correct version of the message with one arm raised in the air, index finger pointing at the stars.[27]

The sheer number of students involved in wartime educational programs and the diverse backgrounds from which they were drawn helped plant the seeds of change in Southern higher learning. The precedent of educational democratization established by the war was significant from both a psychological and a political standpoint. In the face of a dire national emergency the Federal government had made higher education a national priority and had provided both the means and the incentive for ordinary citizens to pursue advanced training. Those with the talent for college were unlikely to forget even a brief encounter with higher learning; and they were all but certain to remember that when their services were most needed the government had been willing to foot the bill for the entire cost of college instruction.

Without the wartime experience it is difficult to imagine that the normally conservative American Legion would have made higher education a key element in the omnibus package of veteran's benefits enacted as The Servicemen's Readjustment Act of 1944, better known as the "G. I. Bill of Rights."[28] Indeed, the Legion's uncharacteristically liberal stance becomes even more striking when it is counterposed to the more outwardly conservative position taken by America's educational establishment, with strong influence and support from Southern members. The earliest proposals for federally sponsored postwar educational benefits came not from veterans groups but from the Roosevelt administration's Committee on Postwar Educational Opportunities for Service Personnel, a body chaired by General Frederick H. Osborne and composed of various figures connected with wartime education including U. S. Commissioner of Education John W. Studebaker, Columbia Law School Dean Dexter M. Keezer, and Tulane University President Rufus Carrollton Harris who served as the Committee's Vice-Chair. Working in an environment of Congressional hostility to postwar centralized planning, sensitive over wartime infringements upon the autonomy of academic institutions, and fearful that open-ended federal subsidies would attract weak students and tempt colleges to lower academic standards in order to maximize revenue, the Osborne Committee proposed a limited veteran's aid program that would, in effect, have restored the pre-1942 educational status quo by providing just enough federal support to eliminate the war-related "educational deficit" in college graduates.[29]

The closest thing to an official "Southern" position on the issue of postwar educational aid was set forth in a series of resolutions probably written by President Harris of Tulane and adopted in December, 1943 by the Executive Committee of the Southern University Conference, a forty-three member group that included virtually all of the region's major universities and stronger liberal arts colleges. Without directly addressing the issue of how large the federal aid program should be the Conference urged that the individual veteran receive college benefits large enough to cover the "necessary cost of maintenance and education in the school of his choice." The Conference also declared that each veteran should be free to determine his own course of study and "have the right and privilege of selecting the institution which he will attend," provided that the school had been duly accredited by a recognized agency. The South-ern Conference position, which stressed that individual veterans rather than colleges should be the contracting parties with the federal government, gained support from the National Conference of Church-Related Colleges and from the Association of American Colleges, headed by former Birmingham-Southern President Guy E. Snavley.[30] The final "G. I. Bill" legislation incorporated all of the principles enumerated in the 1943 resolutions.

The men who endorsed the 1943 resolutions (women were conspicuous by their absence from the ranks of Southern academic leadership) were reacting, in part, to the disruptions of a wartime situation and the corresponding wish to regain institutional equilibrium by keeping the government at arms length in a postwar setting. Behind the seemingly straightforward recommendations lay a keen awareness of the challenges Southern colleges and universities would face in the postwar era as they sought to accommodate egalitarian and modernizing influences within the context of a regional political culture that was remarkably impervious to both. Such an environment made the entire question of higher education's relationship to federal authority a delicate matter. With contractual relations under the "G. I. Bill" limited to an agreement between individual students and the federal government, Southern schools could avoid, for the moment, being caught in a direct clash between opposing political and social tendencies. Until the mid-1950s they would have space to maneuver in a fluid environment which allowed for the rapid expansion of higher education's social base without direct or immediate legislative challenge to racial segregation (that would come from the courts), and with a renewed emphasis upon academic quality through the expansion of research and the creation of new institutional hierarchies.

The "G. I. Bill," once enacted, did not operate in a vacuum. In the South neither African-American veterans nor women had a range of educational choices equal to those of white men, academic resolutions to the contrary notwithstanding. Although a separate paper, if not a major book, would be necessary to do justice to either the racial or the gender components of Southern higher education during the years in question, a few observations may help suggest the outlines of a larger inquiry. In education, as in so many other areas of American life, the war years were less a turning point for women than a temporary detour in the road to resurgent peacetime domesticity. From time to time during the two years in which undergraduate women constituted a majority of the civilian students on most Southern campuses there were glimpses of the kinds of change that would take place a generation or more later with the rise of the modern feminist movement. In some cases the absence of civilian men placed female students in unaccustomed roles of leadership when, as at the University of Tampa in 1943, a woman was chosen student body president for the first time in the school's history. But at other schools such as North Texas State Teachers College where women outnumbered men by a ratio of 6:1 in 1944–45 numbers seemed to produce no change in female status.[31]

On balance, however, there is little to suggest that the wholesale militarization of Southern campuses enhanced the prospects for gender equality. If anything, the exclusion of women from the draft underscored their subordinate social status and left them in the same category as physically unfit men—the much maligned "4-Fers"—and draft-exempt ministerial students who received few accolades in a war atmosphere. Perhaps more to the point, there is little evidence that wartime conditions worked to the advantage of female faculty members whose career prospects might logically have been expected to improve with the departure of male colleagues. In a rare study of the question published in 1946 Eoline Wallace Moore, a professor of education at Birmingham-Southern College, compared employment data for Alabama colleges during the war years with statistics gathered in 1926, 1931, and 1939. She found that despite a substantial increase in the number of graduate degrees awarded to women during the interwar decades, and notwithstanding an acute wartime shortage of male faculty, "Little significant change in the ratio of women to men teachers in Alabama colleges has resulted from war conditions."[32]

The GI Bill did little to alter the gender disparities in Southern higher learning. Across the region, as throughout the nation, adult veterans and their families imparted a more serious tone to campus life and helped legitimate the practice of student marriage within a framework that gave primacy to male career goals. In the South conservative religious dogma and a feminine ideal built largely around the experiences of a leisured upper class lent powerful reinforcement to the view that marriage and motherhood were the most appropriate outcome, if not the stated goal, of female college attendance.[33] For Southern women, therefore, the late 1940s marked the beginning of a pronounced remasculinizing of higher learning which saw female influence recede as the number of women students remained relatively stable while male veteran enrollments exploded. Nearly three decades would elapse before gradual increases in the proportion of women attending college produced roughly equal numbers of male and female undergraduates on Southern campuses of the 1980s. Although the upturn in female enrollment can be traced to the mid 1950s, its impact upon the gender climate of postwar college life was minimal.[34] In the virile world of Southern universities during the two decades after 1945, a setting replete with high spirited "panty raids," close order drill by awkward ROTC cadets, and ritualized combat in intercollegiate football, white college women encountered a range of less than subtle cues concerning their perceived status as ornamental husband-seekers.

Some of the clearest messages came from the admissions offices of leading Southern institutions like the University of North Carolina at Chapel Hill which established a "Coed Quota" of 1,000 in 1946 in order to accommodate more male veterans and announced that "additional student body increases in the next few years will be made by men students." A policy of restricting female admissions to "especially well qualified" applicants remained in force until overturned by federal law in 1972.[35] Policies at the South's leading private schools were equally unfair to women. At Vanderbilt where the Board of Trust had refused to permit the enrollment of additional women during the war, a postwar gender quota lifted female enrollment to one-third of the College of Arts and Sciences student body, a percentage that translated into 125 entering women each year and roughly 25 percent of the total undergraduate student body. Vanderbilt's quota system also remained in force until 1972.[36] At Rice University "a quota of sorts" limited female enrollment to the number of men in the liberal arts curriculum. Until 1966 the University provided only one female dormitory and few other facilities. These conditions led historian Fredericka Meiners, a Rice alumna, to characterize her alma mater during the postwar era as "primarily a man's school, with women enrolled."[37]

On its face the GI Bill was color blind, providing the same package of fixed living expenses plus full tuition at the school of one's choice to both black and white Southerners. Yet, when applied within the framework of rigid inequality created by Southern segregation, veterans' college benefits can scarcely be regarded as the kind of nationally uniform educational voucher system conjured up by nostalgia prone historians of the 1980s.[38] Throughout the life span of the GI Bill the majority of black college students attended segregated Southern institutions that were vastly inferior to their white coun-terparts. Chronically impoverished and excluded from the larger processes of educational policy making, Negro colleges were poorly situated to accommodate a sudden influx of veterans, much less provide for their educational needs.[39] Roughly half of the black colleges had less than 500 students and only a handful offered serious graduate work.[40] Apart from Howard University in

Washington, D. C., opportunities for advanced graduate work and professional training scarcely existed for blacks in the South. Across the entire region in the late 1940s there were but two accredited black medical schools, one provisionally accredited law school, one program in pharmacy and none at all in engineering. Professional schools at Howard had ten times more applicants than available places and elsewhere less prestigious black schools turned away some 20,000 veterans during 1946 and 1947 because of limited space. Probably few of these individuals would have concluded that the doors of higher education were fully open.[41]

When due allowance is made for Southern higher education's gender and racial inequities, the Second World War must still be regarded as the catalyst for an unprecedented drive toward educational democratization. The connection between the war and college expansion was especially clear in Alabama where the influx of veterans in the late 1940s prompted the opening or expansion of University of Alabama branch campuses in Birmingham, Montgomery, Mobile, Selma, Gadsden, and Huntsville. Aggregate registration at these "extension centers," as they were initially called, temporarily surpassed enrollment at the main Tuscaloosa campus. And in the next two decades several of the centers would become permanent institutions.[42] The late forties also witnessed a major push for the expansion of trade schools, a cause championed in the Alabama legislature by one George C. Wallace, a young and seemingly liberal protégé of Governor James E. ("Big Jim") Folsom.[43] For Wallace the trade school issue was a harbinger of the ambitious program of junior college expansion that would take place during his extended political reign in the 1960s. Beginning in 1963 Alabama created a network of two-year schools virtually from scratch, with Governor Wallace eventually dispensing the construction contracts, architects' fees, real estate opportunities, state payrolls, and choice administrative posts associated with no less than forty-one new junior colleges and technical schools scattered for optimum political effect across the length and breadth of a state in the throes of court-ordered legislative reapportionment. During the 1960s when national enthusiasm for junior and community colleges reached a peak, other Southern states exhibited a strong commitment to what Wallace would later describe as "higher education for the average working man."[44] During the two decades after 1948 the number of two-year institutions in the South grew by almost 150 percent while enrollment in those schools increased five-fold, a growth rate slightly higher than the national average. What distinguished the South from most other regions was the relatively higher proportion of beginning students who attended two-year rather than four-year schools. By 1968, more than one-fifth of all deep South under-graduates outside of South Carolina and Louisiana enrolled in community or junior colleges. Only the far West, led by California, reported a higher percentage of two-year enrollment.[45] The South's expenditures on junior and community colleges, mired as they often were in political patronage, constituted the region's most serious attempt to realize, albeit imperfectly, the vision of universal education through the "13th and 14th grade" advocated by the Truman administration's Commission on Higher Education in 1947.[46]

If one could somehow ignore the fact that the racial politics of the 1960s caused figures like George Wallace to undermine the upper echelons of higher learning even while expanding its base, it would be accurate to say that the broad outlines of postwar Southern college expansion resembled the larger national pattern.[47] After the early 1950s institutions of all types—large and small, public and private, religious and secular, old and new—experienced annual increases in the number of student applications. As was true in other regions, enrollment grew most dramatically in the South's public institutions which, by the early 1970s, contained nearly four-fifths of those attending college. At that juncture Southern higher education enrolled almost 2,000,000 students, a 700 percent increase since 1940 and a figure three times greater than the peak veteran enrollment of 1948. During the single decade of the 1960s the South's college population doubled.[48] During the postwar growth era some schools seized the opportunity to become more academically selective while others mingled egalitarian principles with budgetary expedience to derive the greatest fiscal benefit from tuition revenues and public funds allocated on a *per capita* basis. The result was a larger and vastly more diverse institutional network encompassing postsecondary vocational schools, research universities, and a broad range of two and four year colleges and comprehensive universities falling between the two extremes.

If junior colleges carried forward democratizing tendencies that were rooted in the wartime experience, the development of research universities attested to the Second World War's importance in stimulating qualitative improvement in Southern higher learning. At the heart of the postwar expansion of Southern research universities was the pattern of federal support for scientific research set during World War II through the work of the National Defense Research Committee and the Office of Scientific Research and Development, the agencies which mobilized much of the scientific and technological talent needed for work on projects ranging from the development of radar, napalm, and the proximity fuse to biological warfare research and the initial stages of the Manhattan Project.[49] At the time of Pearl Harbor American scientific talent was heavily concentrated in the network of research universities created through private foundation philanthropy during the 1920s and 1930s. These schools—basically the Ivy League institutions plus the strongest state universities in California and the Midwest—accounted for the great bulk of OSRD research.[50] Although many individual Southern physicians and scientists (including some, like Alabama's Robert Van de Graaff, who had already migrated to the North) made valuable contributions to the war effort both in and out of uniform, Southern universities played only a minor part in war research, primarily because they lacked the facilities and the top talent found elsewhere. Medical schools accounted for many of the South's contracts with OSRD as did applied engineering projects such as the development of aerial bomb sight testing at the University of Texas and work on electronic communications amplifiers at Georgia Tech.[51]

In the short run research actually suffered at many Southern schools during the war because of the heavy demands on faculty who were called upon to teach large numbers of military trainees in what was basically an introductory scientific curriculum. Graduate work languished as students and faculty entered the military while professors who remained on campus took on new responsibilities. Between 1941 and December, 1943 the number of students enrolled in Southern graduate schools declined from 12,590 to 6,864—or only 5972 if one eliminates the 1351 students at the Catholic University of America in Washington, D. C. Some two thirds of the South's roughly 6000 wartime graduate students were found in seven schools: the state universities of North Carolina, Texas, Louisiana, Kentucky, and Virginia together with Duke and George Peabody College for Teachers in Nashville. Only "skeleton" graduate programs remained at Emory, Vanderbilt, and Tulane where 1943 enrollments ranged from 25 to 39 students. As Tulane's Graduate Dean observed, his program had reached a state of "suspended animation" while professors devoted their energies to Naval instruction of "a very elementary grade"[52]

This picture would change dramatically in the postwar era as plans unfolded to preserve and nominally "civilianize" federal science patronage. The principal line of bureaucratic descent ran from the moribund OSRD to the embryonic Office of Naval Research created in 1945 with a mandate to pursue basic research that was "pure and imaginative." Like the OSRD the new ONR operated primarily through project grants to individual investigators on university campuses and set the pattern for research arrangements by similar agencies within the Air Force and later the Army. Government medical research continued without interruption as the newly expanded National Institutes of Health absorbed much of the activity previously underwritten by National Defense Research Committee, while the ONR and its Army and Air Force counterparts sponsored many additional biomedical projects. Again the mechanism for government funding of university research was the project grant system. In the field of nuclear science the legacy of the Manhattan Project fell to the Atomic Energy Commission, a civilian agency which after its creation in 1946 evolved as a "skeletal bureaucracy" overseeing extensive contract research at universities and in the private sector.[53]

Slowly at first but more rapidly as the Cold War heated up Southern schools became competitors for a share of the federal research budget. During the seven year period from 1948 to 1953 no less than thirteen Southern institutions, mainly state universities and engineering schools, granted their first earned doctorates, while at least three additional campuses revived Ph.D. programs after decades of quiescence. From the early 1950s through the early 1960s the South's annual production of Ph.D.'s in the liberal arts and sciences (excluding education degrees) averaged 23 doctorates per institution. The University of Texas led the way with an average of 125 new Ph.D.'s per year followed by the University of North Carolina with 82, Duke University with 69 and the University of Florida with sixty-five.[54] Although the South produced no research universities of truly preeminent stature during the quarter century after 1945, a number of institutions positioned themselves for emergence onto the national scene. By the mid-to-late 1960s peer ratings placed major Southern universities such as the University of Texas, North Carolina, Duke, Florida, Rice, Virginia, Vanderbilt, Tulane, Emory, and Florida State somewhere in the middle third of the national research hierarchy.[55]

More than any other single factor the increased emphasis on graduate training and research led Southern institutions to adopt a more realistic and self-critical posture as they began to measure themselves against national rather than local or regional standards. Inevitably the new outlook produced tensions between modernizing universities and their alumni. One symptom of the contrast between older and newer ideas of what Southern universities should represent was the struggle over the place of intercollegiate athletics—particularly football—in postwar college life. Once again the story begins in 1942–43 when conscription, ASTP regulations, wartime travel restrictions, and a certain uneasiness with frivolity in the midst of death led many colleges and universities to suspend or de-emphasize intercollegiate football for the duration of the conflict. Advocates of suspension included small schools which found the game burdensome and large football powers whose Army affiliations stood in the way of fielding competitive teams against rivals that were well stocked with V-12 and other Navy players.[56] In the South football was suspended at major Southeastern Conference schools such as Auburn, the state universities of Alabama, Tennessee, and Kentucky, and the publicly supported colleges of Louisiana and Mississippi. Less powerful competitors including Vanderbilt, Washington and Lee, William and Mary, Mercer University, Howard College, the University of Tampa, Virginia Polytechnic Institute, and East Texas State Teachers College also dropped the game.[57] In the long run the vigorous effort in Navy preflight programs to link competitive athletics to combat training helped set the stage for a new era of postwar excess in intercollegiate sports. Naval flight trainees at the University of Georgia and North Carolina learned that football was analogous to war. The 83 coaches assigned to each group of 1500–2000 trainees followed a syllabus that aimed to strip young men of socially acquired inhibitions against aggression, and to impress upon them that for "ruthless, determined competitors" there could be "no substitute for winning" and that "gracious defeat should be forgotten." A number of postwar football coaches including Charles "Bud" Wilkinson and Paul "Bear" Bryant served as Navy physical training instructors on land or at sea.[58]

During the 1940s, however, the paramilitary fanaticism of Southern college football still lay in the future. Wartime curtailment of college athletic schedules and the reduced importance attached to football by spectators during the war raised hopes in some quarters that once peace was restored Southern schools could avoid a return to past athletic excesses. In a speech to the Southeastern Conference that was subsequently published in the April, 1944 issue of the *Southern Coach and Athlete* Tulane President Rufus Harris urged colleges to take advantage of diminished public pressure and seize the opportunity to reorganize intercollegiate sports upon a "sane, reasonable basis." Among the specific changes he advocated were the elimination of scouting and spring training, the restriction of fall practice sessions to one hour per day, a reduction in the number and amount of athletic scholarships, and the hiring of coaches whose vocabularies were "rich in something besides profanity" and whose literary interests extended beyond the content of "sport pages and comic strips."[59]

The best chance, and probably the only real hope, for reforming intercollegiate athletics in the South lay in regulatory measures imposed from outside the region. For a brief moment after the war such a solution seemed within reach when nationwide concern over controlling expenses and preserving, or restoring, amateurism in college sports led the National Collegiate Athletic Association to adopt its 1948 "sanity code" limiting student athletic grants to the cost of tuition and incidental fees and requiring that awards be based upon need. Under the new regulations athletes would not receive grants covering room and board and were expected to seek part time employment to defray personal expenses. For the first time the NCAA seemed ready to enforce its own rules and, in theory at least, schools that violated the code could be expelled from the national organization.[60]

Southern institutions led the way in evading or openly defying the new rules and by the time of the 1950 NCAA convention seven schools including the Citadel in South Carolina, the University of Maryland, the University of Virginia, Virginia Military Institute, and Virginia Polytechnic Institute were officially charged with sanity code violations. An unsuccessful attempt to expel the offenders revealed that small colleges and Northern schools including many "Big Ten" representatives generally supported the sanity code while large Southern schools vociferously opposed it. During the following months Dixie's football spokesmen unblushingly called for a return to the time honored principle of "institutional integrity," a philosophy that would leave enforcement of NCAA rules entirely in the hands of individual schools or local conferences. Other Southern proposals attacked the sanity code directly by seeking to eliminate the restrictions on aid to student athletes. At the NCAA's 1951 convention it was Southern historian Albert D. Kirwan, faculty representative from the University of Kentucky, who went furthest in claiming the moral high ground for unlimited aid. "If it is not morally wrong to grant a student his institutional fees so that he may be able to go to college, and play football," Kirwan asked rhetorically, "why should it be evil to give him three meals a day and a bed to sleep in . . . ?"[61] Quite possibly Professor Kirwan looked upon generous athletic grants as the lesser of evils since his own institution was, even then, embroiled in a major national scandal over sports gambling and basketball "point shaving," moral lapses which a few months later would cause a trial judge to describe Kentucky's athletic program as "the acme of commercialism and over emphasis." At the 1951 convention, however, Kirwan's position easily prevailed and, amid "cheers and much back slapping," the sanity code was effectively emasculated.[62]

The failure of athletic reform at the national level left Southern leaders of the de-emphasis movement—primarily Harris and Vanderbilt Chancellor Harvie Branscomb—in a lonely position. In 1951, after trying unsuccessfully to persuade Tulane, Duke, Rice, Washington University and the University of Virginia to join Vanderbilt in forming what would have been tantamount to a Southern version of the Ivy League, Branscomb wryly observed that Vanderbilt was "located in a spot where Ivy does not seem to flourish."[63] Later that year reform proposals in the SEC went down to a resounding defeat. For the remainder of the decade Tulane and Vanderbilt remained isolated critics of the win-at any-cost philosophy that prevailed at major public universities. The most either school could do was to set a good example. Alone among SEC institutions Tulane and Vanderbilt endorsed a 1952 report of the American Council on Education advocating faculty control of athletic policy, a shortened football season, new limitations upon athletic grants-in-aid, an end to bowl games, recruiting payments, paid campus visits, and special admissions standards for athletes.[64] For a few years both schools managed to rein in big time sports on their own campuses by reducing the number of football "scholarships," limiting the size of coaching staffs, eliminating or refusing to provide a physical education major or other special courses for athletes, and giving faculty a direct role in the formulation of athletic policy. These changes, in conjunction with the NCAA's more restrictive substitution rule designed to end platooning and reduce the level of specialization among college players, did briefly check the momentum of football's plunge toward professionalism. Throughout the 1950s Tulane and Vanderbilt awarded fewer athletic grants-in-aid than any other SEC schools, but initial efforts to reduce the annual number of football stipends to seventy-five could not be sustained. After a second effort to create a Southern Ivy League failed in the early 1960s it was apparent that research and Division One athletics were destined to occupy conspicuous if antagonistic positions in the political economy of Southern higher learning.[65]

Like colleges and universities throughout America, Southern institutions were moving inexorably from the periphery toward the center of national life in the postwar decades. Beneath the rhetoric of regional pride and institutional autonomy that was still served up to Southern alumni during the 1950s and '60s lay an increasingly intricate pattern of relationships with government, private enterprise and large scale philanthropy. The new pattern of interdependence had implications that were far reaching. As most universities had discovered during World War II federal, and particularly military, sponsorship of research favored the sciences at the expense of the humanities and left even the favored scientific disciplines subject to the vagaries of changing governmental priorities. Wartime priorities had produced severe curricular imbalance within Tulane University's College of Arts and Sciences where the humanities languished after 1943 while the Schools of Engineering and Medicine were able to strengthen offerings in war-related specialties.[66] A different problem confronted the University of Alabama's School of Engineering which saw enrollments and fields of concentration fluctuate wildly between 1940 and 1944 in response to the Army's changing policies and curricular requirements. Similar patterns would manifest themselves during the 1960s when engineering enrollments at Alabama and other Southern schools rose and fell with the fortunes of the American space program.[67]

Southern higher education's junior partnership with the federal government began during World War II and continues through the present moment. The ultimate meaning of the relationship transcends questions of research funding, disciplinary rivalry, and changing power relationships between externally sponsored researchers and their host institutions—matters ably explored by University of California Chancellor Clark Kerr in his 1963 volume *The Uses of the University*. For many colleges within and outside the South the war marked the beginning of a prolonged identity crisis in which the purely utilitarian aspects of higher learning were weighed against more traditional conceptions of the university as center of disinterested inquiry and independent social criticism. No one grasped the war's deeper implications sooner or more vividly than Robert M. Hutchins, the brilliantly iconoclastic President of the University of Chicago. Writing in 1943 Hutchins, who was best known for his advocacy of the Great Books program and an approach to teaching rooted in classical metaphysics, warned against the perils of what he described as a dawning era of "education by contract." During the war, universities like Chicago were being "supported to solve problems selected by the government and to train men and women chosen by the government, using a staff assembled in terms of requirements laid down by the government." Hutchins had no illusions that "education by contract" would end with the war. He was convinced, on the contrary, that "a government which has once discovered that universities can be used to solve immediate problems is likely to intensify the practice as its problems grow more serious." But, as usual, Hutchins was not finished with the subject. "Since the government is establishing in the public mind the doctrine that technical training is the only education for war, the public mind will eventually conclude that technical training is the only education for peace," Hutchins predicted.[68]

Although spoken originally in a forceful Yankee cadence Hutchins's words resonate powerfully in the academic South of the late twentieth century. At a time when Southern, or nominally Southern, Congressmen and Senators, holding Ph.D.'s from Southern institutions, are seeking to "zero out" the already minuscule levels of public funding available for the arts, the humanities, educational television, and presumably any other activity that might please a literate Democrat, Hutchins's warnings take on a disturbing note of contemporary relevance. Coming on the heels of what is often described as a managerial revolution in higher education during the 1980s, a period when the vocabulary and techniques of commercial marketing, as well as a business corporation approach to institutional decision making found ready acceptance among financially hard pressed schools in search of paying customers, the current political assault on liberal learning is not so much a new departure as a consolidation of incremental changes that have long been under way.[69]

But contemporary public criticism of American universities represents more than a simple triumph of instrumentalist values over the true spirit of liberal humanism. In an era of shrinking blue collar employment, weak labor unions, and ruthless corporate "down sizing," economic insecurity has strengthened the hand of those cultural conservatives within and outside academia who long for an end to the troubling re-examination of America's egalitarian faith that was set in motion by the civil rights struggle and which continues on campuses of the 1990s in the form of debates over affirmative action, faculty tenure, and the racial and gender aspects of college curricula. Universities and tenured professors offer tempting targets for ideologues who seek to exploit public frustration over the loss of economic security while diverting attention away from the destructive forces unleashed by the wholesale deregulation of free enterprise. Seizing upon the shrill particularism of a few extremist figures in the ongoing (and entirely legitimate) academic arguments over feminism, gay rights, and ethnic studies, modern critics of the liberal university have become specialists in what F. Sheldon Hackney has termed "assassination by anecdote." The technique finds its fullest expression in a large body of polemical literature distinguished by a ready willingness to substitute rumor for fact when the inclusion of a particular episode will depict liberal professors in a manner that confirms popular prejudice and reinforces negative stereotypes concerning intellectuals and the nature of academic life. Untroubled by contradictions between professed aims and the means employed to achieve them, conservative critics often present themselves as defenders of academic freedom while seeking to mobilize political pressure for external interference by governing boards into the most sacrosanct domains of faculty authority including matters of curriculum, hiring, and promotion.

None of the tactics now being employed is entirely new but the challenge facing those who genuinely believe in the university's primary obligation to foster free inquiry and cultivate critical intelligence has seldom seemed more formidable than at present. Southern colleges, by reason of their long experience in combating the forces of intolerance, belong in the vanguard of any effort to defend the essence of higher learning from the threat of political intimidation or subservience to any creed or dogma that stands in the way of free inquiry—a process which depends ultimately upon the willingness of the individual investigator to ask the unwelcome question or to confront the most unpalatable truth. For a full generation after 1945 the combined effect of strong academic leadership, rising qualitative standards, and a professorate aroused to defend basic principles against external menace proved sufficient to maintain the vigor and integrity of Southern academic life. This was no small accomplishment in a region known for its susceptibility to what Wilbur J. Cash called the "savage ideal." Meeting present day threats will require an equally resilient dedication to protecting the inner life of universities.

For the student of Southern academic life World War II must inevitably cast a long shadow. The war and its aftermath brought Southern schools into the national mainstream and in the past quarter century Southern colleges and universities, freed from the burdens of segregation and chronic poverty, have achieved something approaching genuine parity with peer institutions through-out America. These gains were not achieved easily or without a considerable cost in money and human effort. It would be ironic and deeply tragic if the accomplishments of the postwar era should be diluted or slowly eroded in the coming decades through a failure of vision or a collapse of internal will and sense of purpose. As Southern higher education approaches the next millennium it will be necessary to recall the lessons of World War II and to apply them creatively in a world which seems suddenly bereft of familiar economic and geopolitical signposts. There will, of course, be bills to pay. But the likelihood of squaring accounts will be vastly improved if the basic prerequisites for serious scientific and intellectual work are kept clearly in view. This will require, among other things, that universities resist the temptation to rush headlong into a post-industrial drama which casts educational institutions in the role of high-tech corporations whose professor-employees market specialized skills to the highest bidder and dispense knowledge as a commodity to be purchased by customers called students. As economically rational as corporate-university partnerships may often appear to be, the university per se cannot and must not remake itself in the image of IBM. In any such Faustian bargain fiscal solvency would have been purchased at much too high a moral price. The "spirit of the seminar" would become an empty cliché and there would be little hope of ultimate salvation for any of the contracting parties.

IV SOUTHERN WOMEN IN A WORLD AT WAR

Judy Barrett Litoff

> Women of the United States from Revolutionary [War] days have had a
> high tradition of courage and steadfastness under the shock of war. . . .
> World conditions demand even more of women today. . . . You are the
> voice of multiplied thousands of women in the homes and kitchens,
> in fields and factories, in cloistered college and public ways. It is for
> you not only to think and act, but to stir those whom you can reach to
> thought and action.[1]

The well-known Mississippian, Lucy Somerville Howorth, a senior attorney
in the Office of Legislative Counsel at the Veterans Administration in Washington, D.C., and a member of the New Deal women's "network," delivered
these remarks during her keynote address to the June 14, 1944 White House
Conference on How Women May Share in Post-War Policy Making.[2]

The architect of the conference, Tennessee native Charl Ormond Williams,
had served as chair of the ratification committee when Tennessee became the
thirty-sixth state to approve the Nineteenth Amendment—the woman suffrage
amendment—to the Constitution. A devoted public servant who had held
leadership positions with the National Education Association, the National
Congress of Parents and Teachers, and the National Federation of Business
and Professional Women's Clubs, Williams spearheaded the movement for
the White House Conference in response to numerous requests by Eleanor
Roosevelt that "women . . . be represented at the peace table . . . [and] in every
international conference."[3]

At the suggestion of Williams, the First Lady hosted a May 11 White House
luncheon for a small "exploratory group" to discuss the feasibility of holding

a conference on women and postwar planning. The women at the luncheon expressed enthusiastic support for the idea, and they selected June 14 as the date for the proposed conference.[4] For the next four weeks, Williams immersed herself in planning for the conference. Writing to Roosevelt just three days before the meeting convened, she remarked: "We have worked like beavers on this conference, Mrs. Roosevelt, but it has been a labor of love."[5]

Invitations to the conference were sent to more than 200 distinguished women, including leaders of seventy-five women's organizations, representing "every section of the country." Among the 213 conference participants were several notable southern women.[6] Mary McLeod Bethune of Sumter County, South Carolina, founder and president of the National Council of Negro Women, member of the New Deal's "Black Cabinet," and special advisor to Colonel Oveta Culp Hobby (a southerner from Killeen, Texas), the Director of the Women's Army Corps (WAC), participated in the conference. Harriet Elliot, an Illinoisan by birth who served as the Dean of the Woman's College of the University of North Carolina for much of her adult life and whose wartime responsibilities included coordinating the many war bond campaigns promoted by women's groups throughout the nation, took part in the day-long proceedings. Missourian Margaret A. Hickey, chair of the Women's Advisory Committee of the War Manpower Commission from 1942 through 1945 as well as president of the National Federation of Business and Professional Women's Clubs from 1944-1946, also attended the conference.[7]

Sharing the speaker's podium with Howorth was another Mississippian: Ellen S. Woodward, a close friend and associate of Howorth. As a Democratic Party stalwart and the leading advocate of programs to advance women's economic security and social welfare within the Roosevelt administration, Woodward earned a place as an advisor to the U.S. delegation at the first conference of the United Nations Relief and Rehabilitation Administration (UNRRA), held in Atlantic City, New Jersey, in November 1943. Drawing on her experiences at Atlantic City, Woodward's address to the White House Conference emphasized the importance of determining ways that "women may have greater opportunity to participate in weaving the pattern of the post-war world."[8]

In an effort to ensure that commensurate numbers of qualified women would be appointed to postwar policy positions, conference delegates heeded a suggestion made by Lucy Howorth in her keynote address that a roster be compiled of "the names of able, intelligent, personable women, qualified to serve in conferences to come." Over the next six months, a Continuation Committee, headed by Charl Williams, solicited information on 730 nominees to be considered for inclusion on the proposed roster. From this number, 260 women were named to the official "Roster of Qualified Women," which was presented to President Franklin D. Roosevelt and Secretary of State Edward R. Stettinius, Jr., in January 1945. In Williams's letter of transmittal to Stettinius, she expressed the hope that "one or more qualified women . . . [would] be appointed to serve on all commissions looking toward the establishment of peaceful relations in this wartorn world."[9]

The press provided substantial coverage to the work of the White House Conference. Eleanor Roosevelt devoted parts of two of her "My Day" columns to the meeting. An editorial writer for the *New York Times* endorsed the conference, noting that there had been "few such appointments [of women]. There should be more. . . . It would be for the good of the country that their representation be larger." Ellen Woodward reported to Charl Williams that "the men have all been asking questions about the meeting and I think they know that women mean business—that they intend to have a share in the planning of the post-war world."[10]

During the late summer and early fall of 1944, as Charl Williams and the Continuation Committee hastened to gather information for the "Roster of Qualified Women," the Dumbarton Oaks conversations were held in Washington, D.C. These pivotal negotiations, conducted by representatives from the United States, the Soviet Union, England, and China, led to the proposals that provided the outline for the United Nations organization. Much to the chagrin of Charl Williams and the White House Conference participants, U.S. women were excluded from the Dumbarton Oaks talks.[11] However, the hope that women would eventually have the opportunity to take their rightful place at the peace table was rekindled with the State Department announcement of February 13, 1945, that Virginia Gildersleeve, Dean of Barnard College, would be one of eight U.S. delegates to the United Nations Conference to be convened in San Francisco in April. Charl Williams attributed Gildersleeve's selection to the development of the "roster," and Gildersleeve, herself, acknowledged its importance, commenting in an interview that "I feel I was appointed because American women made a drive for representation and my name was on the roster they compiled. Therefore I do represent our women, but I hope I also represent my fellow citizens as a whole."[12]

Despite the hard work of Charl Williams and the women who supported the White House Conference, the nation's political leaders, consumed with military, strategic, and geopolitical concerns, demonstrated only lukewarm support for the inclusion of women on postwar councils. Women were excluded from the influential Dumbarton Oaks conversations, and they were woefully under-represented at other postwar conferences and councils. Writing to Margaret Hickey from the 1943 UNRRA conference, Ellen Woodward observed: "I do not want to be trite but I want to say and with all due emphasis—this is still a man's world."[13] At the end of the war, women who continued to push for full participation in national policymaking councils and international peace assemblies had little cause to dispute Woodward's statement.

Prominent southern women, such as Lucy Howorth, Ellen Woodward, Charl Williams, and Mary McLeod Bethune, joined with Eleanor Roosevelt, Frances Perkins, Mary Anderson, Molly Dewson, Margaret Chase Smith, Mabel K. Staupers, Edith Nourse Rogers, and other well-known public women from outside the South to help lead the successful battle against Fascism and plan for the postwar world. Yet, without the energy, courage, fortitude, wit, and ingenuity displayed by millions of unsung heroines of the South—and their counterparts throughout the nation—the war could not have been won. Early in 1942, the prolific writer, Margaret Culkin Banning, emphasized the important role to be played by ordinary American women in the winning of war. "Women by themselves cannot win this war," wrote Banning. "But quite certainly it cannot be won without them. For aggressive defense in this total war against the democracies not only can use women's help but it needs all they can give."[14]

D-Day historian Stephen Ambrose has persuasively argued that it was democratic, citizen soldiers—junior grade officers and enlisted men—taking the initiative and making quick, on-site decisions, who were ultimately responsible for the break through Hitler's Atlantic Wall and the military defeat of Nazi Germany.[15] By the same token, it was the grit, determination, and resourcefulness of ordinary American women that made it possible for wartime food production to increase by an astounding 32 percent over the Depression years; permitted the percentage of women in the work force to leap from 24 percent at the beginning of the war to 36 percent at the war's end; enabled young war brides to become self-reliant, assertive individuals; provided mothers, wives, sisters, daughters, and sweethearts with the courage to cope with the tragedies of war's carnage; and, challenged some 350,000 pioneering women to serve their country by joining one of the women's branches of the Army, Navy, Coast Guard, or Marines.

No where is the indomitable spirit of southern women better depicted than in the millions of morale-boosting letters they wrote to loved ones and friends during the war years.[16] These letters, as well as those written by women from other regions of the United States, are candid accounts written "at the scene" for a limited audience and with little idea that historians would one day be interested in their content. They demonstrate the many important ways that women contributed to the winning of the war, and they vividly illustrate women's growing sense of self and their place in the world.[17]

Scholars, in their efforts to determine whether World War II served as a major force for change in women's lives, have paid considerable attention to the public record. They have sifted through the archives of many wartime agencies as well as other government reports and documents, examined the records of labor unions, analyzed public opinion polls, scrutinized popular fiction, read widely in contemporary newspapers and magazines, and investigated perceptions of womanhood in popular culture. Although the specific conclusions of these scholars differ, they agree that the wartime changes that affected women were not lasting.[18]

By contrast, an examination of the private correspondence of United States women, rather than public records, suggests that the events of World War II had a much more dramatic and far-reaching effect on women than has previously been thought. Women's wartime letters provide an important missing piece to the World War II puzzle; they offer the first significant opportunity to incorporate the actual wartime voices of women into accounts of the Second World War.

Lieutenant Monica Conter of Apalachicola, Florida, was one of two Army nurses on duty at the Station Hospital, Hickam Field, Hawaii, at the time of the Japanese attack on Pearl Harbor. She described the chaotic events of December 7 in a December 22 letter to her parents:

> The wounded started coming in 10 minutes after the 1st attack. . . . Well, the sight in our hospital I'll never forget. No arms, no legs, intestines hanging out. . . . In the meantime, hangars all around us were burning—and that awful "noise." Then comes the second attack. We all fell face down . . . in the halls, O.R.[operating room], and everywhere and heard the bombers directly over us. We . . . had no helmets nor gas masks—and it really was a *"helpless"* feeling. . . . You know, I [have] always loved activity and excitement—[but] for once, I had "enough."

The events of December 7 were also the subject of a letter that Lt. Conter wrote to Major (later Colonel) Julia O. Flikke, Superintendent of the Army Nurse Corps. Acknowledging that "there were parts of that day I can hardly account for," Conter concluded her letter with the comment: "There are days like December 7 when a nurse can fully appreciate her profession as never before, and deep inside there is a feeling of satisfaction and thankfulness that she was able to do her bit to help 'Keep 'em flying.' "[19]

Following the devastating events of December 7, 1941, an aroused American citizenry began rapidly mobilizing for war. Men flocked to recruiting stations while women inundated Red Cross and civilian defense offices with offers to help. Throughout the nation, women volunteered, organized, planted, conserved, collected, and recycled in behalf of the war.

In the South, both black and white women rushed to support the war effort. Given the harsh segregation laws and oppressive discriminatory practices embedded in the "southern way of life," it is especially significant that black women came to the aid of their country in its time of great need.

Four days after Pearl Harbor, Mary C. Harris, an African American nurse from Athens, Georgia, wrote a poignant letter to Judge William H. Hastie, the Civilian Aide to Secretary of War Henry L. Stimson, informing him of her desire to serve her country. Hastie, a former dean of the Howard University School of Law, was responsible for issues concerning the fair treatment of African Americans within the segregated military. Harris explained that she was "urged and moved by the hour of trial which has visited our country" to serve as a "nurse, clerk or social worker." She emphasized that she was "ready and anxious to serve in any branch of the government service" and that she was "willing to serve anywhere in or out of the country."[20]

Southern black women like Mary Harris, eager to support the war effort, faced prejudice and discrimination at almost every turn. African American Army nurses wrote letters to Civilian Aide William Hastie and his successor, Truman Gibson, describing how they were required to perform menial jobs in place of and in addition to their nursing assignments. Black WACs traveling through the South reported that they were forced to ride on filthy, segregated coaches and denied admission to dining cars. They also told of being pushed and shoved by white railroad workers who hurled angry racial epithets at them. Black WACs stationed at Camp Nathan Bedford Forrest, Tennessee stated that they were treated as "labor detachments" and "tossed about like a chip on a sandy shore by *white civilians* working on the post." One African American WAC wrote of how a "white civilian [at Camp Forrest] went to the extreme to strike (slap) a colored WAC and endeavored to pour hot grease on her in one of the messes."[21]

Black women throughout the South also faced enormous difficulties in their mostly unsuccessful efforts to secure good-paying jobs in shipyards and defense plants. In Mobile, Alabama, as white women rushed to secure jobs in the booming war industries, black women's share in the labor force actually declined from 54 percent in 1940 to 46 percent in 1944. Although the Alabama Dry Docks and Shipbuilding Company in Mobile began hiring women as early as July 1942, the company never allowed black women to work as welders or burners. In fact, shipyard work for black women was limited to low-paying jobs such as cleaning out the ships, gathering up scrap iron, and loading boxcars. In sharp contrast to the expanding job opportunities in manufacturing and government that opened up for southern white women during World War II, the only job mobility experienced by southern black women was the shift from agricultural and domestic work to the service trades.[22]

Southern black women, long accustomed to a life of economic hardship and instability, understood better than most the importance of adhering to the wartime admonition, "Use it up, wear it out, make it do, or do without." Nanny H. Burroughs of Orange, Virginia, the well-known black educator and founder of the National Training School for Women and Girls in Washington, D.C., traveled throughout the rural south encouraging African American women to "Produce, Conserve, Consume for Victory."[23]

In Bolivar County, Mississippi, the *Bolivar Commercial* reported in April 1943 that two young black women had "made six bales [of cotton] on several acres of their land." In addition, the *Commercial* reported that Winnie Anderson, a graduate of Tuskegee Institute, had been hired by the Bolivar County Farm Bureau to help black farm families develop ways to increase wartime agricultural production.[24]

After traveling by train across Arkansas during the late summer of 1944, Mabel Opal Miller wrote a letter to her Army Air Forces boyfriend describing the special contributions southern farm women were making to the war effort: "I noticed on the farms, mostly the little ones with just a shack for a home, there seems to be no one but the women left to do the work. You see them out taking care of cattle, etc. It makes one proud to see how the women have picked up where the men left off and are keeping the home fires burning."[25]

Yet even as farm workers, southern black women encountered discrimination and prejudice. Following the establishment of the Women's Land Army (WLA) of the Department of Agriculture in the spring of 1943, several southern states acknowledged that they had deliberately bypassed efforts to recruit and train black women for the WLA. South Carolina officials reported that "it was thought best to start the Women's Land Army in the State with white women only . . . as, if it became known first as a [N]egro program, it would have been impossible later on to interest white women in participating." In Virginia, black women who were recruited for farm work were simply "not considered a part of the Women's Land Army."[26]

Despite all of these obstacles, southern black women remained steadfast in their support for the war effort. A. Philip Randolph's March-on-Washington Movement used as its motto, "Winning Democracy for the Negro Is Winning the War for Democracy." The "Double V" campaign, adopted by the black press in March 1942, called for victory over totalitarianism abroad and racism at home. It was in this context that many black women embraced the ideals for which World War II was fought.

African American women often linked the war for democracy abroad with the war for democracy at home. One black WAC, in a letter to the *Chicago Defender*, succinctly remarked: "As a member of the Women's Army Corps, I am deeply conscious of this war against fascism and have dedicated myself to do all possible to bring the day of victory closer. In order to win a war against fascist ideas, I feel strongly that the same ideas at home must be combatted [and] that a discriminatory racial policy can only interfere with the winning of the war." In her opening remarks to the 1944 Annual Workshop of the National Council of Negro Women, Mary McLeod Bethune utilized the workshop theme, "Wartime Planning for Post-War Security," to call for "one long strong pull altogether, toward the integration of and participation in the new found freedoms and opportunities that are opening daily to the women of America and the world." At the same meeting, Mary Church Terrell of Memphis, Tennessee, the author, educator, and civil rights advocate, asserted that there "is only one way . . . to establish and maintain peace. To succeed in doing this each and every government must treat all its citizens justly, no matter what their color may be, nor in what kind of religion they may believe, nor where they were born, nor in what social class they may move."[27]

Mary McLeod Bethune, Mary Church Terrell, and Nannie Burroughs often used the exigencies of war as an opportunity to advance interracial cooperation among women. In their public speeches and writings, they routinely emphasized the importance of black and white women working together for the war effort. Bethune made a special effort to invite white women, such as Virginia Durr of the Southern Human Welfare Conference, to speak to the annual workshops of the National Council of Negro Women. Early in 1943, when a black woman sent Nannie Burroughs a "flag for the Negro race," she sternly retorted: "Negroes do not need a special flag. We are American citizens. We have fought, bled, died and sacrificed for Old Glory and we are going to stay by this flag and go up or down with the nation. We are a definite part of the American people, and we are not going to be put off under any other banner."[28]

The war work of southern black women did not go unnoticed by their white counterparts. Mrs. Keith Frazier Somerville of Cleveland, Mississippi, author of a bi-monthly "Dear Boys" letter column for the *Bolivar Commercial,* took special care to report on the contributions of the black residents of Bolivar County to the war effort.[29] In her column of September 8, 1944, she related the story of Annie Tutwiler, a black six-star mother from Merigold, Mississippi, whose children were showing "the world that all races, creeds, and colors in America are in there fighting for that victory which today seems almost in sight." Somerville made several trips to the all-black town of Mound Bayou in order to gather firsthand accounts of how African Americans were aiding the war effort and being affected by the war. Prescient of the impending changes in southern race relations, she told her readers:

> In Mound Bayou, I found America dreaming again. Dreaming of the day her sons will come marching home; dreaming of better housing and hospitalization; dreaming of the day when education will really "educate". . . . Dreaming too, of absolute fairness . . . when our boys of all races, creeds, and color come home again to peaceful years, [and] we may all work together to make our dreams come true.[30]

Wartime women, such as fifty-five year old Keith Frazier Somerville, defied the stereotype of the "southern lady on a pedestal."[31] As Somerville noted in her journal, writing the letter column, correcting the proofs, and addressing newspapers to hundreds of "dear boys" stationed around the world was "almost a full time job." In her "spare" moments, she rolled bandages for the Red Cross, collected scrap-metal, served as a hostess at the local U.S.O., curtailed food consumption beyond the limits imposed by rationing, and did a great deal of mending "so as to be more patriotic and make things last for the duration." That she may have slighted her housework for war work bothered her not at all. "I'm not lazy," she confided in her journal, "but honestly, I am so much more interested in this than in everlasting sweeping and dusting."[32]

Young war brides who "grew up" during the wartime emergency also challenged established norms as they traveled alone to distant places to be with their husbands, discovered how to live on meager allotment checks, learned how to maintain and repair automobiles, coped with raising young children alone, and grappled with worry, loneliness, and despair. Early in 1945, Frances Zulauf of Nevada, Missouri, wrote to her Army Air Forces husband and discussed how the events of the war had contributed to her growing sense of self:

> Personally, I think there's no doubt that this sacrifice we're making will force us to be bigger, more tolerant, better citizens than we would have been otherwise. If it hadn't been for all this upset in my life, I would still be a rattle brained . . . spoiled "little" girl in college, having dates and playing most of my way thru school. . . . I'm learning—in this pause in my life—just what I want for happiness later on—so much different than what I wanted two years ago.[33]

Frances Zulauf's assessment of how the war had made her a more self-confident individual was shared by Barbara Wooddall Taylor, a war bride from

Fairburn, Georgia. Writing to her Army husband in Europe late in 1944, she asserted: "This War has certainly made me realize just how foolish I was about a great many things. Guess I just hadn't really grown up before."[34]

The lives of women employed in shipyards, aircraft plants, chemical industries, and other assembly lines, where they wore overalls, worked on the swing shift, and even became "lead men," extended far beyond the bounds deemed appropriate for the "southern lady." The working women of the South expressed great pride in their war jobs and often commented, with enthusiasm, about the new sense of responsibility and independence they were achieving.[35]

Polly Crow, a young mother living during the war with her parents in Louisville, Kentucky, explained in a June 1944 letter to her Army husband why she wanted a war job. She also highlighted the advantages of swing shifts for working mothers:

> I'm thinking seriously of going to work in some defense plant . . . on the swing shift so I can be at home during the day with Bill [their young son] as he needs me. . . . Of course, I'd much rather have an office job but I couldn't be with Bill whereas I could if I worked at nite which I have decided is the best plan as I cain't save anything by not working and I want to have something for us when you get home.

After securing a job at Jefferson Boat and Machine Company in nearby Anderson, Indiana, Polly Crow proudly proclaimed: "You are now the husband of a career woman—just call me your little Ship Yard Babe!" She described the "grand and glorious feeling" of opening her own checking account, gas rations and automobile maintenance, the many "wolves" on the swing shift, and what it was like to join a union. Late in 1944, upon learning that the work of building Landing Ship Tanks at the shipyard would be completed within the next few months, she wrote a letter in which she bemoaned the fact that "my greatly enjoyed working career will come to an end."[36]

Coping with the tragedies of war further contributed to the southern woman's growing sense of self. The news that loved ones were prisoners of war, missing in action, or killed in battle required women to draw upon an inner strength that many did not know they had. In DeQuincy, Louisiana, Christine Cockerham agonized for more than three years over the fate of her Army Air Forces son, taken prisoner by the Japanese following the fall of Bataan in the spring of 1942. The relief and joy that she felt upon learning that he had survived the war years as a prisoner of the Japanese were expressed in a letter written to him on October 1, 1945:

> Just received your letter and you don't know how happy we were. . . . Mother is so excited and nervous I can't think of anything to write. . . .

Everybody is well and so happy about our hearing from you. . . . The whole town was like wild fire—the phone rang all the time to see if it was true. . . . Looking every day for a phone call or telegram from you that you are in the states and are home. Everybody sends their love.[37]

Among the many new opportunities extended to women during World War II, probably none presented a greater challenge to conventional notions of "southern womanhood" than that of service in the military. Letters written by southern women who donned military uniforms contain vivid descriptions of the ways in which their wartime experiences greatly expanded their horizons and afforded them a new appreciation of their abilities.

WAC Private Maud Turner Cofer of Atlanta, Georgia, served with the Motor Transportation Corps in England where she drove trucks and worked as an automobile mechanic. In a November 5, 1944, letter to her parents, she described the "dirty work" and "grime" of her job. She also noted that "the garage has responded wonderfully to what work I am able to get done, [but] lacking brute strength . . . I do not keep the place as well as it should be kept."[38]

Helen K. McKee of San Antonio, Texas, an Army nurse anesthetist with the 300th General Hospital in Italy, was assigned to evacuation hospitals during the Anzio landing and the Cassino drive. Writing to her family about those difficult days early in 1944, she confided that "our patients came to us with only first aid care. We debrided their wounds, did the amputations, took slugs out of the livers and removed their shell fragments from all vital organs. We cleaned them up—killed the maggots in their wounds, and *put them to bed between clean sheets.*"[39]

Army nurse Ruth Hess of Louisville, Kentucky, arrived in France in late June 1944. In a long retrospective letter to friends and colleagues at the Louisville General Hospital, she described the challenges she encountered during her first days as a combat nurse in Europe:

> We embarked by way of a small landing craft with our pants rolled up—wading onto the beach a short distance. . . . We marched up those high cliffs . . . about a mile and a half under full packs, hot as "blue blazes"—till finally a jeep . . . picked us up and took us to our area. . . . For nine days we never stopped [working]. 880 patients operated; small debridement of gun shot and shrapnel wounds, numerous amputations, fractures galore, perforated guts, livers, spleens, kidneys, lungs, . . . everything imaginable. . . . It's really been an experience. At nite—those d—d German planes make rounds and tuck us all into a fox hole—ack ack in the field right beside us, machine guns all around—whiz—there goes a bullet. It really doesn't spare you—you're too busy—but these patients need a rest from that sort of stuff.[40]

Marian Stegeman of Athens, Georgia, was one of approximately a thousand women who received the silver wings of the Women Airforce Service Pilots, a quasi-military organization loosely affiliated with the Army Air Forces. Her vivacious letters to her mother, dated from many cities as she ferried aircraft throughout the United States, recount her joy of flying and the tremendous sense of independence she experienced as a pilot. In an April 24, 1943, letter to her mother, she exclaimed:

> The gods must envy me! This is just too, *too*, to be true! (By now you realize I had a good day as regards flying. Nothing is such a gauge to the spirits as how well or how poorly one has flown.) . . . I'm far too happy. The law of compensation must be waiting to catch up with me somewhere. Oh, God, how I love it! Honestly, Mother you haven't *lived* until you get way *up* there—all alone—just you and that big beautiful plane humming under your control.[41]

Rita Pilkey of Dallas, Texas, was one of the first American Red Cross women to be assigned to China. Flying from Calcutta, India, over "The Hump," she arrived in Kunming in late January 1944. In letters to her parents, Pilkey wrote about learning to fire guns in small arms class because "when you drive any place away from the base you are on, you always take a gun because of the bandits." In November 1944, after being selected to set up the first tent facility at Luliang, she told her parents that "I like it here [in Kunming], but I feel honored to be chosen to go there because it is supposed to be the hardest place here." She wrote that with "hard work we were able to open two of our tents for an Open House on Christmas. . . . It was a big success and the boys all seemed to appreciate our efforts so much that we decided to keep those two tents open while we continued to work on the rest of the club." The grand opening of Luliang's Canvas Cover Club occurred on January 30, 1945. Pilkey reported that the Red Cross doughnuts are "the talk of the base" and our "tents are so small and there are so many men that the sides literally bulge."[42]

As the war drew to a close during the spring and summer of 1945, the question of the larger meaning of the conflict weighed heavily on the minds of many southern letter writers. Following the end of the war in Europe in May 1945, Keith Frazier Somerville was quick to remind readers that "we are only just half happy" as "we must await the complete surrender of Japan [and] the coming home of all you boys." Writing from Italy three weeks after V-E Day, Army nurse Helen McKee confided to her parents in Texas: "You know at times I still feel sort of numb to anything except the fact that casualties have ceased to be. I don't think anyone felt closer, or shared the pain of these boys than we, the

A.N.C. Now we have finished our jobs, we've seen the war thru. We are tired and ready to come home."[43]

After the atomic bombs fell on Hiroshima and Nagasaki in early August 1945, the war in the Pacific and the Second World War finally came to end. In her last "Dear Boys" column, Keith Somerville wrote: "It seems almost unbelievable, doesn't it, that Peace has come again to the world? We have lived with war so long—it almost seems forever." She told her readers of how she had gone to thanksgiving ceremonies and "wept some happy tears and said some prayers." Yet she also described how the news of the "awe-inspiring and terrifying" atomic bomb had stunned the world. She continued by saying, "Perhaps we have unloosed a Frankenstein, which may eventually destroy us, but it's here, and we should be thankful its secrets were discovered first by a peace loving nation! What if Germany had beaten us to it!"[44]

In her "victory" letter to her Army Air Forces fiance in India, Constance Hope Jones of Kirkwood, Missouri, included thoughtful comments on the end of the war that continue to resonate with meaning:

> I guess our family has been lucky in that both of our "warriors" are safe and sound. There are thousands of families not so lucky. . . . Now, I suppose President Truman and Congress really have a big job of getting things and people adjusted to peace time ways of hiring and doing! Perhaps the biggest job is yet ahead. Over the radio yesterday . . . I heard the starting of another war! All about how the U.S. was developing new and secret weapons and how we should keep our secrets from the Russians! . . . Talk like that is a betrayal of those who died or were wounded in this war and of those who are working to make it possible for nations to live in peace with each other.[45]

Of course, ebullience and love filled many of the "victory" letters penned by southern women. Writing to her Army husband in France on August 16, war bride Barbara Wooddall Taylor exclaimed: "THE War IS OVER—oh, Charlie baby, this is what we waited for so long. Even yet, I can't believe it. I'm so grateful to God. . . . Mother and I were listening to the radio when the news first came on—and we were laughing and crying together." Taylor described how she attended a "community meeting" at the local Baptist church where she "sat in the choir . . . and felt good all over singing 'My Country 'Tis of Thee.'" After the church service, she and several other war brides went to a "real ole fashioned square dance" in the middle of town. They topped off their celebration by having a "short drink" of whiskey at a friend's house where they cooked bacon and eggs and talked until 2:00 a.m. Capturing the euphoria of the day, Barbara Taylor concluded:

Everyone has a holiday today of course, so we're going swimming this afternoon. And, gasoline is NOT rationed—man, that's wonderful. Honestly, things are happening so fast, well, I just can't grasp it all.[46]

Southern women in a world at war joined with women from throughout the nation to plant victory gardens, roll bandages for the Red Cross, contribute to war bond drives, seek war jobs, volunteer for military service, and write millions of morale-boosting letters to loved ones and friends stationed far from home. They got married, had children, crisscrossed the continent as they followed their husbands to distant postings, agonized about loved ones stationed at "far flung fronts," planned for the postwar world, and became stronger, more self-reliant individuals in the process. While the southern woman's experience of war was marred by the racism and prejudice that pervaded the region, the wartime exodus of blacks from the South also caused these issues to take on a new national dimension.

For southern women—as well as for women throughout the United States—the events of the Second World War served as a major force for change in their lives. The war transformed the way women thought about themselves and the world in which they lived, expanding their horizons and affording them a clearer sense of their capabilities. Although the postwar decade witnessed a renewed interest in motherhood and family that resulted in a return to a more conventional way of life for many women, the immense changes wrought by World War II were not forgotten. A generation later, these changes would provide the foundation for the rejuvenation of the woman's movement.

Life would never be the same for the southern women who lived through World War II. With fortitude and ingenuity, they had surmounted the challenges posed by total war. As the women of the wartime generation are quick to acknowledge: "We knew that if we could overcome the trials and tribulations of the war years, we could do anything."

V AFRICAN AMERICAN MILITANCY IN THE WORLD WAR II SOUTH

Another Perspective

Harvard Sitkoff

It is now commonplace to emphasize the Second World War as a watershed in the African American freedom struggle, as a time of mass black militancy, and as the direct precursor to the civil rights protest movement of the late 1950s and 1960s. Even most textbooks today dramatize the wartime bitterness of African American protests against racial discrimination in the defense industry and the military, and highlight the phenomenal growth of the National Association for the Advancement of Colored People and the beginnings of the Congress of Racial Equality, which practiced direct-action civil disobedience to desegregate places of public accommodation. They quote the sardonic statement, supposedly popular during the war, of a black man, just drafted, who seethed: "Write on my tombstone—Here lies a black man, killed fighting a yellow man, for the protection of a white man." The individual military experience of a Jackie Robinson or a Medgar Evers is portrayed as representative of the turning point for African Americans as a whole; and virtually all devote the lion's share of space on blacks in the war to A. Philip Randolph's March-on-Washington Movement. Commonly described as the foremost manifestation of wartime mass black militancy, and singularly credited with forcing a reluctant President Franklin Roosevelt to issue Executive Order 8802 banning racial discrimination in defense and government employment, the MOWM is invariably pictured as the forerunner of the later Black Freedom Struggle's tactics and strategy. Most accounts also assert that the African American press during World War II was militantly demanding in a way it had never before been, and that the black masses, who actively, aggressively, even violently confronted Jim Crow, were yet far more militant. The war years, in sum, are depicted as a time when mass militancy became characteristic of the African American, when blacks belligerently assaulted the racial status quo, and when this watershed in black consciousness and behavior ignited the Negro Revolution that would later blaze.[1]

Perhaps. Maybe. It is comforting to think that the destructiveness of mass warfare can have redeeming virtues; it is good to have forebears to admire and emulate. But if by a watershed in militancy we mean a crucial turning point in the aggressiveness of black actions, a far greater combativeness than previously exhibited, then the evidence to prove this argument conclusively has yet to appear; and major questions concerning this interpretation remain unanswered. This is especially so concerning the South, particularly the rural South, where most African Americans continued to live during World War II. Total war did, of course, generate major ruptures and upheavals in American life. Japan's sudden attack on the U.S. Pacific fleet at Pearl Harbor on December 7, 1941, evoked a widespread wave of patriotism and national purpose. Few Americans, black or white, dissented from the war spirit, intensified by media publicity and government-orchestrated campaigns to rally 'round the flag. Support for the war effort placed a premium on loyalty and unity. Even those who wished to protest had to tread carefully.

The angry demonstrations by African Americans against racial discrimination in the defense industry and in the armed services, the flurry of petitions and protests, so common in 1940 and 1941, diminished after the United States entered the war, and received decreasing attention as the war dragged on. In fact, the most militant editorials in the Negro press, the virulent threats by African American protest leaders and protest organizations, the indignant portents of black disloyalty or of tepid support by blacks for the Allied cause, almost without exception came *before* Pearl Harbor, *before* the United States entered the war. Pre-war actions are not instances of *wartime* militancy.[2]

Indeed, soon after the attack on Pearl Harbor, Edgar G. Brown, director of the National Negro Council telegraphed President Roosevelt that all African Americans pledge 100 percent loyalty to the United States. The National Urban League promised total support for the war effort. The Southern Negro Youth Congress raised money for defense bonds, sponsored an Army Welfare

Committee to establish a USO Center for Negroes, and created its own Youth V for Victory Committee. W. E. B. Du Bois and A. Philip Randolph spoke at "Victory Through Unity" conferences. Father Divine donated a hotel to the Navy, and Paul Robeson travelled to training camps to entertain the troops. Dr. Charles Drew, whose research made blood transfusions possible, proclaimed that the priority of all Americans, "whether black or white, is to get on with the winning of the war" despite the scientifically unwarranted decision of the Red Cross to segregate the blood of black and white donors. Joe Louis promised the entire profits of his next two fights to the Army and Navy relief funds. Langston Hughes wrote plays for the War Writers Board and jingles for the Treasury Department. Josh White sang "Are You Ready?" promising to batter the Japanese "ratter till his head gets flatter," and Doc Clayton sounded a call for revenge in his "Pearl Harbor Blues." African Americans working in Hollywood formed a Victory Committee, headed by Hattie McDaniel. Richard Wright, who had earlier denounced American involvement in the war, immediately offered his literary services to the government for "the national democratic cause," and African Americans in the Communist Party hierarchy sought to aid the war effort by ordering that the attacks on racism in the script for the Broadway play based on Wright's *Native Son* be toned down.[3]

The first issues of the Negro press after Pearl Harbor proclaimed in banner headlines "Mr. President, Count on Us," and "The Black Tenth is Ready." Major newspapers that had once excoriated Du Bois for penning his First World War "Close Ranks" editorial now repeated his very imagery to restate his plea that Negroes put aside their special grievances for the duration. The Norfolk *Journal and Guide* called upon African Americans to "close ranks and join with fervent patriotism in this battle for America." "The hour calls for a closing of ranks, for joining of hands, not for a widening of the racial gap" echoed the Chicago *Defender*. The California *Eagle* promised to shift its campaign from full citizenship rights to full citizenship duties. A study of twenty-four Negro newspapers in the first several months of the war found that only three harped on the grievances and complaints of African Americans; the other twenty-one stressed the necessity of racial cooperation to avenge Pearl Harbor and the common goal of both blacks and whites of defeating the United States' foreign enemies. Columnists who before the attack on Pearl Harbor had accentuated the similarities between Nazism and American racism, stressed their differences after Pearl Harbor; essayists who had trumpeted that the Black Yanks Are Not Coming changed their tune to the Need to Do Everything to Win the War. And the Negro Newspaper Publishers Association, at its first meeting after the entry of the United States into the war, unanimously pledged its unequivocal loyalty to the nation and to the president.[4]

In marked contrast to the First World War, the Post Office Department did not suppress black publications in WW II, the Negro press suffered no special censorship restraints, and there were only a few short-lived bans on African American newspapers at army and navy installations. Even Patrick Washburn, whose research most extensively emphasizes the *threat* of suppression, states that by June 1942 consideration of even this had ended. By then, the opening of hiring gates to blacks had quelled militant political activity adds Herbert Garfinkel: "The fighting bite had gone out of the Negro protest."[5]

Only a tiny, numerically insignificant, number of African Americans initially opposed the entry of the United States into the war, and an even smaller number maintained such opposition. But even the actions of these few should not automatically be equated with wartime racial militancy. Some blacks had sincere religious objections to war; some were truly pacifists. And those who did base their opposition on the racial discrimination and segregation rampant in the armed services, and had the support of some mainstream African American groups and newspapers, like the Conscientious Objectors Against Jim Crow, disappeared with American entry into the war. But whatever the reasons, there were only thirty-three black conscientious objectors in 1941, less than 2 percent of the total number of COs, and only 166 in the following four years. Between 1941 and 1946, when over 1,154,000 blacks joined the military just two thousand African Americans went to prison for not complying with the Selective Service Act. Most were members of the Ethiopian Pacific Movement, the Pacific Movement of the Eastern World, and the Nation of Islam. Hardly supported by those in the forefront of the Freedom Struggle, those groups opposing the drafting of African Americans were labeled "the lunatic fringe" by A. Philip Randolph, referred to as "agents of fascism" by the Chicago *Defender*, and described as "Japanese agents" by the black journalist Roi Ottley. Moreover, the almost infinitesimal number of African American "conscientious objectors, delinquents and evaders or seditionists" during World War II, concluded a study of the wartime selective service system, was "little short of phenomenal" given the extent of racism in American society. As Lester Granger of the National Urban League maintained throughout the conflict, African Americans want "full partnership in the war," they "desire to assume full citizenship responsibilities." Apparently agreeing, a higher proportion of blacks volunteered for service, despite discrimination and segregation in all the branches of the armed forces, and a lower proportion sought to evade service, than did whites, or did African Americans in the First World War.[6]

Equally telling, the Negro press during the war continually downplayed or denounced as "fools and fanatics," as "crackpots and starry-eyed cultists who are without influence or intelligence," those few African Americans who refused induction. Dissociating "the traitors" from the mass of loyal blacks, the Negro press admonished African Americans that patriotic service to the nation was the path to eventual equality. Not a single mainstream African American newspaper, organization or spokesperson supported draft resistance by blacks. In the most publicized case, that of Winfred W. Lynn, who refused induction to protest segregation in the military, no Negro newspaper or black rights group backed him. Not only did the leading protest organization, the NAACP, refuse to aid Lynn, but its most prominent attorney, Thurgood Marshall, went to the American Civil Liberties Union and pleaded that they not take Lynn's case. They did not. Similarly, when Edgar B. Keemer, a black physician in Detroit, refused induction because the navy would not accept African Americans as doctors, no major black organization would take his case.[7]

Instead of militant protest, the dominant theme of African American organizations and journals during the Second World War was that patriotic duty and battlefield bravery would lead to the Negro's advancement. The notion that blacks would gain from the war, not as a gift of white goodwill but because the nation needed the loyalty and manpower of African Americans, had been sounded in every one of America's previous armed conflicts, and it continued to reverberate throughout World War II. "War may be hell for some," columnist Joseph Bibb exulted, "but it bids fair to open up the portals of heaven for us." Whites will respond positively to the needs of African Americans if Negroes do their part as 100 percent loyal Americans declared Lester Granger. In order for African Americans to benefit later they must fight for the United States now, "segregation and Jim Crowism to the contrary notwithstanding," announced the New York *Age*. Full participation in the defense of the nation, claimed the Baltimore *Afro-American,* is the path to eventual equality. And the NAACP declared the slogan for its mid-1942 convention to be "Victory is Vital to Minorities."[8]

In this vein, African Americans took up the call of the Pittsburgh *Courier* for a "Double V" campaign. Originating with a letter to the editor from James G. Thompson of Wichita, Kansas, who sought to join the army "to take his place on the fighting front for the principles which he so dearly loved," the *Courier* urged blacks to "fight for the right to fight" because wartime performance would determine postwar status. Opposing the war effort, or sitting on the sidelines, argued the *Courier,* would be the worst possible course for blacks to follow. Rather than calling for a massive attack on the Jim Crow system, the *Courier* added, African-Americans must join in the defense of their country. "The more we put in," argued columnist J. A. Rogers, "the more we have a right to claim." That notion was re-stated in hundreds of ways, as the *Courier* and the Negro press overall harped on the necessity of African Americans serving fully and faithfully so that they could prove their patriotism and later gain concessions. With cause, the Socialist Workers Party denounced the Double V as "a cover for unqualified support of the war." Yet even a fight for the right to fight could be misunderstood, and the space devoted to the Double V in the *Courier* declined by half between April and August 1942. By the end of 1942 the Double V campaign had been wholly superceded by less ambiguous, more positive, declarations of African American patriotism; and the *Courier* would go on to urge black soldiers to "insist on combat duty." "The most significant achievement of the Negro press during this crisis, in our estimation," bragged African American publishers in 1944, "lies in the fact that the Negro newspapers have brought home to the Negro people of America that this is their war and not merely 'a white man's war.' "9

However much the great majority of African Americans desired the end of racial discrimination and segregation in American life, only a minority thought that their fight for rights should take precedence over defeating Germany and Japan, and far fewer flirted with militant protests that might be considered harmful to the war effort. Thus A. Philip Randolph's March-on-Washington Movement, generally depicted as the epitome of mass black militancy during the war, truly held center-stage in the Negro community only for a few months in 1941, before American entry into the war, and then gradually withered away. Shunned as "unpatriotic" by many of the mainstream Negro organizations and newspapers that had earlier supported it, Randolph's group labored in vain to rebut accusations of employing the "most dangerous demagoguery on record" and of "Marching Against the War Effort." Polls in the Negro press during 1942 revealed a steady diminution of black support for a March on Washington to demand a redress of grievances. When Randolph called for mass marches on city halls in 1942, no blacks marched. When he called for a week of non-violent civil disobedience and non-cooperation to protest Jim Crow school and transportation systems in 1943, a poll indicated that more than 70 percent of African Americans opposed the campaign, and no blacks engaged in such activities. And when he called upon the masses to come to his "We Are Americans, Too!" conference in Chicago in the summer of 1943, virtually no blacks other than members of his Sleeping Car Porters union attended. By then, as Randolph admitted, the March-on-Washington Movement was "without funds." Unable to pay the rent for an office or for the services of an executive secretary, the organization existed only on paper.10

Asa Philip Randolph's brief shining moment had passed quickly. The March-on-Washington Movement ended with Randolph having never led a wartime mass march or a civil disobedience campaign. When he described the program of his organization in Rayford Logan's *What the Negro Wants* (1944), Randolph barely discussed mass militant protests. Instead, most of his essay was devoted to attacking American Communists, to explaining why racial change in the South must be gradual and piecemeal, and to advocating race relations committees that would take the necessary measures to prevent or stop race riots. Quite at odds with the image of the wartime Randolph in most current accounts, his wartime agenda for the March-on-Washington Movement in fact differed little from that of the NAACP. Randolph, moreover, devoted the greatest amount of his time and energy during the war to criticizing discrimination within the American Federation of Labor and heading the National Council for a Permanent Fair Employment Practices Commission, a traditional legislative lobby which never advocated mobilizing the masses and which was controlled by an elite group of mainly white New York socialists and labor leaders. Penning the moribund March-on-Washington Movement's epitaph in 1945, Adam Clayton Powell, Jr., described it as an "organization with a name that it does not live up to, an announced program that it does not stick to, and a philosophy contrary to the mood of the times." Its former headquarters in Harlem had already been converted into a bookshop.[11]

The Congress of Racial Equality suffered much the same fate as the March-on-Washington Movement during the war, but it did so in relative obscurity. The white media barely mentioned it, and the Negro press did so even less. A tiny interracial, primarily white, elite group of pacifist and socialist followers of A. J. Muste, CORE mainly engaged in efforts to counter discrimination in places of public accommodation and recreation in northern cities where those practices were already illegal. It did little to try to desegregate schools and housing, or to expand job opportunities for African Americans, or to influence civil rights legislation, and its wartime efforts proved negligible. Because its dozen or so local chapters took to heart the reconciliatory aspects of Gandhian non-violence, the vital importance of changing the consciousness of those engaged in racist practices, few of its Christian pacifist members went beyond negotiations to direct action in the streets. CORE's hopes of becoming a mass, broad-based movement lingered as only a dream during the war, and blacks at Howard University and in St. Louis who, independent of each other, thought they were inventing the sit-in in 1944, did not even know that CORE, too, sought to employ the tactics of the CIO's famous "sit-down" strikes to the fight against Jim Crow. Faced with public apathy, unstable chapters, and a budget of less than $100 a month for its national office, CORE did not even contemplate entering the upper South until 1947, when eight blacks and eight whites decided to test the compliance with the Supreme Court's 1946 ruling in the Irene Morgan case, declaring segregation in interstate carriers unconstitutional. Even then, CORE would not try to establish a chapter in the South for another decade.[12]

The NAACP, on the other hand, saw its membership grow from 50,556 and 355 branches in 1940 to over half a million and more than a thousand branches in 1946. Yet, it essentially remained middle-class in orientation and bureaucratic in structure, abhoring radical tactics and adhering to a legalistic approach that did not countenance collective action. This was especially so in the South, the site of three-quarters of the new wartime branches. None of the southern branches sanctioned confrontations, direct action, or extralegal tactics. Ella Baker, who visited local chapters of the NAACP throughout the wartime South, first as an assistant field secretary of the Association and then as its national director of branches, never ceased hectoring the national office that most of those branches were little more than social clubs with no interest whatsoever in pursuing local protests. Thurgood Marshall also chafed at the reluctance of the southern branch officers to attack Jim Crow, and their tendency to devote themselves solely to teacher-salary equalization suits. Such suits "aroused little excitement, even in the Deep South," maintains George B. Tindall: "The tedious pace, the limited results, the manifest equity of the claim" muted white alarm. And that suited the NAACP's southern leadership of black academics, businessmen, and ministers just fine. The issue of inequitable salaries for Negro public school teachers would remain their top priority even in the immediate postwar years. The pursuit of traditional objectives by restrained tactics remained the hallmark of the Association in the South. As they had in the 1930s, the wartime southern branches lobbied and litigated against the poll tax, the white primary, and lynching, and requested a more equitable share of educational facilities and funds.[13]

Continuity also characterized the work of the seven southern affiliates of the National Urban League. They held firm to their social work orientation and to their reliance on negotiations to expand employment, recreational, and housing opportunities for African Americans. Such matters as African American juvenile delinquency and family disorganization took precedence over the fight for equal rights. Their wariness towards demonstrations and protests reflected their fear of losing funding from the Community Chest and local philanthropies, their faith in being able to make progress by working in conventional channels, and their hostility toward the NAACP—which they viewed as a competitor for financial contributions. Confrontation and disruption, even harsh talk, did not fit the Urban League's pursuit of gradual and limited racial change. When Benjamin Bell, the newly appointed executive secretary of the Urban League in Memphis, angered white politicians and businessmen by denouncing Jim Crow, the national office quickly replaced him with someone more compliant.[14]

Much as southern black leaders did not support direct action protests or forthright attacks on segregation during the war, the editorials of southern Negro newspapers rarely echoed the demands for racial equality of those in the North. Several African American newspapers in the South followed the wartime lead of the Savannah *Tribune* in discontinuing the practice of reprinting editorials from northern black newspapers. Most of the southern Negro press had never done so, and they continued, as did most southern black church and community leaders during the war, to stay on the sidelines of the civil rights struggle, to advocate upright behavior and individual economic advancement within the existing order, and to preach paternalism and "civility." Even when calling for "fair play" or an end to disfranchisement, they did so in a manner that posed no clear and present danger to white supremacy. Lest criticism be construed as unpatriotic, they accentuated African American loyalty and contributions to the war effort above all else. Surveying the Negro press in Mississippi during the war, Julius Thompson concluded: "Submission to the system was the watchword."[15]

True to form in wartime Dixie, the leaders of the South Carolina African American Democratic and Republican clubs both declared that the Negro wants only "a man's chance"—not integration or social equality. And when a young black applied to the all-white College of Charleston in 1944, the local NAACP repudiated him, accusing him of an "exaggerated ego." The opinion studies of African Americans conducted during the war continued to reveal significant attitudinal differences between blacks in the South and in the North. One mid-1943 survey indicated that just 13 percent of southern blacks expressed dissatisfaction with wartime employment opportunities as opposed to 32 percent of northern blacks; that only 10 percent of African Americans in the South complained about the treatment of blacks in the armed forces versus 19 percent in the North; and that a mere 3 percent of southern blacks were bothered about social discrimination, compared with 14 percent of northern African Americans. Yet another poll reported in the Negro press claimed that only one out of ten southern blacks felt that segregation should be attacked during the war. Other polls noted that blacks in Memphis did not care as much about civil rights issues as did those in New York, and, while a majority of African Americans, both North and South in 1943, did not think that the March-on-Washington Movement would accomplish any good, in Atlanta only one in five blacks thought African Americans would benefit from Randolph's proposed protest.[16]

Despite the many transformations and upheavals triggered by the war, there would be no mass militancy in the World War II South. There, proportionately, fewest blacks joined the NAACP or supported Randolph's March-on-Washington Movement, much less CORE or the National Negro Congress. The bitterness and resentments toward the pervasive color line, which flared occasionally in sporadic acts of aggression or passive disobedience and more frequently in covert "gum-beating" or "taking it out in talk," was largely held in check by a sense of impotency and insecurity, which cautious southern African American leaders did little to combat. Indeed, many such spokespersons, like the Committee of 100 in Mississippi, preferred a separate black community, however unequal, as the base for their careers and profits. Many of the African American educators and teachers, often the mainstay of the NAACP's southern branches, particularly feared the loss of their positions as a consequence of attacking and eliminating the segregated public school systems. Consequently, not until 1950 would the NAACP Board of Directors adopt a resolution stating that all future education cases would seek "education on a non-segregated basis and that no relief other than that will be acceptable." Until then, separate-but-*really*-equal remained the long-standing goal of its Dixie affiliates. And the preferred strategy continued to be working within the South's biracial system, meeting behind the scenes to seek improvements on the black side of the color line—that line which not only separated the races but determined rights and modes of conduct, and sustained subordination and exclusion, as well.[17]

The Negro leaders who met secretly in Durham, North Carolina, October 20, 1942, purposefully excluded northern African Americans to avoid agitation of the segregation issue. That ruse and the initial suggestion for their meeting had come from Jessie Daniel Ames of the Commission on Interracial Cooperation and the Association of Southern Women for the Prevention of Lynching. A white reformer and adversary of the NAACP who insisted that the status of African Americans could be improved within the separate-but-equal framework, Ames believed that the key to her goal was cooperation by the "better class" of southern whites and blacks. She found an ally in Gordon B. Hancock. The president of Virginia Union College in Richmond, Hancock was a black moderate who sought to build bridges between the races while conserving a separate African American community. He agreed to organize a conclave of like-minded black educators and editors, men who would draft a statement of "minimum advances," a "Southern Charter for Race Relations" that would, as Ames urged, "avoid bringing in segregation, white supremacy and other loaded ideas." The seventy-five black professionals who assembled in Durham were eager to reduce racial tensions and prevent racial violence, and at the same time to appear assertive enough to forestall being supplanted by northern black firebrands. Accordingly, their "A Basis for Interracial Cooperation and Development in the South," better known as the Durham Manifesto, formally opposed the principle of compulsory segregation but deemed it "both sensible and timely" to defer that thorny matter for the present. Rather than a call to arms to battle Jim Crow its rallying cry was for improved race relations in the South—"not only a moral matter, but a practical necessity in winning the war." In a most conciliatory tone, it reiterated demands for African American voting rights and end to the mistreatment of blacks by police, for equality of access to public services, the armed forces, and educational and employment opportunities, and for a federal antilynching law. "No case was made against segregation," charged Benjamin Mays, the president of Morehouse College who had pleaded in vain for an unequivocal denunciation of this "basic evil in the South."[18]

The some one hundred white liberals—the Other South, the largely Invisible South—who met in Atlanta on April 8, 1943, to respond to the Durham resolutions, as well as the additional two hundred who later signed their conference statement, similarly, tepidly, side-stepped the central issue of segregation and all that it implied. Having to contend with rotten borough legislatures, entrenched conservative machines, one-party politics, and truncated electorates, these journalists and academics had long-perfected the art of caution and evasion on racial issues lest the white masses be "enraged into resistance." Wartime changes, uncertainties, and fears accentuated this tendency, and seeking safe middle ground, they equated and damned those they considered the irresponsible extremists at both ends of the spectrum: A. Philip Randolph and the racist Mississippi Congressman John Rankin, the NAACP and the Ku Klux Klan. To counter the equally small bands of those described as "Negro agitators" and "white rabble-rousers," the southern liberals agreed to a statement effused with visions of fair play and mutual cooperation, yet one that depicted Jim Crow laws as "intended to minister to the welfare and integrity of both races." Insisting that solutions to the race problem must "be found in evolutionary methods and not in ill-founded revolutionary movements which promise immediate solutions," they envisioned racial reform without ending Jim Crow. Because the Durham Manifesto is "so free from any suggestion of threat and ultimatum, and at the same time shows such good will," the white southerners proclaimed, "we gladly agree to cooperate."[19]

These similar commitments to gradualism and moderation became the basis for a biracial meeting of representatives from both conferences in Richmond on June 16, 1943, and then, in Atlanta on August 14, the founding of the Southern

Regional Council. Primarily a vehicle for anti-militant southern journalists and educators, the SRC sought a liberalization of race relations without fundamental change. It wanted trade unions and businesses to act fairly toward African Americans, supported the FEPC and the anti-poll tax bill, favored improving the living conditions of minorities, and approved of experimental racially-mixed units of volunteers in the army and navy—but not desegregation in the South. It would not publicly condemn segregation until 1949. When chastized by Lillian Smith for this failure, the Council's wartime executive director replied that the SRC preferred "to capture the foothills" rather than "storming distant peaks." Booker T. Washington would have approved.[20]

Lillian Smith also had harsh words for the Southern Conference for Human Welfare, which she quit because it too refused to oppose segregation during the war. Instead, the SCHW resolved to work "toward the development of the friendliest of relations" between the races. The title of its new magazine, *Southern Patriot*, reflected its wartime priorities, as did the many articles and editorials beating the drums of war and stressing the necessity of racial unity for victory. Essentially mirroring the overall de-emphasis of civil rights by the Left, and unlike the pre-war SCHW, which had conducted its annual meetings without segregating the races and had loudly trumpeted its support for civil rights, the SCHW devoted its wartime energies to "Win the War" rallies, to abolishing the poll tax—by keeping it from being identified as a racial issue— to denouncing Roosevelt's domestic opponents as "traitors," and to promoting labor unionization, particularly by the Congress of Industrial Organizations. The SCHW would not even hire its first black field representative until after the war.[21]

Nor did the SCHW criticize the CIO's wartime acceptance, in the main, of a biracial unionism which acquiesced in Jim Crow meetings of its southern locals and in their selection of union representatives. Dependent upon the CIO for financial support, the SCHW did nothing to oppose discriminatory job classification systems and racial wage differentials in the majority of plants the CIO organized in the South. The fear of losing the support of white workers, who far out-numbered black unionists in almost all of the unions organized by the CIO in the South, meant no commitment to racial equality, no attacks upon traditional racial etiquette and practices, no fight against segregation by the majority of southern CIO affiliates. Anti-communist CIO leaders, particularly prominent in the South, regarded racial integration and communism as related, pernicious evils; and leftist unionists, in the main, neither contested racism within their ranks nor in the larger southern society, for the same anti-fascist reasons that they zealously promoted the no-strike pledge and advocated speedups and incentive pay to maximize production. Consequently, the CIO in the wartime South, despite the portentous pronouncements of its national officers and its Committee to Abolish Discrimination, essentially left intact the color line pervading both shop floor and union life—as did the American Federation of Labor which had a larger southern membership than the CIO. Nevertheless, few southern liberals or leftists dissented from the notion that the union card was the most effective way to undermine white supremacy. With few exceptions, the once more racially radical elements of the Popular Front in the South either ceased to exist during the war or subordinated all matters to victory abroad. Commonwealth College expired and the Southern Tenant Farmers Union barely managed to stay alive as it changed names. Myles Horton's Highlander Folk School retreated from its integrationist practices to concentrate on training labor union organizers; and Howard Kester dissolved his revolutionary Committee on Economic and Racial Justice and sought fulfillment in the Fellowship of Southern Churchmen's battle against materialism and modernity. Both the Southern Negro Youth Congress and the National Negro Congress folded their tents in various southern states, and neither organization would be in existence when the 1940s ended.[22]

Even more so than their counterparts in the CIO, African American Communists soft-pedaled their censure of racism in the United States during the war. Executing an about-face from the period of the Nazi-Soviet Pact, when they took the lead in exposing Jim Crow in the armed forces, the Communists opposed efforts by blacks to embarrass the military after Germany invaded the Soviet Union in June 1941. They even sought to prevent African American legal challenges against discrimination from coming before the courts. The party's wartime policy was to do nothing that might erode the unity necessary for prosecuting the war. Ben Davis vigorously denounced both the March-on-Washington Movement and the NAACP for placing the interests of blacks above the needs for "national unity, maximum war production, and the highest possible morale in the armed forces." Having opposed civil disobedience by blacks and mass protests against racism, and defended the military against its civil rights critics, Davis confessed after the war that he had "often lost sight of" the black liberation struggle. Communist leader and social scientist John Williamson later concurred. "Neglect of the problems of the Negro people," Williamson wrote, "and the cessation of organizing efforts in the South undoubtedly slowed the pace of the freedom movement which arose later."[23]

As did most black Communists, Georgian Angelo Herndon and his *Negro Quarterly* followed Earl Browder's wartime policy of refraining from public censure of Jim Crow. Its articles and editorials downplayed racial militancy, emphasized the need for patriotic unity, dispelled the "dangerous fallacy" that this is "a white man's war," and subordinated all racial issues to victory over fascist aggression. Similarly, chapters of the National Negro Congress metamorphosed into Negro Labor Victory Committees; Southern Negro Youth Congress cadre mainly worked within NAACP and CIO affiliates to promote victory abroad; and local party members in St. Louis hounded that city's March-on-Washington Movement and accused it of "disrupting the war effort" when it attempted to organize a demonstration to get more blacks jobs in defense plants. The response of the *Daily Worker* to the race riot in Detroit was to condemn the NAACP for making such a fuss and to urge everyone to get back to work quickly. Such actions and the many articles written by James Ford, Ferdinand Smith, Doxey Wilkerson, and Max Yergan insisting that black protest must remain subordinate to the drive for victory even led the leftist *Negro Digest* to publish a debate entitled "Have the Communists quit fighting for Negro rights?" Symptomatic of the Left's preoccupation with wartime unity, and concomitant abhorrence of potentially divisive racial issues, Adam Clayton Powell, Jr., went so far as to suggest that the NAACP change its name to the National Association for the Advancement of *Common* People.[24]

With the Left neither prodding them to greater militancy nor challenging them for leadership and membership, mainstream black and interracial organizations tacked to starboard. Many new interracial committees had been established to prevent or control outbreaks of racial violence, the predictable consequence of increasing black hopefulness and the forceful insistence of whites to maintain the racial status quo, and these committees decried black assertiveness as much as white intransigence in their efforts to contain conflict. Rumors of race warfare, of African Americans forming "pushing clubs" and stockpiling ice picks, of "Eleanor Clubs" and blacks "taking over" white women, however unsubstantiated, were rife throughout the wartime South—so much so that the Julius Rosenwald Fund financed the Institute of Social Studies at Fisk University to prepare a study of racial friction areas. Clearly, both talk of violent retaliation and racial violence did occur. But whether sporadic African American belligerency and the apprehensions of those whose views appeared in print during the war constitute a watershed in militant black protest remains problematic. African American and white American soldiers had also repeatedly clashed in the First World War; and Bigger Thomas was not a product of World War II. "Multiply Bigger Thomas twelve million times," Richard Wright had written well before American entry into the war, "and you have the psychology of the Negro people."[25]

Moreover, although the interracial violence within the armed forces is often cited as evidence of wartime black militancy, the largest number of violent clashes on military installations occurred in 1941, prior to the United States entry into the conflict, and these were primarily instigated by whites against individual blacks. During the war itself, racial strife crested in mid-1943, and then rapidly receded. For the entire period of America's involvement in the war, less than a score of the hundreds of military camps in the United States and abroad reported racial brawls, and many of those had nothing directly to do with African American protests or racist conditions. With a critical mass of a million black servicemen, several hundred thousand of whom had been raised in the North, one may wonder why there were so relatively few outbreaks of violence given the conditions they had to endure during the war. While a relative handful responded to segregation, inferior training and facilities, officers calling them "niggers," and brutal control by hostile military police by attacking whites, others resorted to forms of covert hostility, to violence against other blacks, and to extraordinary efforts to prove their worth. Still others expressed no dissatisfaction with their lot. Only fifteen thousand joined the NAACP, the organization most vocally critical of the insensitivity of the War Department toward the problems of black GIs. Surveys during the war indicated that only a minority of blacks in the army opposed separate post exchanges, and more African Americans favored racially segregated units than integrated ones. Although some wished to let "the Whites fight their own war," many more thought that the war was as much their affair as anybody else's, and served eagerly and proudly, leaving those not considered fit enough or too old to serve to express their disappointment.[26]

Especially after mid-1943, the Negro press, sensing the explosive potential of the race problem, downplayed the remaining incidents of racial violence in the military that transpired, hailed the achievements of African American servicemen, and castigated those blacks who defied military authorities. When the navy courts-martialed fifty blacks for refusing to report to work in Port Chicago on San Francisco Bay, following an accidental explosion that killed three hundred African American seamen, the *Defender* insisted that blacks should obey military orders whatever the circumstances. "None of us condones disobedience of miltary orders," opined the *Courier*, "no matter how unjust an order may appear to be." And the *Journal and Guide* added: "No right thinking person can excuse desertion, disobedience, mutiny." The Negro press expressed the same editorial views when four African American WACs were courts-martialed following their refusal to do the dirtiest jobs at a military hospital in Fort Devons, Massachusetts. Summing up the sentiment of the

Negro press and leadership toward the actions of the black women, the *People's Voice* claimed that "no matter how serious the provocation, they should not have defied military discipline."27

The Second World War, as well, failed to ignite the widespread racial rioting by African Americans seen in the 1917–1919 or 1964–1968 periods. Despite the legitimacy of African American aspirations and disillusionment with minimal changes during the war, despite the rising level of both expectations and frustrations, and despite the expansion of settings that brought blacks and whites into close contact and thus possibly into conflict, there were far fewer clashes in the Second World War than in those two other periods. Civilian African Americans during World War II rarely initiated attacks on whites, rarely responded in kind, rarely fought back. Commentators during the war, in fact, singled out the 1943 riot in Detroit, in which 25 blacks and 9 whites died, and more than a thousand were injured, as the sole truly race riot of the period. The two riots in the South, in Mobile and Beaumont in June 1943, now often cited as manifestations of black militancy, resulted from white resistance and hatred, not black aggression. In Mobile, the attempt by FEPC officials to have the Alabama Dry Dock and Shipbuilding Company upgrade twelve of its seven thousand African Americans holding menial positions at the yard to racially mixed welding crews caused white workers to go on a rampage, assaulting and injuring some fifty blacks, and forcing the FEPC to back down and accept traditional Jim Crow arrangements in all work assignments. Likewise, in Beaumont, opposition to black aspirations at the Pennsylvania Shipyards, sparked a false rumor that a black worker had raped the wife of a white employee and led to six hours of rioting by whites that injured several hundred African Americans and destroyed parts of Beaumont's black ghetto. The Negro press described both outbreaks as white pogroms against defenseless African Americans who neither resisted nor retaliated violently.28

That same summer, when a false rumor of a black soldier being killed by a white patrolman ignited Harlem blacks to plunder more than a thousand white-owned stores in the ghetto, African American leaders and columnists with virtually a single voice repudiated the looters as criminal "hotheads," lauded the New York police for quickly quelling the rampage, and maintained that the "orgy of vandalism" was not a race riot! The *Courier* opined that "the prepondering majorities of law-abiding American colored people are deeply downcast and humiliated" by the irresponsible disorder of a minority of blacks in Harlem, and an opinion poll revealed that fewer than one in three Harlem residents thought the riot justified. The NAACP's *Crisis* compared the disorderly in Harlem "to a Southern lynch mob." Adam Clayton Powell, Sr., blamed the disorder on "criminal subhuman savages" who wanted something for nothing rather than wanting to right racial wrongs. His son agreed. Adam Clayton Powell, Jr., whose image had changed from the Great Depression man on the picket line to the war-booster selling bonds at "victory rallies," emphatically insisted that the "wanton violence" was wrong, had not accomplished anything, and "was not a race riot." "I don't think it's a race riot," added Richard Wright. "I had the feeling it was a spontaneous outburst of anger, stemming mainly from the economic pinch."[29]

Langston Hughes similarly gave an economic explanation for the wearing of zoot suits by young black males—another supposed sign of racial militancy, of black self-determination, of a subversive response to white oppression. Depression kids who had too little in the 1930s, wrote Hughes in 1943, loved the excesses of material in the outfit: "It made them feel good to go to extremes. In the light of the poverty of their past, too much becomes just enough for them. A key chain six times too long is just enough to hold no keys." However understandable as a sign of young blacks' economic yearning, the zoot suit and all manifestations of disrespectful or anti-social behavior received little but condemnation during the war from those considered to be the voices of the black community. They denounced zoot suits as synonymous with bad conduct and those who wear them as strutting fools. "Zoot suits no more represent the Negro than watermelons, dice, switch-blades, or muggings," claimed the *Defender* in one of its editorials beseeching African Americans not to wear them. Rather than flaunt behavior that confirmed white stereotypes, African American editors and civic leaders advised blacks to buy war bonds, plant victory gardens, do their utmost to spur war production, and serve bravely in the armed forces in order to qualify for equal rights. The two most-read Negro newspapers, the Chicago *Defender* and Pittsburgh *Courier* carried numerous articles lecturing blacks on their manners and morals, their loud clothes and loud talk. The African American publisher of the Cincinnati *Union* proposed adding to the Double V a third V for "victory over ourselves." He instructed his black readers that "as long as we tolerate and condone among ourselves public misconduct, impoliteness, spendthrift habits, slovenliness, uncleanliness, we need never hope to attain the standards that white American citizenship endorses, the rights that the U.S. Constitution accords." In Cleveland the Vanguard League, which had led militant protests by blacks in the 1930s, conducted a wartime Good Conduct Campaign. Emphasizing the necessity of African Americans being respectable to gain the respect of whites, it displayed posters and handed out cards to those in the black neighborhoods it considered guilty of misconduct proclaiming: "Watch your conduct on the streetcars,"

"Fix that door; cut that grass; pull those weeds," and "Zoot suits, the mark of irresponsibility."[30]

The many African American ministers, educators, and civic leaders who served on the some two hundred interracial committees established after the Detroit race riot went still further in demanding a "piping down on stentorian drives for equality" and in importuning blacks to behave properly. Mindful of the "practical wisdom of gradual adjustment in dealing with the race problem in the South," the Richmond Ministerial Union adopted resolutions on interracial cooperation which put a lid on potential militancy. So did the Nashville Committee of 50, the Portsmouth, Virginia, Council of Racial Amity, the Birmingham Good Neighbor Club, the Memphis Council for Americanism, the Washington D.C. Citizens' Committee on Race Relations, and the Baltimore and St. Louis mayors' commissions on race relations. All functioned as impartial mediators to minimize tensions, not as advocates for black rights.[31]

Throughout the last two years of the war the moderate interracial committees set the tone and dominated the discourse on racial matters in the United States. Blunting confrontation and allaying conflict became their strategy and goal. In the South, which had 14 percent of the new interracial committees, more time was spent on requests for more frequent garbage removal in African American neighborhoods and for the hiring of black policemen to patrol those segregated enclaves than any other matters. Virtually all sought to foster goodwill by initiating interracial contacts and exchanges among students. Many set up rumor-control bureaus and hired consultants in human relations. Race relations suddenly became a cottage industry: interracial committees begat commissions against bigotry which begat councils for unity; there would be more than a thousand such groups dealing with tolerance for minorities by 1948. In return for not directly attacking racial discrimination and segregation, they had the support of such newly organized national groups as the Race Relations Division of the American Missionary Association, the American Friends Race Relations Committee, the American Jewish Congress Commission on Community In-terrelations, and the American Council on Race Relations. Given the backing of such prestigious company and the official status many of the commissions had by virtue of being municipal agencies, as well as the endorsement of leading African Americans, promoting tolerance became voguish in 1943. Brotherhood Week supplanted protests against white supremacy.[32]

With so many former allies in the fight for equal rights now counseling "go slow," most African American advocates of aggressive tactics to achieve fundamental racial change either trimmed their sails or foundered. Battling Hitler largely terminated the encouragement to black assertiveness that had been supplied in the 1930s by the Communists, militant labor union activists, supportive progressive government officials, and by the beliefs and sympathies spurred by the reform liberalism of the Great Depression-New Deal era. During the 1930s, at least ten cities had experienced NAACP-supported school boycotts protesting segregation. To demand employment, African Americans, with the support of major community leadership, had mounted sustained campaigns of picketing and boycotting retail establishments in at least thirty-five cities, including Atlanta, Baltimore, Durham, Houston, Memphis, New Orleans, and Richmond. In Charlotte, Greensboro, and Norfolk, as well as in Chicago, Philadelphia, and New York, blacks had sat-in at relief bureaus, conducted rent strikes, and led mass hunger marches. They had engaged in direct action protests against racial discrimination at restaurants, hotels, beaches, and theaters in both the South and North. In comparison, there was only one boycott against school segregation during the war, in Hillburn, New York, and not another one in the South until 1951; there were just a handful of direct action protests against Jim Crow in public accommodations, primarily by the largely white CORE in Chicago and Denver; and there were no sustained boycotts or mass demonstrations against job discrimination in World War II. As Meier and Rudwick state, in the only study to enumerate African American protest activities: the Depression—not the war—is the "watershed in Afro-American direct action." Militant black activism in the Thirties "achieved a salience in black protest that would not be equalled or surpassed until the late 1950s and 1960s." Indeed, they conclude, there "was less actual use of direct action tactics during World War II than in the 1930s"; the number of protest "demonstrations declined sharply during World War II compared to the 1930s"; and, overall, "the amount of direct action was minor compared to the Depression era."[33]

These facts do not in the least suggest that African Americans wanted equal rights any less in 1944 than in 1937; or that blacks during the war complacently accepted second-class status. Discontent is ever-present among those who are discriminated against and oppressed. Indeed, as has been amply described, the war against Hitlerism intensified the civil rights consciousness of the New Deal years, raised the expectations of blacks considerably, and had a significant impact on American racial opinions, especially in heightening perceptions of the discrepancy between the democratic ideals of the United States and its undemocratic racial practices. But compared to the Depression decade, and far more to the 1960s, blacks in World War II faced greater resistance to change, in a milieu less hospitable to disruptive protests, with reduced internal wherewithal and external support. The constraints imposed by a nation at war, the dwindling resources for sustained confrontation, and the genuinely patriotic response of most African Americans to the dangers their nation faced all inhibited militant protest activity. The NAACP, which had faced challenges throughout the 1930s from more radical, contentious African Americans urging direct action against Jim Crow, for all practical purposes now became *the* civil rights movement.

The largest and most influential of the black rights organizations, and far more so in 1945 than in 1940, the NAACP during the war gained the support of many of its former leftist critics, such as Ralph Bunche, E. Franklin Frazier, and W. E. B. Du Bois, who rejoined the Association in 1944 as its Director of Special Research. That year, the NAACP's Supreme Court victory in the white-primary case legitimized and gave yet further impetus to its legal-redress campaign. Litigation, always important to the NAACP, now became the keystone of its strategy. Its battle against racism would be fought by lawyers, not the black masses. At the same time, the NAACP became evermore a part of, and bound by, the liberal-labor Democratic coalition, campaigning against the poll tax and lynching, and for federal aid to education and an increase in social security coverage, but avoiding direct assaults on Jim Crow. With prominent white liberals, as well as A. Philip Randolph and other African American leaders, the NAACP also made the drive for a permanent FEPC a major priority after the war, and close cooperation with the American Jewish Congress and like-minded reform groups who supported NAACP cases with "friends of the court" briefs its main *modus operandi*.[34]

The most widely noted (if not actually read) wartime book on racial matters, Gunnar Myrdal's authoritative *An American Dilemma* (1944), gave its imprimatur to the NAACP strategy. It judged the NAACP the most effective of all black protest groups, celebrated the success of its legal campaign, and presented a moderate agenda for action almost identical to the NAACP's. Instantly hailed as a "classic," rarely criticized outside the recalcitrant white South, *An American Dilemma* warned against the folly of black militancy in the South, accentuated the role of white liberal allies in the campaign for racial equality, and insisted that the key struggle was the moral one within the white conscience—and not a struggle for power between the races. Myrdal's placid prognosis fit the needs of a moderate African American leadership dreading racial conflict, or challenges to its own hegemony within Black America, and set the tone and the premises of action by the civil rights movement in the postwar decade.[35]

As LeRoi Jones would later write, "the psychological hypothesis which informed the Negro's attitude toward America in the mid-forties" was that by relying on legal redress, education, and collaboration with white liberals, blacks would achieve their aspiration: equality of opportunity. And hardly any black intellectuals or leaders dissented. Across the spectrum from W. E. B. Du Bois

to George Schuyler, from Richard Wright to Dean Charles H. Thompson to
E. Franklin Frazier, African Americans initially lauded *An American Dilemma*,
and approved of its pragmatic tactics and strategy as the course for blacks
to follow. The fourteen southern and northern, conservative, moderate, and
radical black contributors to the Howard University historian Rayford Logan's
landmark *What the Negro Wants* (1944) further implanted and legitimated
Myrdalian means and ends in civil rights thought by giving an African American
stamp of approval to Myrdal's meliorist approach to the race problem.[36]

While now seen by some as a major break with previous African American
thinking, largely because of W. T. Couch's intemperate reaction and defense
of segregation in his "Publisher's Introduction," most of the contributors to
Logan's compendium took pains to emphasize that what Negroes wanted closely
matched Myrdal's rank order of discriminations. What blacks especially desired,
equal economic opportunity, whites could easily accept; what blacks least cared
about, intermarriage and miscegenation, whites emphatically resisted. Scorning
the contention that blacks wanted entree into the drawing rooms of whites,
Logan's contributors all stipulated that blacks wanted the same political rights
and economic opportunities possessed by other citizens—no more and no less
than what African Americans had traditionally wanted. Charles H. Wesley of
Wilberforce College underlined this point by entitling his essay "The Negro Has
Always Wanted the Four Freedoms." The goals of blacks for equality remain
the same, wrote Doxey A. Wilkerson for the Left. "Negroes are demanding
nothing new," added the NAACP's Roy Wilkins: equal rights has been the goal
of the NAACP since 1909. But neither Wilkins nor any of the others issued a
call to arms against the southern Jim Crow system. Believing that it could not
be gained "in the near future," Logan favored "the eventual abolition of public
segregation." Wesley placed the end of segregated education in the category of
"ultimate, long-range proposals" rather than "immediately approximate ones."
Sterling Brown, chastizing both southern African American leaders who think
segregation too deeply rooted ever to be eradicated and those in the north who
"believe it can be easily uprooted by speeches and governmental decree," concluded that it must be "eventually abolished"—but not "overnight." A. Philip
Randolph also counseled that the racist barriers "in the Southern section of
the country cannot be abolished overnight and that they must be approached
in terms of the conditions of the racial climate of the community." With still
less bravado, Gordon B. Hancock advised blacks to concentrate on eradicating
prejudice, not segregation, and to make the most of separation, "gaining strength
for the long tomorrow," rather than exhausting their "energies struggling for
integration." So did the Tuskegee Institute's Frederick D. Patterson, claiming

that blacks prefer to live among their own race and that they need to make the most of segregated opportunities. Neither the conservative Leslie Pinckney Hill of Cheyney College nor the CIO's Willard Townsend and the Communist Party's Doxey Wilkerson even addressed the issue of segregation.[37]

Logan's contributors also urged blacks not to attempt to take advantage of the war to gain their rights. The Negro must "unconditionally" support the war effort and do nothing to hinder a rapid and total Allied victory said Wilkerson. "The Negro race in America must give to the nation its unreserved allegiance" stated Hill. "Even at the cost of the preservation of the *status quo*," intoned Brown, "this is still the Negro's war." And Logan affirmed: "We have no wish to obstruct the war effort." To that end, none of the fourteen contributors advocated mass marches or protest boycotts. While Wilkerson groused that it would be a grave mistake for "Negroes to organize mass struggles *as Negroes*" rather than place their faith in President Roosevelt, Townsend averred that the organized labor movement was the medicine for complete recovery from "the Negro problem."[38]

Most emphatically and specifically, however, the southern black contributors affirmed solutions that harkened back to Booker T. Washington. Hancock advised self-help and vocational education. Decrying radical protests, Patterson called for "sound, practical and realistic programs" that recognize the limitations of blacks, employ "the most feasible methods," and aim at slow, steady improvement in African American life. Hill, claiming that no protest strategy "that produces racial hatred and antagonism can advance the common good," proposed that blacks gain the indulgence of whites by demonstrating "strong personal self-control, good manners," respect for law, obedience to authority, and "faith in the proved leaders and spokesmen of both races." And Langston Hughes suggested replacing Jim Crow with a system of first, second, and third class transportation that would "let the whites who wish to do so ride in coaches where few Negroes have the funds to be." Neither a militant call to arms nor an innovative strategy for black advancement, *What the Negro Wants*, like Myrdal's *An American Dilemma*, concentrated more on eradicating white prejudice and avoiding racial conflict than on storming the ramparts of racial discrimination and segregation.[39]

Militant protest never entirely abated during the war, but it never assumed dominance in either black strategy or action. To the extent that it is now possible to gauge the amount and strength of the rupture, or the transformation, in civil rights protest activities, World War II does not appear to be a watershed. Change, of course, occurred. But in a limited manner. The status and protest cognition of southern blacks in 1945, their organizations, leadership, language, and strategies for reform were neither exactly the same nor fundamentally different than they had been in 1940. The goals considered a distant dream in the 1930s had not suddenly appeared attainable. The traditional tactics of African American protest groups had not suddenly become unacceptable, nor had new, more disruptive ones come into widespread use. Why? In part, because the nearly million young black men who might have been expected to be in the forefront of more militant forays against racist practices had been uprooted from their communities to serve in an armed forces which cramped organized protests. In part, because the optimism of African Americans for postwar progress, induced by the sudden prosperity of those who left mule and plow or domestic work for a job in a defense plant and by the din of democratic propaganda during the war, mitigated against a radical turn in practices. And, certainly in part, because wartime America proved an infertile ground for the seeds of protest planted in the 1930s. The needs of war came first. Period. The domestic unity, as well as manpower and production efficiency, required for victory took precedence over all else, for the Roosevelts, and for virtually every prominent African American, labor leader, white liberal, and progressive proponent of civil rights. And if that meant holding the color line, defusing conflicts, eschewing confrontation for compromise, well, the expected rewards for African Americans would come after the war. Furthermore, social, economic, and demographic alterations, no matter how vast or rapid, in and of themselves do not generate mass movements for social change by the aggrieved or oppressed. The resources for sustained mass confrontations with the Jim Crow system in the South were gestating but still embryonic, and the political climate that would facilitate rather than inhibit militant collective action had not yet emerged. The war had driven old Dixie downward, but not down and out.

The hopes of some, and dire warnings of others, "that a New Negro will return from the war," willing to fight and die rather than accept the traditional structure of white dominance in southern society, proved premature. Indeed, it appears that many of those southern African Americans most "modernized" by military service soon left the South in the greatest numbers to pursue their individual ambitions in northern cities, or re-enlisted in the armed forces, depleting the pool of potential southern black activists. The insurgent struggle for racial justice to come in the South would eventually draw sustenance from the many fundamental transformations in American life and world affairs catalyzed by the Second World War, but that mass movement would hardly be just an extension, a continuation, of previous civil rights reform efforts. Those militantly fighting for change in the 1960s would not look to the agenda and actions of World War II blacks and racial organizations as models to emulate.

VI FIGHTING FOR WHAT WE DIDN'T HAVE

How Mississippi's Black Veterans Remember World War II

Neil R. McMillen

In November 1993 I began interviewing some of the 85,000 black Mississippians who served in uniform during World War II.[1] Conducted on the fiftieth anniversary of allied victory over the Axis Powers, these conversations did not neglect what might narrowly be defined as "military history," but they focused more fully on the social meaning of the war. The emphasis throughout was on matters of race: the more painful aspects of black service in a Jim Crow military, the connections between soldiering and citizenship, the relationship between wartime patriotic sacrifice and postwar racial struggle, the ultimate American wartime irony: the conscription of blacks to fight abroad for the very liberties they were denied at home. By interviewing survivors in a thinning population of World War II veterans, I hoped to document both how ordinary black men and women from one southern state remembered their service in the last Jim Crow war and how that service may have influenced their understanding of the black place in what white Mississippians once called "a white man's country." By gathering life experiences from the historically nameless, I hoped the better to distinguish between the wartime aspirations and agendas of the nation's black leadership elite and those of rank and file black conscripts from the lower South.

What I found was consistent with, but rather more complicated and more interesting than, what I had expected. These oral accounts, I believe, illuminate aspects of wartime experience that might otherwise escape notice. No writer could fabricate stories quite so compelling as these; no academic narrative could speak so eloquently of the American dilemma as the plain words chosen by these Mississippians.

The civil rights movement, it is now widely believed, was borne on the wings of war, World War II.[2] The remote origins of this modern freedom struggle, of course, are remote indeed, traceable through more than three centuries of black protest and striving, back to the early period of the slave trade. Its immediate catalyst, moreover, may have been any one or a combination of specific postwar developments: the southern bus boycott movement that began, almost unnoticed, in Baton Rouge, Louisiana, in 1953, and then reached critical mass two years later in Montgomery, Alabama; the Supreme Court's landmark school desegregation ruling of 1954; or the black rage that overflowed nationwide following the unpunished murder in 1955 of teenager Emmett Till in Money, Mississippi.

For fundamental first causes, however, many scholars now look to the Second World War, to home-front dislocations and overseas sacrifices, to the moral contradictions of a war for "four freedoms" fought by a democratic nation with a segregated workforce and a Jim Crow military. They look to a series of interrelated economic, demographic, political, cultural, and other changes in the structure of American society that emanated from (or were accelerated by) total war and that collectively created a context favoring racial progress. Not least, they look to the returning black troops who, as Woman's Army Corps veteran Luella Newsome explained, "wouldn't take it any more."

Transformed by wartime experience, African Americans of the World War II generation, soldier and civilian, often could not immediately act on their emergent convictions. Yet they entered the postwar period more determined than ever to become full partners in the American democratic experiment. Not a few of them, even many who lived in the darker reaches of the Deep South, announced for all to hear that the United States must now live by its own ideals. Not all black southerners literally "returned fighting," but many of them shared as never before the conviction that the humiliations of Jim Crow were intolerable. "It had to change," the Mississippi WAC explained, "because we're not going to have it this way anymore."[3]

Stated so baldly, the argument that the postwar black awakening flowed more or less directly from wartime black militancy may seem problematic on its face.

There is, after all, the problem of that apparently quiescent ten-year interlude between war's end and the rise of anything that can reasonably be described as an effective, mass-based black movement capable of stirring a nation's conscience and changing a region's laws. Moreover, as Harvard Sitkoff suggests elsewhere in this volume, the reductionism of the "Double-V" argument may well have led historians to overstate the case for an unconditional black two-front war for freedom abroad and freedom at home. We should be wary of a determinism that reads every squall on the wartime color front as a storm of racial militancy. It does seem at least arguable that historians, by and large as committed a group of "continuitarians" as can be found anywhere, could have been led into teleological error and, by reading history backwards, could have found more continuity between wartime yearning and postwar confrontation than there may in fact be.

It is arguable. But the war narratives collected for this project suggest that while the Second World War in the short term left the structure of white control in Mississippi very much intact, it nevertheless touched the lives of Mississippi's black service men and women in ways their white oppressors both feared and underestimated. Most veterans in this sample believed that though the war may not have changed their hometowns, it nevertheless changed them. It gave them new perspectives and new aspirations they could not always act upon immediately, but that influenced the subsequent course of their lives.

"Oh, it changed a great deal of things," Wilson Ashford said of his two years in the army. "It changed the individual." Shouting to be heard over the din of the small automotive garage he had operated since returning to Starkville in 1945, this 70-year-old Oktibbeha County NAACP leader told me that the black soldier learned from wartime military service "that he was able to compete":

> That's where the change come in. That was the first step in change, where you would feel that you could do it. You were always taught that you can't do, you can't do. [Whites] they'd always tell the negative side. Nothing positive. From that standpoint it gave you an opportunity to see things in a different light.

Then looking squarely at his interviewer—the nearest emblem of racial oppression—Ashford closed the subject: "I believed you was wrong all of the time, the way blacks were being treated. And after I got out [of the army] I *knew* you was wrong."

His entire postwar life seemed testimony to that conviction. Soon after his discharge, Ashford became a founding member of the local NAACP; he paid his poll taxes unfailingly and in 1950 became one of the first black registered voters in his county. Thereafter, as the freedom struggle unfolded, he became active in county voter registration drives and a persistent advocate of school integration; eventually he was appointed to the local school board and to the state School Board Association, became a lay minister in his church, served on a citywide bi-racial committee and on the board of trustees of a local community college, and became president of the local Habitat for Humanity. In 1993, the Starkville Area Chamber of Commerce honored this veteran with its Community Service Award, in recognition of an exemplary lifetime of civic responsibility.[4]

For this white interviewer, old enough barely to remember the war but fully a generation younger than these interviewees, one of the more striking aspects of the stories I collected is the shock of *non*recognition. I grew up listening to the war stories of white men, older friends and family who served in Europe and the Pacific. I began this oral history project, moreover, as a historian with some knowledge of wartime racial discrimination. Yet the memories I recorded moved and disturbed me in unexpected ways. So different were those white stories of my youth from these black stories that they might well have been from a different war. And in fact, in important respects, they were.

War, as those who study it often say, is not experienced by everyone in the same way. For the disempowered and the marginalized, for segregated black men and women, the shape of war is dictated by their secondary status. The American defense establishment of World War II was not, as these veterans frequently explained, Colin Powell's military. As the war began, black participation either in civilian war work or military training was rigidly circumscribed by race. Shut out of the better defense jobs and restricted largely to non-combat military assignments, African Americans were initially excluded from both the Marine Corps and the Army Air Corps; they were accepted by the Navy, but only as messmen, and by the Army only in segregated units. The Red Cross at first refused "black blood" and the War Department planned to train few African American military officers. Under the pressure of extreme national emergency, some adjustments were made and blacks were more fully utilized in the defense of their country. But from first to last, Uncle Sam was not during World War II an equal opportunity employer, and black troops were often subject to the embarrassment and humiliation of separate and unequal military service.[5]

Some black veterans, however, clearly had the time of their lives in the military. "I enjoyed every minute of it," a Laurel women said of her two years in the Women's Army Corps. "We were given opportunities to do all the things I never would have done had I not gone to the army."[6] Others believed that military service gave them pride and purpose they might otherwise never have experienced. "I had low self esteem," said former supply sergeant Nathan Harris of his youth in the Mississippi Delta. "The army built me up and made me proud of myself. It sounds stupid. But that's the way it was. And I've still got it in me."[7] In a third example, Dabney Hamner, a veteran combat soldier, remembered action during the German counteroffensive of December 1944 as a defining moment in his life. "I'm about the only black that I know was in the infantry," he said. "The biggest pride I ever had in my life [was] when the guy put that combat infantry badge on me."[8]

Yet black memories of the war years are rarely star-spangled memories. The war these veterans recall bears little resemblance to the so-called "Good War" of romanticized American white popular memory. Although these narratives document the diversity of black wartime experience and perception, one thread running through all of them speaks to the pain of a pariah race—to the humiliations and the burdens that were all too often visited upon African Americans in a Jim Crow military. In nearly every case, the veterans described how the white soldiers who preceded them abroad had tried to export American racial values to civilian populations in England, the European Continent, or the South Pacific. In one version of a story that reflected common black experience, Charles H. Jones, Sr., a soft-spoken retired Clarksdale school teacher who had served in the European Theater of Operation as a medical corpsman, remembered that the first obstacle he confronted overseas was the idea, deeply implanted in the English mind by white GIs, that blacks were so low on the evolutionary scale that they had tails that came out at night. The English, as he said, had never known black people:

> I met a very interesting family. This man and his wife befriended me and I was very appreciative because I didn't know anybody. The first time they invited me to dinner his daughter put a large pillow in my chair. I just figured what the heck, to make me nice and comfortable. So one day I asked her [the wife] and she said, "Well they had told us you had tails and I didn't want you to sit on it. The whites had told us that you had this tail and you were monkeys."

"Oh that embarrassed me," the veteran recalled. "This is what we had to face." In time, Jones said the British learned otherwise: "they found out that we were good people too."[9]

Slanderous white accounts of black character were perhaps still more wounding. Henry Murphy, a veteran from a Piney Woods county who as a supply sergeant had been wounded in Germany in 1945, laughed a little as he related his personal encounters with the tail myth. "After we got on through," he said of the black men in his company, "we laughed about it. It just didn't catch hold to us at all." Murphy pretended no amusement, however, when he recalled, "They [American whites] also said that we was rapists, murderers, and thieves. That bothered me. I don't know of anybody in my outfit [who] raped anybody. I imagine there are some people who probably was raped by black folks and [others] by some white folks. I don't know. But I know in my outfit we didn't go around raping or rob[bing] anybody."[10]

Some veterans remembered that just wearing their nation's uniform could cause problems in a Deep South town. WAC volunteer Brunetta Garner, who served in the medical corps, recalled that what she wore mattered little to whites in the village of Ellisville. They regarded her, she thought, "the same way they did before I left: 'There's a nigger with a uniform on'."[11] A Scott Countian, a retired handyman and sometime custodian, insisted that no white ever dared challenge his right to appear in khaki: "You're looking at one black man here never been scared of white folks. Eugene Russell is his own man. Don't nobody tell me what to do. Wore my uniform till it got too small for me."[12] Still others, however, thought that white resentment was palpable. Whites often feared, they recalled, that service in the armed forces, especially service overseas, might elevate black status, might make blacks "uppity." Clemon Jones, an elderly Jackson native who as a postwar emigre had once been commander of the American Legion in New Jersey, still remembered half a century later the hostile stares his uniform attracted when he was on leave in his home state: "You could tell they resented it because if you met one or two of them on the streets they'd look at you like you was an alligator or something. You could tell they was talking about you."[13]

The case of Rieves Bell, the soldier who went home to Starkville on furlough in 1943 only to be imprisoned following an encounter with whites who objected violently to his military attire, is well documented in military archives and still remembered by local blacks. Outnumbered on a city street by three young white men who taunted, pushed, and then tried to strip off his uniform, he fought back, wounding one of his tormentors with a knife. Despite the efforts of the military to handle the matter through army channels, civilian authorities tried and sentenced him to three and a half years in the state penitentiary at Parchman for what was surely self-defense.[14]

Other examples, perhaps less dramatic, are remembered only by the soldiers themselves. In one of the most affecting of these, Henry Murphy, a purple-heart winner who served in two wars, recalled that when he returned to Hattiesburg in 1946, his father, a local minister, met him at nearby Camp Shelby with a change of civilian clothes, lest he invite trouble from white residents and police: "He told me not to wear my uniform home. Because the police was beating up [black] GIs and searching them. If they had a white woman's picture in his pocket, they'd kill him." Although Murphy had no pictures, he did as his father wished. His was no hero's welcome; as the older man drove the family Chevrolet to Hattiesburg, the returning soldier slipped out of his olive-drabs and put on overalls and a jumper, the uniform of a field hand.[15]

Incidents of open racial conflict, including deadly fire fights between black and white troops, recur in these narratives. The hidden, or perhaps forgotten, history of the American soldier during World War II includes a disturbing number of bloody encounters, some of them full-fledged race riots, on or near military training centers, particularly at southern camps, posts, and stations where roughly 80 percent of all black enlistees were trained. Mississippi, as one might expect, had its full measure of such conflicts. Fifty years after the fact, one can hardly imagine the horror many northern black soldiers felt when they learned they had been assigned to a Mississippi base, to their minds not unlike being sold south into slavery.[16]

The worst examples of GI racial conflict, however, seem to have occurred overseas where, as some interviewees explained, the black soldier had two enemies: the Wehrmacht and white American troops. One veteran actually remembered that he feared the Germans rather less than the men of what he called "the Bloody 1," the First American Division he encountered near Nuremberg:

> They was the worst of all. The most prejudiced. Most of them came out of—you're going to be surprised—like California, New York, Ohio, [as well as] Arkansas, Mississippi and they were hell-double-breasted. If you faced that "Bloody 1," you'd better be ready, you hear me, or you would not survive. They would kill you and throw you in the middle of the street. They didn't care anything about blacks at all. Do you hear me?

He described fist fights, knife fights, fire fights—open warfare between white and black Americans in the army of occupation that in some cases resulted in death. Fearing he'd be killed or mutilated, Sergeant Murphy learned to avoid any contact with the men of the First Division: "I wasn't going to let them castrate me because you understand they were castrating—hit your seeds with a razor. I didn't want no part of that, so I decided to stay in camp. That wasn't no rumor, that was true."[17]

Of course it must be said that many black veterans remembered warm friendships with white soldiers, and some of these friendships survive to the present day. Napoleon Evans, a retired Laurel police officer who as a young draftee had been attached to the 96th Engineers Regiment in the Philippines and New Guinea, believed that the war fostered interracial understanding in ways that civilian life had not. "You might not have had all of the rights you wanted," Evans remembered, "but some of them did treat you like you was a human being. A lot of blacks and whites in service together, I think they learned to have respect for each other. The whites I know learned to have more respect for blacks than they did at first."[18]

Not a few other veterans, on the other hand, recalled virtually no contact with white Americans, other than with their officers who were nearly always white and very often southern. As these men and women put it, growing up in color-conscious Mississippi was good preparation for military life, for being what some called "half a soldier": "Everything was segregated then, everything— different water fountains, different bathrooms, different camps."[19] "Black folks on this side of the track, and white people on their side of the track. That's the same thing within the Army: All your blacks over here, and all your whites over there."[20] The two races were fully as isolated in northern camps or overseas as they had been at home. They did not train together. They generally did not play together. They rarely served together.

Inevitably, however, other veterans told deeply moving stories of interracial friendships made and interracial friendships shattered as wartime emergency gave way to peacetime normalcy. In one version of this all-too-common memory, Ben Fielder, a retired hotel bell captain who served in both Europe and the Far East, recalled a last long train ride across the country from California to Mississippi at war's end. This staff sergeant and his white traveling companion had for days exchanged stories of family and sweethearts; they had shared their meals, their dreams, their hopes for the future. They had gotten, Fielder believed, beyond "this race nonsense," and "become tight"—until the train crossed into Dixie. Then everything changed, as the white soldier assumed his traditional role of dominance and, without a trace of subtlety, informed the black soldier that the war was over, that they were back home, that—as the black soldier remembered—"I was still just a nigger. Not an American soldier anymore. Just a nigger."[21]

Other interviewees related similar experiences amid the ebb and flow of War itself. "When the bombs were falling," Dabney Hamner said of Hitler's desperate Ardennes offensive of December 1944, there "wasn't no black or white— we was just the same, black soldiers and white soldiers, all Americans." Napoleon Coney of Pike County, another infantry veteran who proudly displayed his five bronze stars, remembered his years in the European theater as "the only time in my life I felt like a man. It's perfect. When you're in combat those folks forget that you're black. When the shells start, incoming mail—BOOM—your whole self is shaking. [Color] don't make no difference."[22]

Another man, a twelve year veteran with a remarkable gift for recreating the historical moment, first described a racial "hornet's nest," a bloody stand-off between himself, another black soldier, and two white GIs in Germany, a conflict that resulted in serious injury and perhaps death to one of the whites. Threatened by the armed white Americans and fearing the worst, this soldier's companion lashed out with the butt of his M-1 rifle: "We had no choice because they was fixing to do us in. I mean blood flew everywhere. I don't know whether he's living or dead. We left." Then, as if to put the story in some larger context, the veteran explained that during the thick of things, race rarely divided American fighting men: "Yes, we supported them during the war. We gave our hearts to them during the war, and they gave theirs to us." A non-commissioned officer assigned to a trucking unit, he remembered close quarters and easy relations with whites in the early aftermath of the Normandy invasion, amid the fog of battle in France. "We picked up their dead. We even hauled them on spearheads. We slept in the same areas they slept in. We shared the rations." Although some whites initially resisted an integrated mess, troops of both races quickly discovered that racial convention was impractical at the front: "they decided that oh, what the hell, everybody eat together, work together, and get along." "When we was supplying them, they needed gasoline, food, ammunition. Everything was lovely. They welcomed us until after the war." During the German breakthrough, he remembered, his unit got out of their trucks, "to fight the Germans for them and with them." But once the war was over, he recalled, "everybody went back into their little old world. They decided we was the scum of the earth after the war. They never did decide we was equal, you know that. But they needed us when the Germans [were] giving them hell." Asked how such could be, he thought a moment and said: "Well, it was just a mirror of our civilian life, that's all. The way of life that we've been living all them many years."23

Perhaps the deepest meaning of such memories is to be found in the very singularity of the interracial moment. Combat allowed a shared American experience, one not circumscribed by race; the Jim Crow army was never so color-blind as when it was in a foxhole under fire. Wilson Evans of Harrison County, for example, explained that he never felt so accepted, so free from the burden of color, as he did during the Battle of the Bulge: "That was the first time during twenty-seven months in the service that I was an American soldier. For those what six, maybe eight, ten days there was no black or white soldiers. We was all soldiers. White was afraid of dying as blacks. And there was no color. During the breakthrough I did see that Americans could become Americans for about eight or nine days."24

Among the questions of most interest to this project were those that centered on the American wartime dilemma, on the moral paradox of a democratic nation deploying a Jim Crow military to liberate Europe and Asia. Few of the interviewees came from families that then voted. Most scoffed at the very idea that their parents enjoyed the protection of the Fifteenth and Nineteenth Amendments. "When we went in World War II, we didn't have no rights. We couldn't vote," remembered Sam Jackson, a retired custodian who had served in the South Pacific. "Man, you'd get killed [just] talking about voting."[25] Most recalled brutal treatment by white police ("If you were a black violator you got a beating first. After they got you handcuffed you got a whipping before they'd take you in").[26] All, when asked, recounted the humiliations of Jim Crow public transportation, of being forced to sit at the back of the bus, behind a screen—what William Nicholson of Wayne County called "an iron curtain," "a Jim Crow curtain," positioned to shield white eyes from black passengers.[27]

"Conditions here was ridiculous," Jonestown native Nathan Harris said of the Mississippi Delta. The example this veteran non-commissioned officer used was one that had been painfully seared into the memory of virtually all African Americans of the World War II generation: the status of black American citizens relative to the nearly 250,000 white German prisoners of war interned in the South. "I'll tell you what," he said, "if you was a black boy here in Mississippi, when they brought those Germans over here as prisoners they got more privilege than you did as a citizen—German prisoners! Right here around this country." "Blacks didn't have nothing" and the worst part, Harris thought, was that "at the time we didn't know any better. We thought that's the way it was supposed to be."[28]

Veteran after veteran used virtually the same words—"we thought it was supposed to be that way"—explaining, often, that even in the North they encountered in more subtle forms the racism they were accustomed to in Dixie,[29] and that not until they served overseas did they fully understand the depths of their own degraded citizenship. Growing up separate and unequal, Clarksdale navy veteran Haywood Stephney recalled, was like "living in a closed circle":

> Because you grow up in this situation you don't see but one side of the coin. Having not tasted the freedom or the liberty of being or doing like other folks then you didn't know what it was like over across the street. So we accepted it. When you're not exposed to much you don't get much. But after seeing what some of the other world was doing then I realized how far behind I was. As we began to move and stir around and learn other ways then we had a choice—a comparison. I could contrast this with that.

With a new sense of himself and his race, Stephney remembered thinking: "Now its going to be difficult to get me back in total darkness. That was my attitude. Deep within me I made up my mind I've got to move out of the situation that I'm in to something better."30

A self-described Scott County jailhouse-minister detailed a similar process of growth and enlightenment:

> We were young men. We all knew the treatment we already had been getting here in Mississippi and everywhere else. So we don't think nothing about that. We thought that was just the way it was supposed to be. We was dumb to the facts and didn't know.

Thirty-three months and nineteen days in the Pacific theater, however, opened Eugene Russell's eyes. "It started coming to me after we got to Australia," he said. "I noticed the difference right then. The Australians called us the 'tan Yanks', not niggers and monkeys." "There wasn't nothing but white people [in Australia]," he remembered, "but you was welcome. And the farther you go up [finger raised, tracing an imaginary map]—the Dutch Indies, I don't care how white you was or how black you was, you were still treated right. You was just a man. When you went on to the Philippines, you were just a man there." "I wouldn't take nothing for it," he said of such experiences. "I got a better understanding in life and my destiny and where I'm headed to. I saw how folks can live. It opened up a new world to me, opened up [my eyes] to the racial problems."31

These memories of changing personal perspectives and transforming encounters overseas, of new and revealing light shed on old injustices, become more poignant still when paired with memories of return and reunion in the immediate postwar period as GI became civilian. Consider but a single story, this one told by Dabney Hamner, a veteran of the 125th Infantry Division who had been wounded in Germany and who believed that "the only time in my life I [had] felt like a man was in Europe." He returned to Clarksdale, Hamner remembered, with a chest full of decorations and not a little pride that, as he put it, "I'd been hopping in and out of foxholes in five battles for American democracy." One of the first whites he met stopped to admire his medals: "Ow-w-w look at the spangles on your chest. Glad you back," the white man said. "Let me tell you one thing though, don't you forget." Forget what? the veteran inquired. "That you're still a nigger."32

The message was not always so blunt, but time and again one finds evidence in these narratives of black homecomings spoiled by pointed reminders that this was still Mississippi, that the old rules still applied.33

Why then did these Mississippians fight? What were they fighting for? Did they think this might not be their war? Or did they expect that the uniform might be a ticket to full citizenship? At a conscious level, did they then embrace the ideology of the "Double V"? Do they now believe—did they then suspect— that for blacks World War II was a "War on Two Fronts" and thus a staging point for the modern freedom struggle?

The answers found in these narratives are so diverse, the expressions of personal motivations often so complicated and ambiguous, as to defy confident analysis. Human diversity is the oral historian's most vexing challenge; the men and women represented in this sample did not speak with one voice on these or any other issues. Some few veterans admitted that they didn't know why they went to war or, until much later, what they were fighting for.[34] Others reported that they were not eager to fight in Europe or Asia for what their own people did not have at home, that they put on a uniform only because they were drafted or because military pay was better than that of any other job then open to black Mississippians.[35] "I wasn't thinking about volunteering," one conscript remembered. "Most of my people always said that it was a white war and blacks didn't have no business going."[36] Another declared that after weighing the alternatives he had concluded he would fight for the lesser of two evils: bad as Theodore Bilbo was, Adolph Hitler was worse.[37]

From a somewhat different perspective, an infantry veteran from the Gulf Coast said that his prewar experiences with Jim Crow had stripped him of all patriotic feeling for his country. He was unmoved by the Japanese attack on Pearl Harbor: "I figured that if the Japs took America that I would fare better." Even after he was drafted, even as he slogged across Europe from Normandy to Berlin, he saw little difference between German and American racism. He rather hoped, he said, that the Nazis didn't want his mother's Harrison County home, but if they wanted downtown Gulfport, "hell, they could have it."[38]

That bitter memory aside, most of these men and women insisted that, however resentful of social injustice, they served in uniform because this was their country too. "We were second class citizens," said James Briwder Jones, a veteran of the 761st Tank Battalion said. "We were called niggers, and we were deprived of certain privileges. We lived as a nation within a nation." Still indignant that his unit never got the recognition it earned for cutting off a German spearhead, for as he believed "saving Bastogne," this Jones County NAACP branch president nevertheless remembered the black tankers' pride "in just being Americans. We always felt that someday that shackle that held us down would be broken. We had faith in this country. This is the only country we had."[39]

Such hopes and sentiments were widely, if not universally, shared. One finds in these narratives rich layers of counterpoint: shocking accounts of interracial bloodlettings and wounded spirits balanced by the uncomplicated love of flag and country that seems so natural to the World War II generation. Twenty-year veteran flyer Alva Temple, one of the celebrated Tuskegee Airmen, was perhaps more forceful than most when he declared that his wartime patriotism was unconditional. By war's end he had flown 120 combat missions over Italy and East-Central Europe and been awarded the Distinguished Flying Cross. Acknowledging that some African Americans "said that blacks should not participate in that war because we weren't getting a fair deal," this retired lieutenant colonel nevertheless insisted: "Well, I never felt like that. I felt it was my job, and I did it the best that I knew how. I was going to make my contribution. I did think that the contribution would have some effect on things being equalized, blacks getting a better deal in the United States." "On the other hand," Lt. Col. Temple said, "that was not a condition why I went. I would have gone regardless of what happened. I felt it was my duty to do that."[40] None said it more eloquently, but the thought recurs in interview after interview: I went because I loved my country.

Expressions such as these might invite derision in some circles today, but these interviewees did not seem naive. Few admitted to any illusions; none truly expected a hasty change of racial heart back home.[41] None of them—not even those who reported weekly wartime contact with the Pittsburgh *Courier*, the most militantly anti-segregation black newspaper published in the United States—remembered hearing the protest slogans of the "Double-V" and the "War on Two Fronts." Not one professed to have had what Dr. David W. White, Mississippi's first black optometrist and a veteran of the 1895th Engineers, called a "crystal ball," a clairvoyant understanding when they answered the call to arms that the war marked the beginning of Jim Crow's end.[42] In fact some reported that they expected nothing when they went to war and, so well schooled were they then in Jim Crow's ways, that they were neither surprised nor even particularly disappointed to learn upon their return that nothing had changed, that, as German Levy of Brookhaven expressed it, "the pancake hadn't turned over," that "you come back home right into the same world you left."[43]

Three years in the Army Air Corps had made Delta postal worker William McDougal less patient with white injustice, but not a fool. "All the white folks they was worried about the reaction from [black] soldiers," he remembered of his return to Coahoma County; but "we didn't push nothing in that time because they was running everything. We didn't have no say so about nothing then because we weren't voting." Understanding that "one man couldn't do too much," McDougal didn't "think too much about the segregation. I didn't entertain the idea that I was going to change it. No, but I had the idea, look I'm trying to better myself."[44]

Employing the same blend of social realism and personal ambition, retired university Professor Matthew Burks said of his return from three years in the Philippines: "I knew the way conditions were, and I really did not expect them to have changed within that period of time." Discharged in December 1946, he resumed an interrupted education in a segregated Mississippi high school. "It really didn't bother me that much at the time," Burks remembered. "I just went on and fitted into the situation as I had before." In fact, this Neshoba County sharecroppers' son did return fighting, a longtime friend (Arvarh Strickland) remembered, "but fighting to overcome his background." That fight eventually carried Burks to a career as teacher and administrator at Mississippi Valley State University, following degree programs at Tougaloo College (B.A.), Boston University (M.A.), and the University of Virginia (Ph.D.).[45]

Without exception, these returning veterans found more continuity than change in their Mississippi hometowns; there would be no real progress, they patiently explained, until after "the Freedom Riders," until the advent of the "civil rights people"—common metaphors for the upsurge of black activism in the 1960s.[46] In fact, many interviewees affirmed that what they would later call civil rights mattered less to them in 1946 than a decent job. "I didn't know that much about the right to vote," a Brookhaven draftee admitted. "But I did know that I deserved the right to have a job." The moral contradictions of the war had largely escaped his notice, he said, until he returned to a job market that was monopolized almost entirely by whites: "That's when it began to dawn upon me, that's when I began to realize that it was just something wrong in this country."[47] A retired Clarksdale educator, on the other hand, remembered that his father had managed to "sneak in and register" to vote during the war and that he himself had left the military wanting "the same rights as anybody else." His first priority, however, was his family's welfare: "When I came back here the only thing I was looking out to do was to try to survive. I didn't bother about that other [civil rights]. I wanted to make a living for me and my wife and children and that's all."[48]

Others explained that job and wage discrimination in Mississippi, more than any other postwar disappointment, pushed them into either outmigration or reenlistment. "Many veterans in the South came back determined not so much to change things but to get the hell out of here," explained former state Senator Henry Kirksey, who had been a wartime artillery officer. "That was one of the most often expressed intents for those veterans that I talked to. You've got to get out of the South because they can't stand it anymore." After the war Kirksey—who as a major had been Mississippi's highest ranking black soldier during World War II—finished his college education, married, and in 1948 re-entered the army when he concluded that he could support his family in no other way.[49]

Yet, if these Mississippians generally had few short term expectations, their narratives nevertheless document a widely shared hope that black wartime sacrifices would lead eventually, in ways they could not then fully imagine, to a better day. Alva Temple, the Tuskegee Airman who attached no strings to his patriotism, also affirmed that "when you defend your country, I think you were due full citizenship privileges."[50] And, like that Airman, these interviewees more often than not—and very often in the same breath—placed their military experience in a broader context of racial uplift. Asked what they were fighting for, all agreed with a retired shoe repairman from Hattiesburg who said "We were fighting for what we didn't have." Yet veteran after veteran also explained: they fought for the future, for their children and their grandchildren. They went to war hoping that Mississippi might eventually be a better place for all of its people. Not immediately, but eventually.[51]

Their words were as varied, of course, as the men and women who spoke them. But if a single veteran could be said to have somehow captured their collective understanding of the social meaning of the war, it may well have been Douglas L. Conner, a Starkville physician who acknowledged that, though a college graduate when drafted, he never encountered "the expression 'Double V for victory' " until he studied the history of black wartime experience many years after his discharge. Conner thought, moreover, that the men in his unit, the 31st Quartermaster Battalion stationed in Okinawa, did not in any conscious way understand that the war for the Four Freedoms was for blacks a "war on two fronts," a war for democracy over there and back home: "We talked about our hatred for segregation and for the Japanese, but we never tied the two together that way." He also remembered the ambivalence many black Mississippians shared as the war began. Following Pearl Harbor he sensed among his fellow students at Alcorn College no "gung-ho spirit of 'Come on, let's get it over with'. Most of us said that we would not volunteer for a segregated service. If we're called, we'll go. We'll fight this war. We'll do what we can to win, but at the same time we need to do something to make sure that we don't go back to where we were before the war." Once in uniform, he came to think that he was "fighting for future generations because I had a sense that things would get better for African Americans in time." Fifty years after the fact, he remained persuaded that "if there had not been a war, I think it would have been harder to fight segregation and to change Jim Crow laws." "The important thing about World War II," he believed,

> is that there was proof that blacks could enter the service and fight as heroically as anybody else. The air people in Tuskegee, Dorie Miller, and the others gave the blacks a sense that they could succeed and compete in a world that had been saying that "you're nothing." And at the same time because of the world war, I think many people, especially blacks, got the idea that "We're going back, but we're not going back to business as usual. Somehow we're going to change this nation so that there's more equality than there is now."

At war's end, Douglas Conner had no better idea than did any other returning soldier just how that change might be realized. He recognized that "things would not get better on their own" and he now counted himself among those service men and women who were "determined that somehow Mississippi had to do better than it had been doing for black Americans." Yet nothing suggested to him that real change was in the postwar air. When he was mustered out of the army at Camp Shelby in June 1946, his first act as a civilian was not to storm the county courthouse, but to catch a northbound train to a summer job in a Chicago steel mill. That fall he took his savings and his G.I. benefits to Washington, where he entered Howard University Medical School. In 1951, after an internship in St. Louis, Dr. Conner returned to Mississippi to open a medical practice in Starkville. The following year, at the age of thirty-two, he became one of a tiny fraction of adult black Mississippians (perhaps 4 percent) who were registered to vote. Thereafter he was a force for gradual change in his community, and he never forgot the conviction he carried home from the Pacific: "my black skin was not a valid excuse for anyone holding me back—or, for that matter, for holding myself back."[52]

How then shall we understand these narratives? What do these voices say about war as the analogue of reform? What do the narrators tell us about the connections between black participation in the last Jim Crow war and the modern black freedom struggle that engulfed the South in the decade after the *Brown* decision?

However one might choose to read them, these interviews speak directly to the humiliations of separate-and-unequal wartime experience and far more ambiguously about that experience as the genesis of postwar black struggle. One could not persuasively argue from the oral testimony presented here that fifty years ago the generality of black soldiers, much less the generality of black soldiers from Mississippi, returned from the war with radical change on their minds, determined to vote at any costs, determined immediately to challenge the discrimination that for more than three centuries had kept their people down. Although historians understand that wars and their aftershocks very often ultimately unsettle traditional social patterns, these black men and women returned to hometown racial environments that were, as we have seen, depressingly familiar. Much as they hated segregation and disfranchisement, they had known little else and they were not then prepared to fling body and soul upon racial ramparts that were at least as impregnable in 1946 as in 1941. Until the 1960s, few of them found reason to believe that genuine racial progress was imminent—or even possible—in Mississippi.

Some veterans did situate the antecedents of the modern freedom struggle in the World War II years. "We paved the way, we broke the ice, we opened the door," Nathan Harris insisted.[53] Many more, however, saw little relationship between black sensibilities in the 1940s and black protest in the 1960s. In these memories, the war waged for the liberation of Europe and Asia is often described as a defining moment and sometimes a personal turning point, but it does not emerge as America's liberating social divide, the watershed from which flowed a torrent of subsequent social change. Indeed, what seems most remarkable about these narratives is the fact that so many of the aging black men and women who constructed them declined to invest wartime experience with postwar meaning. The narrators, by and large, did not read back into the period before 1946 the attitudes and expectations that in the period after 1954 would be so common to the black community.

That fact is of no small significance, of course. But if the black veterans themselves do not remember World War II as a black war on two fronts, if they seem less prepared than historians to link wartime aspiration to postwar confrontation, does it mean that historians must now radically revise their histories of recent American race relations, severing all connections between the 1940s and the 1960s? The answer is surely No. I do confess that what I expected to hear at the outset of this oral history project was rather different from what I in fact heard. While I did not assume that history makers and history writers would interpret the past in precisely the same way, I expected, nevertheless, greater convergence of perspective than I found between participant observers and scholars. Yet, when read and understood in the context of a larger body of documentary evidence, these fascinating conversations persuade, nonetheless, that because of the war, and the events and circumstances that eventually flowed from it, the Jim Crow system was doomed. In the short term, the war did not massively reshape race relations. In the war's immediate aftermath fearful white southerners were if anything more unyielding, and the color line held for nearly two decades. Despite isolated acts of immense heroism and racial militancy, sustained black protest on a mass scale did not erupt for half a generation.

Nevertheless, though delayed, the war's impact was decisive. As these narratives suggest, patriotic service at home and abroad provided new perspectives on ancient white wrongs and ultimate black possibilities. The war helped shape an emerging racial consciousness; it paved the way for an emerging black awakening. It underscored the moral contradictions of a nation that professed human rights and practiced white supremacy. It illuminated some of the darker places in the American social landscape. It made plain, for all who would see, that in a modern democratic society the citizen soldier, of whatever race, must be both a full soldier and a full citizen. And the war also fostered the development of a larger societal framework within which successful struggle for human rights could be waged. Though never an independent variable in the equation of sweeping social change, World War II nevertheless accelerated political, economic, legal, and intellectual tendencies already in motion. It set in train a combination of international, national, and regional forces that ultimately undermined the legal foundations of segregation, discrimination, and disfranchisement.

And it was precisely this convergence of war-born developments, personal and impersonal—this combination of human agents pushing for social justice and of societal forces conducive to racial change—that brought a Second Reconstruction to the American South. As these interviewees understood only too well, the courage and conviction they attributed in substantial part to their service experiences were in themselves not enough. What they perhaps understood less fully was how the war—their war—contributed to the emergent structural changes in the nation's political and economic life, in its laws and social values, and in its public policy that ultimately opened the way for fundamental racial progress. In this favoring context, black courage and conviction could help transform a system that had once sent these Mississippians to fight abroad for what they didn't have at home.

VII EVERY WOMAN LOVES A FASCIST

Writing World War II on the Southern Home Front

Anne Goodwyn Jones

"Every woman adores a Fascist," wrote Sylvia Plath, "The boot in the face, the brute / Brute heart of a brute like you." This famous line from her poem, "Daddy," connects the apparently distant and public events of World War II to private feelings about a nominally private event: the relationship of a daughter with her father. Plath wrote the poem on October 12, 1962, before the term became a popular epithet (as in "fascist pig" or "male fascist pig") for those of us who came of age in the 1960s. For her readers, then, the emotional impact of the term would have been different—more intense, perhaps more historically inflected. During the same period and earlier, southern women writers wrote about, defined, and used the term "fascist" in writing which, quite like Plath's, appropriated public discourse to analyze private, gendered relationships. I hope to make the case here that these writers' representations of fascism—clearly rhetorical strategies—nevertheless formed the basis for a serious imaginative analysis of the connections between domestic life in the South and an international war overseas. Images from that war and from the 1920s and 1930s, when "fascist" became a household word, seemed useful to these writers, I think, in launching their complicated and risky project of critiquing American manhood while supporting the boys in battle. "Fascist," with its complex and changing American cultural meanings during the two decades before, during, and just after the war, became a term that could usefully join private and public worlds, gender and political wars. It was the linchpin that held together two conventionally separate worlds.

Katherine Anne Porter, Lillian Hellman, and Harriette Arnow respectively wrote a story (1931-40), a play (1941), and a novel (1954), that use the representation of the Second World War as an occasion for reflection about the relationship of domestic, personal, gendered relationships to international military combat. Put differently, they looked for the origins of war in the construction of a particular type of manhood that feeds on war, that requires war for its own survival. Since war could be understood in terms of a sort of masculinity—fascist manhood, perhaps—an analysis of war became at the same time an analysis of gender relations. The masculinity that battened on war was the masculinity of the "Daddy" southern women loved and hated. To understand one was, they wrote, to understand the other. As I hope to show, these writers all felt hopeful that understanding could not only critique but provide ways of resolving conflicts, abroad and at home, short of sustained and systematic violence whether institutionalized as international war or as domestic abuse.

Lest we too quickly elide the terms "fascist," "masculinity," and "southern Daddy," let me situate this argument in the context of the lively current definitional debate over Fascism. Although I am claiming for these writers only that they used the meanings of "fascist" that circulated so widely in English-speaking cultures—not that those meanings were in some sense "accurate"—it is instructive to examine the search for a common denominator, or ideal type, or generic Fascism, among contemporary thinkers. Their lists of *sine qua nons,* although they are by no means identical, intersect with one another and with the meanings southern women found and provided from their own experience. And, I will speculate, they intersect in suggestive ways with the cultural and historical meanings of the American South. It was no accident, in my opinion, that southern women found themselves drawn to, and drawn to critique, the images and concepts of Fascism.

A useful beginning spot is *The Harper Dictionary of Modern Thought.* This volume—edited by Adolf Hitler's biographer Alan Bullock—defines Fascism by locating a term common to various fascisms: "authoritarian." For Bullock and Stallybrass, the ingredients of generic Fascism are the following six: 1. nationalism; 2. anti-Communism & anti-Marxism; 3. hatred for liberalism, democracy, parliamentary parties; desire to replace them with one party, a monopoly of power, and a single leader with charismatic qualities and dictatorial powers; 4. a cult of violence and action, with a para-military exaltation of war; 5. mass propaganda and terrorism; and 6. frequently, racism and anti-Semitism.

Bullock and Stallybrass note also that "fascist" became a term of political abuse for Communists, who lumped together "genuine" Fascists, conservatives, and Social Democrats (228-9). An introductory text for undergraduates, Howard Williams's *Concepts of Ideology*, develops the following list: 1. radicalism; 2. opposition to liberalism; 3. the cult of the leader; 4. nationalism; 5. totalitarianism (playing to the "naive" desire for a "total solution to the problems of social life" [73]); 6. anti-Marxism; 7. and a tendency to glorify violence and struggle for its own sake (all page 61). Williams begins a rudimentary gender analysis, albeit not named as such, when he uses a quotation from Primo de Rivera to capture the meanings of the "cult of the leader." De Rivera describes a Mussolini high up in his lighted study and hard at work at night while others slept, " 'watching over Italy, to whose breathing he listened from there as to that of a small daughter.' . . . [For Williams, this description] captures perfectly the abdication of personal responsibility and freedom which lies at the heart of the acceptance of charismatic leadership" (66). What Williams does not comment on, of course, is the paternalist gendering of the image. However, he later comments that "the Hungarian Marxist, Mikhaly Vajda, suggests that the resort to paramilitary organization was the most characteristic feature of the Fascist phenomenon. . . . As [H. S.] Harris aptly puts it in his book on [Giovanni] Gentile's social philosophy, 'From the very beginning there was in Fascism a strain of romantic violence . . .' " (76) and notes that Fascists associated pacifism with "cowardice, effeminacy, and weakness" (77). Together, these observations suggest a contradictory masculinity that, like a small girl, needs the protection of a strong man, and yet (or therefore?) identifies masculinity with violence and war.

Stanley Payne's thoughtful and deeply informed *History of Fascism, 1914–1945*, points out that as early as 1923 the term "fascist" appeared as a pejorative, usually connoting "violent," "brutal," "repressive," or "dictatorial." These points, however, sadly do not distinguish Fascism from numerous other terms. Payne undertakes a definitional history, beginning with Ernst Nolte, who in 1968 saw "anti-Marxism, antiliberalism, anticonservatism, the leadership principle, a party army, and the aim of totalitarianism" to mark off Fascism(5). Although Payne is drawn to Roger Griffin's pithy and thoughtful 1991 definition of Fascism as "a genus of political ideology whose mythic core in its various permutations is a palingenetic [that is, generating a national rebirth] form of populist ultranationalism." But, Payne observes, other nationalisms can feature rebirth as a goal. In a footnote he cites in full the greater complexity of Emilio Gentile's ten complex points (1992); oversimplified, they are: 1. mass movement; 2. antiideological ideology; 3. mystical thought; 4. totalitarian politics; 5. a civil ethic of virility, [male] comradeship, and warrior spirits; 6. a hierarchy of functions; 7. a corporative economy; 8. imperialism; 9. a single state party; and 10. a police apparatus (5-6).

Payne's own foray into the definitional lists has three fronts. On the first, Ideology and Goals, he enlists the notions of idealism, a new state, a regulated structure, positive attitudes toward violence and war, and a design for empire. On the second front, Fascist Negations, he includes anti-liberalism, -communism, and -conservatism. And on the third, Style and Organization, he places mass mobilization, militarization, and aesthetic structure that creates a "theatrical politics" and a visual culture, and finally "extreme stress on the masculine principle and male dominance, while espousing a strongly organic view of society" (7) that "made a place for women, but in that relationship the rights of the male were to enjoy predominance" (13). Payne continues: "No other kind of movement expressed such complete horror at the slightest suggestion of androgyny." He quotes Roger Griffin on the subject of the Fascist "flight from the feminine, manifesting itself in a pathological fear of being engulfed by anything . . . associated with softness, with dissolution, or the uncontrollable"; and Payne completes his list of Fascist stylistic and organizational patterns by noting the emphasis on youth and on authoritarian/charismatic command (13). If pressed for a single sentence definition, Payne offers the following: Fascism is (was) "a form of revolutionary ultra-nationalism for national rebirth that is based on a primarily vitalist philosophy, is structured on extreme elitism, mass mobilization, and the *Fuhrerprinzip*, positively values violence as end as well as means, and tends to normatize war and/or the military virtues" (14).

Perhaps most helpfully, Payne distinguishes Fascism from other right wing groups in several ways; for example, he points out, ultra-conservatism tends to base itself in traditional religious values rather than to invent its own mystical and mythical rhetoric; it tends, as well, to want to freeze the status quo rather than erase the past to create or "birth" a new nation.

The claim that the South was a site for full-fledged Fascism thus cannot be made with any seriousness. The best recent history of Fascism, Stanley Payne's, devotes only three pages to the United States, and uses them to debunk claims that Huey Long (too egalitarian), the KKK (too religious), Father Coughlin (a priest) and other American phenomena were "fascist." In fact, he writes, "the only theoretical precondition for fascism which existed in the United States was ethnoracial tension, and the only aspects of prefascist culture which flourished were racialist and eugenicist doctrines, fom the 1880s to the 1920s" (351). On what grounds then does a responsible literary theorist like Jefferson Humphries claim that the former Nazi Paul de Man's theories are appropriate for the study of the South precisely because of his Fascist history? And why, if ethnoracial tensions and doctrines were the sole proto-Fascist condition in America, did southern women find the figure of the Fascist so useful an analytical tool?

This is not the place to offer more than tentative suggestions: Humphries, for example, sees the link between the South and the Third Reich in "organicism," a concept available in the work of Elizabeth Fox-Genovese as well. In thinking about Fascism, Payne usefully defines "organic" in a footnote to refer to "concepts of society in which its various sectors are held to bear a structured relationship to each other that serves to define and delimit their roles and rights, taking precedence over the identities and rights of individuals" (note 10, p. 13). For our purposes, however, the more interesting links appear in the notions of "romantic violence," of "charismatic leadership," of a "theatrical politics" as a performance of self, of paternalism, and of dominance, all components of a *masculinity* that both fears and rules over women and the feminine. It is odd indeed that Payne missed the misogyny in his list of preconditions; it is even odder, finally, that not one of these (and other cited) analyses and definitions of Fascism has been organized around questions of gender.

But southern writers have, in a sense, done this for us. I will begin with Faulkner's renderings of the southern tradition of romantic violence, the chivalric tradition; move to his later representations of the links between paramilitary violence, racism, and sexism; and then turn to the texts by women. In those texts, all by white women, the aspects of Fascism that seemed most pressing had little to do with racism, and nothing directly with such definitional components as nationalism, totalitarianism, and a single state party. The images they use draw attention instead to the similarities between southern charismatic, romantic, violent manhood and Fascism; between southern paternalist and overtly dominant manhood and Fascism; and between a southern ethic of virility as honor and Fascism. I will conclude with some remarks about the need for southern historians to take gender into account in their archival work and in their thinking about what they have gathered.

It is a familiar theme in southern writing to link the discourse of southern chivalry, with its courtliness towards women, to the discourse of the southern gentleman at war, the cavalier or "chevalier." Richard Milum has observed that Faulkner (despite the critique of militarism implied in the stories I will soon discuss) was deeply involved in the southern myth of heroic manhood, the cavalier ideal. According to that myth, the Civil War produced the South's chevaliers, calvarymen who brought to war and to love the art of chivalry. Because success in battle and in love meant success as a man, war and gender were intimately linked. Faulkner articulates his yearning for this ideal in the depiction of Civil War hero Bayard Sartoris in *Flags in the Dust*. This Sartoris is one of Jeb Stuart's cavalrymen. In the family myth that ensures his ideological if not his physical survival, Bayard rode with his troop right into the heart of a Union camp in search of (a subtle pause from the storyteller) *coffee*. A romantic nose-tweaking of the Yankees, this successful engagement with the enemy pales beside Bayard's repetition of it, which results in his death: a captured Union officer (so the story goes) taunted Jeb Stuart's chivalric values, saying that in this war "gentlemen" are as anachronistic as "anchovies." As a response, Bayard rode back into the Union camp, this time for anchovies. He was shot in the back by a cook.

Though Bayard dies before he can prove his manhood in chivalric love as well as war, the character of Jeb Stuart suggests the connection between the roles. Aunt Jenny is the character who has been telling Bayard's heroic story, or heroicizing Bayard's story, guaranteeing his mythic survival as a cavalier. She ends her narration by saying, " 'I danced a valse [with Jeb Stuart] in Baltimore in '58,' and [the narrator tells us, perhaps participating in the moment himself] her voice was proud and still as banners in the dust" (FID, 23). The romance of the waltz and the romance of the war are inextricably bound up in the figure of a particular type of manhood. Though Faulkner's World War I Sartoris men show more of the troubles of this southern manhood, its possibility is never finally abandoned, and its ties with the McLendons and Grimms thus never fully confronted. Where for Faulkner, the chevalier's dominance is masked and made seductive by charm and imagination, women writers—who had more of a stake in removing the mask and resisting the charm—found him to be made of the same cloth as his more blatant brothers.

Faulkner's "Dry September" makes these links clear in a pre-fascist setting. The lynch mob's leader, McLendon, has been a hero in the Great War. After the war in Jefferson, Mississippi, he orchestrates the death of an innocent black man. Using the vague claims of an unreliable witness as the excuse, McLendon overrides the single man who opposes him, drives a group of white men out to the ice plant where Will Mayes is night watchman, and stuffs the protesting Mayes down a deep kiln. When the lynching is done, McLendon goes home to yell at his wife for disobeying him and then throws her against the wall. In *Light in August* Faulkner once again develops a "faux" Great War hero who forms a racist paramilitary organization that causes the death of a man they believe is black: Percy Grimm not only makes sure Joe Christmas is dead, but in castrating him makes sure he is feminized as well. The violence of European war, the violence of domestic racism, and the violence of misogyny once again combine to provide energy, motivation, strategy, and goal for these proto-fascist men. Southern historian Pete Daniel makes connections similar to Faulkner's: in his history of the twentieth century South, the chapter entitled "Fascism at Home" discusses the repression of blacks during the Second World War.

Thus far I have focused on representations of the similarities between men at war—whether cavalry or grunts—and men at home, waltzers or wifebeaters. Structural similarities seem at first adequate to explain these continuities: hierarchies of power in the military work together with patriarchal privilege, just as the morality of violence at war may seem to sanction disciplinary violence at home. But more complex analyses from psychoanalytically minded cultural historians such as Klaus Theweleit (*Male Fantasies*, I and II) to Kaja Silverman (*Male Subjectivity at the Margins*) have pointed out the contradictions and ambivalences that undergird such structures. Theweleit's study of the private writings of the German Freikorps in the 1920s argues that, far from feeling power or privilege, these men who formed the core of Hitler's storm troopers were terrified of women, blood, floods, the Red masses—in short, terrified of what appeared to be threats to an already unsteady, even unformed, sense of autonomy. It is Theweleit's contention that these early Fascists felt they needed a sort of "body armor" in various forms. Their power, their violence, their dominance stem, he believes, from terror. Similarly, Kaja Silverman argues that war works not to build men but to deconstruct them, or at least to deconstruct their sense of the "phallus," the illusory sense of male power. Wartime experience of inadequacy, of powerlessness and helplessness, can shrivel men's self-esteem. War can thus provide an opportunity to unravel what Silverman calls American culture's "dominant fiction" of male sufficiency. For her, analyzing the forms of popular culture (such as film) that emerge after World War II provides the opportunity to watch both the possibility of a new "fiction"'s emergence and the efforts to reimplant the old.

Such analyses help to begin to answer questions about the confusing gender implications of war. For men, war has seemed to mean a chance to confirm, or recreate, the traditional sense of manhood as courage and physical prowess, grace under pressure. Particularly in the South, an honor culture where appearances mattered (and still matter) greatly to manhood, war could be an occasion to demonstrate one's masculinity in the view of other men. Yet as Theweleit and Silverman suggest, the actual experience of war might serve the opposite end. This too would seem particularly an issue in the South, where feminization (in whatever form) would have seemed both more horrifying and more likely. The reality of war for a southerner might even be for these reasons *especially* likely to evoke traditional, simplistic, and defensively aggressive manhood— such as McLendon and Grimm. In the Civil War, their own territory had been quite literally invaded and conquered; their cause lost, southern white men suffered what was culturally represented as feminization after the war as well as during it. Ideological feminization was evident in Northern cartoons and writing; the Northern press had great fun with the claims that Jefferson Davis escaped wearing his wife's clothing. But this was easier to resist than the sense of lost manhood that came with losing a war. Southern women, white and black, and black men, of course, saw changes in their experience, their gender roles, and their sense of self in the Civil War, when white women did men's work and all blacks were freed. Yet the soldiers' feeling of emasculation that accompanied the loss of the war seemed likely to lead to a familiar, if deferred conclusion: traditional manhood would be reconstructed. Despite those massive wartime shifts, then, southern women and blacks were on the whole returned to the patriarchal, paternalist, and racialized experience and roles that antedated the war.

The Unvanquished, a Faulkner novel that falls perhaps between the idealization of Bayard in *Flags in the Dust* and the disparaging of Grimm and McLendon, nevertheless offers—I think in spite of itself—a representation of the process of masculine postwar (white) phallic recuperation, recovering for certain male bodies, the dominant fiction of phallic sufficiency. Faulkner's troubling stories of Drusilla Hawk starkly represent this pattern. Drusilla, the best horsewoman in Mississippi, cuts her hair and wears a Confederate uniform in order to serve as a soldier under Colonel John Sartoris. If Faulkner seems to sympathize with Drusilla's apparent gender defiance early in the novel, by the last chapter he appears to be complicit with the ideology that is closing her down. All that is left of her at the end of the novel is an odor of verbena, and her cousin Bayard Sartoris, whom she has earlier bested as a rider, a soldier, and a storyteller, becomes the heir apparent of southern patriarchal culture. Meanwhile, Ringo, the slave who grew up as Bayard's closest friend and more clever than Bayard by half, has likewise exited from the text, all of his wit and spunk with him. In narrowing his multiple stories to one story—that of Bayard Sartoris—Faulkner himself enacts the recreation of white southern manhood that Bayard, as a character, effects in the text.

The First World War produced a similar narrative. We have touched on Faulkner's mixed treatments of postwar manhood, in "Dry September," *Flags in the Dust*, and *Light in August*. William Alexander Percy, the cousin who raised Walker Percy and a prominent lawyer and personage in Greenville, Mississippi, was a non-traditional male before the war in a number of respects. He describes himself in *Lanterns on the Levee* as a poet and a short skinny "pee-wee" of a man. He was also most probably gay. But in his personal narrative Percy shows that he used his First World War experience to consolidate traditional masculinity in a process of self-loathing for his artistic and "feminine" side. After the war he sustained his cultural power, but at significant emotional cost. African-American Southern (and Northern) men who served in and tasted freedom in the First World War were to feel the bars close down again at home. Faulkner's depiction of Caspey in *Flags in the Dust,* for example, details the process by which this black veteran of the War is disciplined back in to the old racial hierarchy.

What about the Second World War, though? Unhappily, the same story seems to prevail. Historian Mary Martha Thomas's *Riveting and Rationing in Dixie: Alabama Women and the Second World War* confirms the paradigm I have been discussing: she concludes that for women's lives the "forces of continuity seem to have prevailed over the forces of change during the war years in Alabama" (121). Thomas wisely refused to look at the question in terms of gender alone: she considered the relationship between gender and race. She examined the impact of the war first on all women, then on black and white women separately, and the outcomes are depressingly predictable. White women—married (one out of ten), older, with children, as well as single—moved into Mobile and took "men's" jobs in manufacturing, government, the shipyards; black women— excluded from those higher paid positions—took over the trade and service jobs the white women had left open. Moreover, though employment for women jumped during the war, when corrected for race, it becomes plain that the significant change is for white women, not black, most of whom had been already working.

Thomas wisely asked how this new employment was represented to white women, and thus what changes women might have experienced in their hopes and plans, their sense of self: "The new economic opportunities were based on a temporary wartime need. The invitations to women to step outside their customary sphere were offered in terms that reinforced traditional ideas about sex roles. Government propaganda appealed to women's patriotism and obligation to their nation rather than to personal satisfaction or financial need . . . it highlighted women's femininity and continued to view women in relation to men. Mothers constantly heard about the undesirable effects their employment might have on their children. With this approach, the public could accept the participation of women in unusual roles without surrendering basic beliefs about those roles" (115-116). And just as we might expect, "in the years immediately following the end of the war, female employment in the state drastically declined" (118).

Katherine Anne Porter's "The Leaning Tower," set in pre-war Germany, Lillian Hellman's "Watch on the Rhine," set in Maryland and awarded Best

Play of the 1940–41 season, and Harriette Arnow's *The Dollmaker*, a novel set in Kentucky and New York that nearly took the National Book Award for 1954 away from Faulkner (he won it for *A Fable*), all define what Pete Daniel calls "Fascism at Home" in terms not of racial but of familial violence, domestic violence, patriarchal violence against women. Moreover, they write about the seductiveness for women of that very "fascism," whether in the bloody violence represented by duelling scars or in the bloodless violence of demeaning and demanding language. Their topic, despite the difference in its focus, is ever the same as Faulkner's and Daniel's: the fascism of the South as seen in the dominance expected of southern white men.

Whether one adopts the positivist structural analysis that focuses on continuing patterns and structures, or the psychoanalytically inflected analysis that focuses on the discontinuities produced by war, a certain "manhood" historically has been reconstructed after war, in what Susan Jeffords called, regarding the Viet Nam war, the "remasculinization of America." If after wars end, men typically sustain or regain traditional manhood, then changes in women's traditional roles that the war has required or allowed have not typically persisted in postwar peace. Historians Carol Berkin and Clara Lovett sum it up: despite the "remarkable fluidity of circumstances and the innovative quality" of wartime experience, traditional roles and structures are typically resilient. If so, were there "gender wars," so to speak, in the South during the Second World War? Did the women who used the figure of the fascist to analyze and critique the very culture that had gone to war "for them" fail in their efforts to move away from the dominant Southern fiction? Were these once again, for women, losing battles?

In Porter's "The Leaning Tower" the fatal connections between war and traditional gender are, by contrast, unequivocal and explicit, unmitigated by charm. Four young men of various nationalities live in a boarding house in Berlin; the widowed landlady's little souvenir tower of Pisa gives the story its name. The American painter Charles inadvertently destroys the (obviously phallic) leaning tower; it collapses at his touch. Thus when the landlady mends the tower in her nostalgia for both her husband and the traditional past, there is a suggestion of the role of women in propping up the leaning and now crushed tower of the patriarchal system. At the time of the story's writing and publication, the tower might more immediately have suggested the power of Fascism, born and then still thriving in Italy.

Such a role for women becomes explicit in the final crucial scene at a local bar. In a lengthy discussion among the four young men in a Berlin cabaret bar on New Year's Eve, 1931, a discussion about race, ethnicity, national character, and

art, the young Polish pianist Tadeusz is arguing for the influence of the Celts.
The German Hans responds. He flaunts a dueling scar on his face, emblem of
the warrior and the patriarchy. And he speaks insolently, arrogantly, about the
next war, when Germany will make no mistakes, and will win. To Tadeusz's
claim about the Celts, he says:

> "Influence?" asked Hans. "A purely oblique, feminine, worthless thing,
> influence. Power, pure power is what counts to a nation or a race. You must
> be able to tell other peoples what to do, and above all what they may not
> do, you must be able to enforce every order you give against no matter what
> opposition, and when you demand anything at all, it must be given you
> without question. That is the only power, and power is the only thing of
> any value or importance in this world." [The others argue with him: power
> doesn't last, the powerful wear themselves out, a new power takes over, it
> doesn't pay. Hans continues:] "It always pays," said Hans; "that is the point.
> It pays, and nothing else does. Everything else is childish beside it. Otto,
> you surprise me, That is a strange point of view for you."
>   Otto sagged, guilty and uncomfortable. . . . (486)

A stunningly beautiful young German woman, a model, has come into the
cabaret on the arm of a "star in the moving pictures" whose mistress and leading
lady she is. Her name is Lutte (the French word for war). Not surprisingly,
Charles finds himself instantly attracted to her. When she begins to dance the
rhumba alone, Charles, who knows the dance, gets up to join her. But they dance
differently; their styles don't fit, and all she wants to discuss is Hollywood. When
Hans cuts in, Lutte's manner "changed completely. She melted towards Hans,
they danced slowly, and as they danced, she kissed him softly and continually
and gently on his right cheek [the cheek with the dueling scar], her mouth
meek and sweet, her eyes nearly closed. Over Hans's disfigured face came [a]
look of full-fed pride, of composed self-approval—of arrogance—" (*Collected
Stories*, 490).

Hans, who has argued for "pure" masculine "power . . . to tell other people
what to do, and above all what they may not do" (*Collected Stories*, 486) is in this
scene the beneficiary recipient of the "worthless feminine" he derides as politics.
Porter gives us so palpable a sense of the complicity between a self-abjecting
femininity and a fascist masculinity that the story becomes virtually an allegory
that shows the relation between gender and war. Two German women, the
landlady in her nostalgia for the leaning tower, and Lutte in her desire for a
dominating man, will sustain the fiction of traditional gender, the leaning tower
that never falls, which Porter connects to patriarchy, to Fascism, and thus to
World War II.

In Lillian Hellman's play, the action turns again on the links between a particular sort of masculinity and the probability of war. A widow, Fanny Farrelly—a conventional, upper middle class southern woman—has two adult children, her son David, who lives with her outside Washington, D. C., and her daughter Sara, who married Kurt Müller, a German, years ago against Mrs. Farrelly's wishes, and now lives in Germany with him and their three children. Mrs. Farrelly and her son David have been entertaining two house-guests for some time now, the daughter of a social friend, whose name is Marthe, and Marthe's German husband Teck de Brancovis. David and Marthe have been carrying on a rather obvious flirtation, which worries the mother, who is concerned about her son's getting involved with a married woman. However, the audience understands Marthe's interest in another man; her husband, Teck, is rather like Porter's Hans. Suspecting that she may have "arranged" to stay longer with the Farrellys, he tells her: "Do not make any arrangements, Marthe. I may not allow you to carry them through. (Smiles.) Come to breakfast now." Teck is apparently a decadent aristocrat, though, instead of a soldier; almost out of money, he plans to win some income tonight gambling at the German embassy in Washington.

The action takes place on the day David's sister arrives with her family from Germany. Teck snoops through their luggage and learns that Kurt has been working since 1933 with a German resistance group, the Anti-Nazi Underground Movement. He is carrying a case with thousands of dollars in cash to be used when necessary for bribes to extricate members from German prisons. At the Embassy, Teck learns of the capture of three major anti-Nazis. The next day he tries to blackmail Kurt, asking for $10,000 of the anti-Nazi money in exchange for his silence about Kurt's identity tonight at the German embassy. But Kurt is not persuaded: he knows that Teck could get even more—a visa—from the ambassador tonight, and he is sure Teck is playing for both cards. He surprises Teck with a blow, and kills him.

Later, he explains the killing: "I sit here. I listen to him [Teck]. You will not believe—but I pray that I will not have to touch him. Then I know I will have to. I know that if I do not, it is only that I pamper myself, and risk the lives of others. [So] do I now pretend sorrow? Do I now pretend it is not I who act thus? No. I do it. I have done it. I will do it again. And I will keep my hope that we may make a world in which all men can die in bed. I have a great hate for the violent. They are the sick of the world. Maybe I am sick now, too." Sara says, "You aren't sick. Stop that. It's late. You must go soon." And Kurt responds, "Maybe all that I have ever wanted is a land that would let me have you."

Kurt will take Teck's body in the car with him tonight on the way back to the airport to return to Germany to rescue his colleagues; he will hide the body and the car, and when they are discovered, the family will blame it all on a fight between two foreigners. Thus he will be unable ever to return to America. Sara expects never to see him again.

Clearly Hellman is at pains in "Watch on the Rhine" to distinguish Nazis from German nationals by developing two such radically different German men. In the love plots, it is the Nazi who dominates his wife, and the anti-Nazi who sees his wife as an equal parent and partner. The linchpin between politics and the personal again is the question of domination. At one point in the play, Teck reads aloud to Kurt, Fanny, and David the newspaper story describing the missing fourth anti-Nazi, who goes by the name Gotter. Clearly Gotter is Kurt himself. Kurt responds by explaining Nazis to Fanny and David:

> All Fascists are not of one mind, one stripe. There are those who give the orders, those who carry out the orders, those who watch the orders being carried out. Then there are those who are half in, half hoping to come in. They are made to do the dishes and clean the boots. Frequently they come in high places and wish now only to survive. They came late: some because they did not jump in time, some because they were stupid, some because they were shocked at the crudity of the German evil and preferred their own evils, and some because they were fastidious men. For those last, we may well some day have pity. They are lost men, their spoils are small, their day is gone. [Then, to Teck, he says] Yes?

Clearly he now has been describing Teck. Teck responds: "Yes. You have the understanding heart. It will get in your way some day." If Teck has been one of those reluctant Nazis, he seems to have learned his new role well.

By contrast to Porter's story and Hellman's play, *The Dollmaker* is very long, an epic of the home front. My students groan and complain when they look at the number of pages they will have to read—nearly 600. But the length of the novel is required by its thematic ambition. In this third and last literary treatment of the Second World War Harriette Arnow provides a sadly neglected but in my opinion major interpretation of the meanings of World War II for the American South. The plot is simple: it focuses on a strong and large mountain woman, Gertie Nevels, who abandons her agrarian dream of owning the Tipton Place, a small farm near Ballew, Kentucky, in order to accompany her husband when he takes a job in the defense industry in Detroit. Thus the novel sets up a division between prewar rural southern life and wartime (and postwar) modernization. They move with their children into a housing project ironically called Merry Hill (it is neither), next to the factories and the train track. In Detroit Gertie encounters cultural, racial, and religious diversity and the hostility of Catholics against Protestants; she moves into a consumer economy where Clovis insists on buying an Icy Heart refrigerator on credit even though it freezes the butter and fills up the tiny kitchen; she watches two of her children adjust by conforming to the images they hear on the radio or see in magazines or at school; and she suffers the loss of two other children, one of whom runs away, and the other of whom is run over by a train trying to find a place to play with her imaginary friend without being called weird.

But the novel complicates what could have been a simplistic thesis by showing the benefits of modernity as well as its costs: the community of women in the project, held together despite their vast cultural differences; the community of men in the labor union that seeks justice for war workers; the chance for an education that the children who "adjust" could never find in Ballew.

Arnow develops Gertie as the prototypical southerner, a yeoman farmer, the woman—to paraphrase Cash—at the center. In tracing the loss of Gertie's dream, Arnow traces the outlines of Allen Tate's and John Crowe Ransom's arguments against industrialism and for agrarianism, published in 1930 in *I'll Take My Stand.* Whereas Gertie loved being in the woods, carving playprettys and working on a huge wood carving of her vision of a laughing Christ, she finds that in Detroit smoke covers everything and that growing even a marigold is difficult. Whereas Gertie and little Cassie loved the freedom to imagine and invent, Cassie's imagination marks her as too different in Detroit to survive. Whereas Gertie ran a self-sufficient and productive farm in Kentucky, in Detroit she lives without producing anything, entirely dependent on truck farmers for food, the milk man for milk, the ice man for ice. Her clothes and her speech mark her as a hillbilly; her children are ashamed of her, and Clovis, her husband, is impatient with her resistance to the brave new world he has found. And whereas in the country Gertie was gaining control over her life, extricating herself from her life-sapping mother's punitive Christianity and saving money towards a dream that would allow her to support her family regardless of Clovis's success or failure, in the city she loses control. Failing to understand the new codes and resisting what she does not understand, Gertie's role in the family shrinks as Clovis's power grows.

Once again, then, we have a southern woman writer who identifies male domination within the family as the linchpin that holds together war and traditional gender. Clovis's control over the family decisions grows as the wartime economy tells him he is the man and that the sign of manhood is being the head of the household. Rather than the "boot in the face" masculinity of the sort that attracted Lutte to Hans in "The Leaning Tower," however, and rather than the overt orders and covert manipulations of Teck in "Watch on the Rhine," this time the man's domination emerges directly from southern tradition and evangelical Christianity. Gertie is at the very point of buying the Tipton Place when Clovis breaks a promise he had made to her and takes a job in Detroit without her knowledge. Gertie does not want to move but finally does so because her mother, her husband, and her minister all combine to tell her the wife's duty is to be at her husband's side and that the children will suffer without a father. Gertie moves to the city out of guilt, not desire, and out of a duty, not pleasure. Once again, the core of the novel's political meanings lies in the realm of the personal.

In the first scene of the novel, Arnow represents a dramatic encounter between Gertie and a man who comes closest to the fascist characters that Porter and Hellman developed in their critiques of manhood as dominance. Gertie's son Amos is near death; he can't breathe and his nails are blue. Riding a frightened mule onto the paved mountain road, she forces a car to stop; it spins and skids, landing on a sandy shoulder near the edge of the bluff. As the rear window of the car slowly rolls down, a "hard and shiny soldier's cap rose above it, then a man's face, straight and neat and hard-appearing as the cap, but flushed now with surprise and anger. The mouth was hardly showing before it spoke, quickly, but with a flat, careful pronunciation of the words. 'You realize you've run me off the road. If you can't manage a horse, don't ride it on the highway. Don't you know there's a war and this road carries . . .'" [it is the road from Oak Ridge].

"'I know they's a war,'" Gertie responds. "'That's why the doctor closest home is gone. It was a mule. I managed him. I had to make you stop. I've got to git my little boy to a doctor—quick.'" She has opened the car door and put her foot inside it. The man bars her way. "His hand moved slowly, as if he wanted her to see it touch the pistol in a polished holster by his side, let the pistol speak to her more than his toneless, unruffled words when he said, 'You must use other means of getting your child to the doctor.'" He jerks the door, but she keeps her foot in it. He threatens to have her arrested in his voice that "still was not a man's voice, but [instead represented] the shiny cap, the bright leather, the pistol." He finally orders the driver to back up quickly and then drive on. "'She'll have to drop off then.'" "'You want him to go over the bluff?'" Gertie asks. Arnow continues: "and her voice was weary to breaking, like an overwrought mother speaking to a stubborn child."

Arnow's rendering of the fascist personality in the form of an American officer differs from Porter's and Hellman's not in the description of his obsession with dominance and control, but in her understanding of the woman's response to male dominance. Where Porter, like Sylvia Plath, represented the fascist's seductiveness to women, and Hellman contested the notion of seduction but had to develop an anti-fascist man to counter fascist power, Arnow exposes it as the posturing of a spoiled child. For Arnow, in this initial scene, the power Gertie has comes from her experience and commitment as a mother in an agrarian setting. After she stops the officer, she performs an emergency tracheotomy on her son, using her whittling knife to let the air in and a hollow reed to keep the incision open while the officer looks on in horror and repugnance. She then shows the soldiers how to get the car out of the sand and they drive together to the doctor. The officer, now impressed and converted to respect, hands her an envelope that has in it what turns out to be enough money to complete the fund for the Tipton Place.

What is truly endangering to Gertie, then, is not the explicitly fascist style and behavior of the officer, seduced by his own clothing. It is the silent southern cultural dominance of Clovis's role as head of household. She does not tell Clovis that she is the one who gave Amos the tracheotomy, a hint of her passivity at the time Clovis tells her to come to Detroit. And in the last scene of the novel, instead of cutting open her child's airways or whittling playprettys or carving the face of the laughing Christ on her beautiful block of cherry wood, Gertie uses an axe to chop the block of beautiful cherry up into little pieces to be used to make production line painted dolls. Her dream of self-sufficiency, her powers as a mother, and her hope of artistry gone, Gertie finally joins the forces of modernity. Though it is complicated by her sudden insight that any of the faces in Merry Hill would have served for the Christ face she has never found, it is in other respects a terrifying conclusion. And it implies that whatever benefits may accrue to the South from the invasion of modernity after World War II, the losses will be irreparable.

Literary critic Richard King has been castigated a thousand times for his remark in *A Southern Renaissance* that he had left women writers out of his book because they did not deal with the "larger issues" of southern life. What King missed, and what I hope I have suggested to you, is that the women writers of the South do in fact deal with those "larger issues." They do so when they look for relationships between the small and the large, the domestic and the public, the personal and the political. Using the occasion of World War II as a time to examine what they most feared and hated—the absolute power of another—these three writers, and many others as well, wrote out prophecies of the postwar South that proved all too true. Men were to reassert their patriarchal prerogatives; middle class white women, seduced by this power or simply forced out of work, were to lose the gains they had made in the war and then be subjected to the feminine mystique of the 1950s. After the war, Miss

Dixie was still alive and well, winning beauty contests and bake-offs, back on her pedestal; her black sister was back in the kitchen and barred from the contest, and her poor white sister was back in the mills. Instead of driving down old Dixie's patriarchy, the South was to drive the Equal Rights Amendment down. It would remain for the civil rights movement in the South, and the feminist movement that emerged from it, to drive Miss Dixie if not down, at least a bit away from front and center in southern ideology.

What about the more general histories of the South? How do they treat the gender wars? A look at two of them will suggest that, although historians of the South tend generally to represent the war as a time of enormous change—marking the shift away from one crop (cotton), one party (Democratic), and one dominant race (white), to drive old Dixie down—few ask questions about a possible shift from one dominant gender. Let's look in conclusion at two recent histories designed for general and teaching use. William Cooper and Tom Terrill focus their discussion of the war in *The American South: A History* (1991) on the big three—the economy, the solid South, and Jim Crow. They spend just under a paragraph on women. Here it is:

> Perhaps 4 million women were gainfully employed in the South in 1940; perhaps 5 million held jobs in 1945, and more of them were married, middle-aged, and mothers. Black women fled domestic service. Their flight may have prompted one of the more exotic rumors of the war. Despite the absence of any firm evidence, stories of "Eleanor [Roosevelt] Clubs" blossomed in profusion. These organizations of black domestics supposedly intended to place "a white woman in every kitchen." A jocular Tennesseean observed that though white women in the South might not feel themselves personally threatened by Hitler, they "certainly recognized what a crisis the loss of a cook is." (692)

In *Standing at the Crossroads* (1986), Pete Daniel entitles his chapter on World War II "The Two-Front War," to give equal emphasis to the battle overseas and the battle at home for racial equality. He discusses the changes the war brought to the "problem of race" for half the chapter, under the subtitle "Fascism at Home." He discusses the changes the war brought to women in two sentences, and here they are: "Women, who a few years earlier had hoed cotton or strung tobacco, worked in defense plants, and even middle-class women joined the work force. Some women flocked to military installations, became camp followers, and, while lifting the morale of troops, also caused concern because of the spread of venereal diseases" (137). Although I expected to find a failure to address the question of women's history in these recent southern history texts—it takes a while, after all, to get all that women's work into the mainstream—

the juxtaposition of these two discussions of women in the South during World War II was both more telling and more depressing than I had feared. A close reader of texts, as we all should be, cannot miss the way each text concludes its all too brief discussion of women with dismissive and degrading remarks: supposedly humorous trivialization, in the case of Cooper and Terrill's little joke about white women, Hitler, and their black cooks, and a male-focused remark about the new openings for prostitution, and the fun and V.D. that southern women brought the soldiers. Is there a relationship between the virtual absence of women's history from these standard texts, and the overtly misogynist frames in which they place what little they do have to say about women? Are southern historians perpetuating the ideology they ought to be analyzing? Is Miss Dixie still standing on her pedestal, propped up by the labor of black women, or groveling in her gutter, serving the sexual preferences of men who degrade her?

Works Cited

Arendt, Hannah. "Ideology and Terror. " Chapter 13 of *The Origins of Totalitarianism.* 2nd ed., enlarged. New York: Meridian Books, 1958.

Arnow, Harriette. *The Dollmaker.* New York: Macmillan, 1954.

Ashton, E. B. (Ernst Basch). *The Fascist: His State and His Mind.* New York: William Morrow, 1937.

Berkin, Carol and Clara M. Lovett, eds. *Women, War, and Revolution.* New York: Holmes & Meier, 1980.

Breen, William J. "Black Women and the Great War: Mobilization and Reform in the South." *The Journal of Southern History* XLIV (August, 1978).

———. "Southern Women in War: The North Carolina Woman's Committee, 1917–1919." *The North Carolina Historical Review* LV (July, 1978).

Bullock, Alan and Olive Stallybrass, eds. *The Harper Dictionary of Modern Thought.* New York: Harper & Row, 1977.

Burchfield, R. W., ed. *The Compact Edition of the Oxford English Dictionary, Volume II: A Supplement to the Oxford English Dictionary Volumes I–IV.* Oxford: Clarendon Press, 1987.

Chafe, William H. "The Paradox of Progress." In *Our American Sisters: Women in American Life and Thought,* 2nd ed., ed. Jean E. Friedman and William G. Shade. Boston: Allyn and Bacon, 1976.

Clarke, Ida Clyde. *American Women and the World War.* New York: D. Appleton, 1918.

Cooper, Helen M., Adrienne Auslander Munich, and Susan Merrill Squier, eds. *Arms and the Woman: War, Gender, and Literary Representation.* Chapel Hill: University of North Carolina Press, 1989.

Cooper, William J. and Tom Terrill. *The American South: A History.* New York: Knopf, 1991.

Daniel, Pete. *Standing at the Crossroads: Southern Life since 1900.* New York: Hill and Wang, 1986.

Elshtain, Jean Bethke. *Women and War.* New York: Basic, 1987.

Faulkner, William. *Collected Stories of William Faulkner.* (1950). New York: Vintage, 1977.

————. *A Fable.* New York: Random House, 1954.

————. *Flags in the Dust.* New York: Random House, 1973.

————. *Light in August.* (1932). New York: Vintage, 1972.

————. *Soldiers' Pay.* (1926). New York: Liveright, 1954.

————. *The Unvanquished.* (1934). New York: Vintage International, 1991.

Gilbert, Sandra, and Susan Gubar. *No Man's Land.* New Haven: Yale University Press, 1988.

Griffin, Roger. *Oxford Reader on Fascism.* Oxford: Oxford University Press, 1995.

Hanley, Lynne. *Writing War: Fiction, Gender, and Memory.* Amherst: University of Massachusetts Press, 1991.

Hartmann, Susan M. *The Home Front and Beyond: American Women in the 1940s.* Boston: Twayne, 1982.

Hellman, Lillian. "Watch on the Rhine." In *The Best Plays of 1940–41.* New York: Dodd, Mead, 1941.

Higgonet, Margaret Randolph, Jane Jenson, Sonya Michel, and Margaret Collins Weitz, eds. *Behind the Lines: Gender and the Two World Wars.* New Haven: Yale University Press, 1987.

Homberger, Eric. "The American War Novel and the Defeated Liberal." In *The Second World War in Literature*, ed. Ian Higgins. Edinburgh and London: Scottish Academic Press, 1986.

Humphries, Jefferson. *Southern Literature and Literary Theory.* Athens: University of Georgia Press, 1990.

King, Richard H. *A Southern Renaissance: The Cultural Awakening of the American South, 1930–1955.* New York: Oxford University Press, 1980.

Kirk, Russell. *The Intelligent Woman's Guide to Conservatism.* New York: The Devin-Adair Company, 1957.

Laqueur, Walter. *Fascism: Past, Present, Future.* New York: Oxford UP, 1996.

Leed, Eric. *No Man's Land: Combat and Identity in the First World War.* Cambridge: Cambridge University Press, 1980.

Milum, Richard A. "Continuity and Change: The Horse, the Automobile, and the Airplane in Faulkner's Fiction." In *Faulkner: The Unappeased Imagination, A Collection of Critical Essays*, ed. Glenn O. Carey. Troy, NY: Whitston, 1980.

Payne, Stanley G. *A History of Fascism, 1914–1945*. Madison: University of Wisconsin Press, 1995.

Plath, Sylvia. "Daddy." In *The Collected Poems*. New York: Harper & Row, 1981.

Porter, Katherine Anne. *The Collected Stories of Katherine Anne Porter*. New York: Harcourt, Brace & World, 1965.

Seldes, George. *You Can't Do That*. New York: Modern Age, 1938.

Shaw, George Bernard. *The Intelligent Woman's Guide to Socialism, Fascism, and Capitalism*. 1924.

Silverman, Kaja. *Male Subjectivity at the Margins*. New York: Routledge, 1992.

Theweleit, Klaus. *Male Fantasies*. Minneapolis: University of Minnesota Press, 1987.

Thomas, Mary Martha. *Riveting and Rationing in Dixie: Alabama Women and the Second World War*. Tuscaloosa: University of Alabama Press, 1987.

Twelve Southerners. (1930). *I'll Take My Stand: The South and the Agrarian Tradition*. Baton Rouge: Louisiana State University Press, 1977.

Williams, Howard. *Concepts of Ideology*. New York: St. Martin's Press, 1988.

VIII FAULKNER AND WORLD WAR II

Noel Polk

On July 4, 1943, William Faulkner wrote to his stepson, Malcolm Franklin:

Dear Buddy:

Mr Robert Haas is vice president of Random House. They publish my books. During the times when I would be broke, year after year sometimes, I had only to write him and he would send me money—no hope to get it back, unless I wrote another book. He's a Jew.

He had an only son, and a daughter. In '40, the son withdrew from Yale and became a Navy pilot. In '41, the girl about 20, joined that Women's Ferry Squadron, is now flying, ferrying aeroplanes from factories to bases. The boy was flying torpedo planes off carriers . . . in the Pacific. He was killed last week. The girl is still flying. All Jews. I just hope I dont run into some hundred percent American Legionnaire until I feel better.

There is a squadron of negro pilots. They finally got congress to allow them to learn how to risk their lives in the air. They are in Africa now, under their own negro lt. colonel, did well at Pantelleria, on the same day a mob of white men and white policemen killed 20 negroes in Detroit. Suppose you and me and a few others of us lived in the Congo, freed seventy-seven years ago by ukase; of course we cant live in the same apartment hut with the black folks, nor always ride in the same car nor eat in the same restaurant, but we are free because the Great Black Father says so. Then the Congo is engaged in War with the Cameroon. At last we persuade the Great Black Father to let us fight too. You and Jim say are flyers. You have just spent the day trying to live long enough to learn how to do your part in saving the Congo. Then you come back down and are told that 20 of your people have just been killed by a mixed mob of civilians and cops at Little Poo Poo. What would you think?

A change will come out of this war. If it doesn't, if the politicians and the people who run this country are not forced to make good the shibboleth they glibly talk about freedom, liberty, human rights, then you young men who live through it will have wasted your precious time, and those who dont live through it will have died in vain. (*Selected Letters* 175–76)

In January of 1947, the city fathers of Oxford proposed a monument to the Lafayette County soldiers who died during World War II. They were well on their way to making it a "whites only" monument until James Silver, a Mrs. Duke, and William Faulkner protested. Moon Mullins, the editor of the Oxford *Eagle* at the time, wrote later that Faulkner came to his office and insisted that black soldiers also be included: "Of course you'll put the Negro names on there," he said: "when they're dead is the only time they are not niggers." He wrote the inscription to be placed on the monument: "THEY HELD NOT THEIRS, BUT ALL MEN'S LIBERTY, THIS FAR FROM HOME TO THIS LAST SACRIFICE." They indeed did list the names of the Negro dead, all seven of them, at the bottom of the plaque, under the heading "OF THE NEGRO RACE" (Meriwether 105).

Faulkner's letter and this minor episode in Oxford history represent in microcosm the tensions that the forces of change during and following World War II set loose in the South, the local skirmishes between those who saw change as inevitable and those who tried to halt it. Faulkner, always a seismograph of social change, very early understood how cataclysmic was to be the effect on the South and on America of World War II. He reacted profoundly to it while it was in progress and at its end hit the ground running fully prepared as a citizen to insist that his fellow white Southerners adapt to inevitability even if not to morality, and was willing to instruct them in how to do so.

In this, alas, he stands quite alone among the canonical, "major" Southern writers and critics: the ones, I mean, that we now identify with the so-called "Southern Renascence." Indeed, it is a matter astonishingly to be noted how little so profound an event as World War II figures in the fiction and poetry of the major Southern writers of the middle of the century. I do not forget Erskine Caldwell's books of *reportage* on fighting at the front, or James Dickey's and Randall Jarrell's powerful poems about their experiences as pilot and bombardier. Katherine Anne Porter's 1962 *Ship of Fools*, though it engages the rise of fascism in Europe, was set in the early thirties, when she began writing it. Robert Penn Warren scholars are now reading his 1946 *All the King's Men* as a commentary on European fascism. William Styron's 1977 *Sophie's Choice* is about World War II only incidentally, as is his 1952 novella *The Long March*, which is set at a military camp in South Carolina in the early fifties, though to be sure it has characters who are veterans of World War II. Carson McCullers's 1941 *Reflections in a Golden Eye* is set on a Southern army base during the thirties. James Agee's 1941 *Let Us Now Praise Famous Men* is about Alabama sharecroppers of the 1930s; his 1951 novel *The Morning Watch* concerns his student years at St. Andrews' School, and his posthumous 1957 autobiographical novel, *A Death in the Family*, is set in 1915 Knoxville. Eudora Welty has said that she set her first novel, *Delta Wedding* (1946), in the early 1920s in order to evoke a time when all the men would be home so she could have a family novel. Shelby Foote finished his first novel, *Shiloh*, in 1947, immediately after demobilization: *Shiloh* is not about his experiences in his own war, but a historical novel about the famous Civil War battle, and his *Love in a Dry Season*, published in 1951, begins in the Depression and concludes in 1941 just as America is about to enter the war. Lillian Hellman's *Watch on the Rhine*, first produced in 1941, is set in Washington, D. C. Flannery O'Connor's long story "The Displaced Person," set in Georgia, appeared in her 1955 collection, *A Good Man Is Hard to Find*. The eight year old narrator of Ernest J. Gaines's lovely story "The Sky Is Gray" is fatherless because of the War, but the War is not otherwise a factor in the story. Doubtless I have missed a novel or story in this list, but none, I think, that would deny my general point that Southern writers produced no novels or stories about the war or its aftermath of the stature of Norman Mailer's *The Naked and the Dead*, Irwin Shaw's *The Young Lions*, James Gould Cozzens's *Guard of Honor*, any of the novels of John Hersey, or even Joseph Heller's much later *Catch-22*.[1]

Save for Faulkner, then, World War II is very nearly AWOL from Southern fiction. Its absence is so glaring as to suggest that the gap is no accident. And we can't help but wonder why the most convulsive, the most revolutionary, event of the twentieth century was so collectively repressed from the "Southern" literary consciousness.

One of the defining moments in the history of Southern letters was the publication, in 1953, of an anthology of criticism called *Southern Renascence*, edited by Louis D. Rubin, Jr., and Robert D. Jacobs, and sporting the auspicious subtitle, *The Literature of the Modern South*. This book almost singlehandedly established "Southern literature" as a legitimate academic field, and helped to insure that the Vanderbilt intellectual circle, rather than those other very interesting literary groups that developed in Richmond and Charleston in the first third of the century, would dominate both academic and non-academic discussions of the South.

Southern Renascence's intellectual roots are devoutly and unashamedly situated in the 1930 Agrarian manifesto *I'll Take My Stand*; indeed, it bears an almost incestuous relationship to that earlier book: many of the essays in the latter were written by the authors of the former and/or in praise of them and their intellectual and spiritual children. Though the book pays homage to the post-War works of Faulkner and Welty (two non-Agrarians the Vanderbilt group nevertheless managed to claim), the essayists in *Southern Renascence* pay almost no attention whatsoever to other writers, whose careers are mostly post-War phenomena—Lillian Hellman, Truman Capote, and Tennessee Williams, for example, get mentioned in a couple of lists of "current" Southern writers, but nowhere to be found is Shelby Foote, who by 1953 had published four well-reviewed novels. Nor, perhaps for other reasons, do they deal with Carson McCullers, except in a list, although she had published five reputation-making major works between 1940 and 1952. Neither do the essayists deal with Agee. We might easily understand the exclusion of Capote and Williams and McCullers, whose works may have portended a different kind of change from the one they overtly feared; it is less easy to understand the exclusion of Foote and Agee, because they seem to be full-fledged and completely masculine members of the Benevolent and Protective Order of Good Ole Boy Agrariana. More astonishing is that the essayists seem not even to have heard of Richard Wright, Zora Neale Hurston, or Lillian Smith, all of whom by 1953 were celebrated national and international literary figures: their exclusion serves to suggest, to be blunt, how perversely lily-white were the interests of the founding and presiding elders of Southern literature at War's end.

Despite its subtitle, then, *Southern Renascence* is rockribbed in its retrenchment; its definitions of "Southern," "modern," and "renascence" are completely shaped by Vanderbilt's agrarian agenda. Most of its essayists seem unaware of the late unpleasantness in Europe and only one or two evoke it, obliquely, as an unnamed and unindicted co-conspirator in the modern world's headlong rush away from those old Agrarian virtues into industrialism and other blights of urban living. Even C. Vann Woodward's essay draws comparisons between the 1830s and 40s and the 1930s and 40s without once mentioning World War II. The Southern writers who merit a place in *Southern Renascence*'s pantheon, in spite of its subtitle, were in fact highly resistant intellectually to anything contemporary, however they defined "modern."[2] Value in *Southern Renascence*, then, is specifically invested in the 19th century and particularly in pre-Civil War culture and economy. In his essay on the spate of Civil War novels and biographies in the 1930s by Southern writers, Walter Sullivan concludes his discussion of Allen Tate's *The Fathers* by attributing to Tate, rightly or wrongly, his own belief that the Civil War "must be understood as the climax of Southern culture, the last moment of order in a traditional society" (116).

That is a monstrous statement, of course, not just for the obtuseness of its rear view, but also for its assumptions about historical privilege and its scarcely-veiled racism. The loss of a stable, traditional, orderly society based in regionalism is a basic theme, even if not so baldly stated, of the Southern literary agenda almost from the day of its inception: the Agrarians, like Faulkner, must have understood the chaos and the disorder of World War II's several simultaneous fronts as a preamble to the chaos and disorder of social change, a threat to the established social order. The War, then, seems to have scared them to death; what it portended was a collective trauma to be collectively repressed.

Agrarians insisted that order and tradition were the defining moral values of *all* great art, and since the Old South (the Older the Better) was ground zero of those values, the loss of the Old South hegemony (which they of course called value) would necessarily mean the death of Southern literature. Sullivan was still carrying on this crusade in his melancholic little 1976 book *A Requiem for the Renaissance.* Tom McHaney, reviewing this volume, responded in simple wonderment, viewing Sullivan's book as perhaps one might have viewed one of those Japanese soldiers who had hidden in South Pacific caves for 30 years and emerged still fighting a war long since over, and quipped that such books as Sullivan's make "one who would write in and about the South afraid to have running water in his house" (McHaney 187).

Moreover, the New Criticism of such Southerners as Warren and Cleanth Brooks suited the Agrarian agenda to a T, by insisting that art was something really apart from life, especially apart from politics, and that to dilute it with political purpose was to debase it. Thus Southerners had permission to read Faulkner's *Light in August, Absalom, Absalom!, Go Down, Moses,* and *Intruder in the Dust* with a morally straight face, praise them as great art, and feel no compulsion to *do something about it.* There is a real sense, then, in which Southern literary studies began as an implicitly racist escape from, a retrenchment against, the implications of the social changes that World War II portended. Quite to the contrary of his fellow Southerners, Faulkner, by his actions, demonstrated that he did not believe that art could exist outside of history or politics or social realities, and I am firmly convinced that his political engagement in the fifties was a direct and courageous and totally admirable response to the racial morality of his own fiction, to America's own racial immorality, and to the practical necessity of dealing straightforwardly with social change. His work and the world he lived in moved in constant, mutually energizing and enriching reciprocity with each other. But Faulkner became the Southerners' and the New Critics' great high priest anyway, as we shall see.

Faulkner's career in the forties bears a curious contrapuntal relationship to the War and its aftermath. His affairs took a steady nosedive from the beginning of the War until its end. He virtually stopped writing fiction. To pay his bills he worked in Hollywood on several propagandistic war films. All his books went out of print, and by War's end he was at an alltime personal and professional low. But during the War French translations of his novels caught the attention of Albert Camus and Jean-Paul Sartre, then active members of the French Résistance and his reputation in France, already high before the war, was beginning to skyrocket. His own country began to rediscover him in 1946 with the publication of *The Portable Faulkner*. In 1947, at least partly in response to the emerging Dixiecrats' revolt against federal civil rights reforms, he wrote *Intruder in the Dust*, about Mississippi's and the nation's racial troubles; his first out-and-out bestseller, it was turned into a movie the following year and he made lots of money for the first time in his life. A brand new industry of paperback publishers began to bring him back into print in cheap editions with lurid covers. In 1950 he won the Nobel Prize and he took some of the prize money and established a scholarship for needy black students to go to college (Blotner [1984] 535).

Lawrence Schwartz has recently argued that at least part of the revival of Faulkner's reputation in the years following the War is directly tied to Cold War politics, to the American cultural establishment's desire to dominate the world intellectually as it now dominated economically and militarily. To make Faulkner the great high priest of American intellectual imperialism was a trick that made curious bedfellows of the two leading movements in the politics of American intellectual life—the retrenched conservative Fugitives and Agrarians (John Crowe Ransom at the *Kenyon Review* and Allen Tate at the *Sewanee*) and those formerly Communist/Marxist intellectuals associated with the now-somewhat chastened *Partisan Review* (Philip Rahv). For the *Partisan Review* crowd the high modernism of Faulkner's early experimental works—*The Sound and the Fury, As I Lay Dying, Sanctuary, Light in August*—made him the perfect exemplar of American intellect at its most creative. For the Southerners, it was precisely Faulkner's presumed Agrarian sympathies, not to say his Southernness, that made him acceptable to bear the load of their regionalism. According to Schwartz, both groups were trying desperately to feed at the generous trough of such funding agencies as the Rockefeller Foundation, which also had their own, similar, agendas. It was a ménage-à-trois made not in heaven but on the battlefields of Europe and Asia.

To be sure, Faulkner was sympathetic with much that Agrarians held. In most ways politically conservative himself, his public statements were filled with the rhetoric of individuality that was based in Jeffersonian localist thought. He was very much at home with the Southerners' rhetoric of resistance to rampant industrialism, technology, consumerism, urban conformity, any form of mass activity, and he hated the idea of federal intervention in local affairs; a part-time farmer himself, he never reconciled himself to the idea of government subsidies or other handout programs. At the same time, however, he obviously believed that for all of its problems, the American paradigm of government offered a better chance for individual fulfillment than the Soviet. In the fifties he accepted Eisenhower's offer to co-chair the President's People-to-People program, and wryly proposed to his committee that the first item of business in the Cold War was "to anesthetize American vocal cords" (Blotner [1984] 626); he then proposed, again wryly, that the best way to win the Cold War was to invite 10,000 young Communists at a time to live in America for a year and go into debt with mortgages and installment-plan purchases. But even though in the 1950s Faulkner became a Cold War warrior who travelled extensively for the State Department as an exponent of American values, he never made the mistake of believing that the Cold War was the simple, horizontal struggle between Us and Them that propagandists in Washington and Moscow would have had it.

Thus in the space of just over a decade, Faulkner went from being a serf in Hollywood's stables of American commodification to being the owner of the stables. He became the ultimate literary and intellectual commodity; at first a despised and rejected critic of America's commercial values, he became an international advocate of post-war American culture. I lay this out in such detail because in all kinds of ways Faulkner's fall and rise during this period is directly connected to the War and its aftermath, his observation of and understanding of the profound social upheaval it brought upon the South, and he was particularly sensitive to the equally profound political and ideological issues that followed the War. Likewise, some of his most important fiction, during the remainder of his life, is a direct response to those social and ideological issues.

Faulkner engaged intellectually and emotionally with the War even as its early tremors began to be felt in the thirties. He tried to get into it; failing to get a commission at the Bureau of Aeronautics in Washington, he worked with Lafayette County Civil Defense. In Hollywood he worked on a series of propagandistic filmscripts about the War, including one about Charles de Gaulle. His 1942 novel *Go Down, Moses* concludes in the late fall before Pearl Harbor. In the early forties he wrote two stories, "The Tall Men" and "Two Soldiers," about class relations in Jefferson—in the latter a wealthy farming family and a sharecropping family both lose sons in battle; they bond, momentarily, in their shared grief, brought together by issues larger than the immediate local ones, but at the same time affirm just how local those larger issues were. His 1951 *Requiem for a Nun* contains five rapturous and heartbreaking pages that poetically summarize the War's effects on Mississippi and the South.

In 1959 he published *The Mansion*, the final novel of the Snopes Trilogy, a work that chronicles the social and economic life of North Mississippi from roughly 1890 to approximately 1947. All three novels analyze a variety of complexly related American themes, but the narrative itself concerns the rise of Flem Snopes from sharecropper to banker and deacon. *The Mansion*'s narrative covers the decade and a half preceding 1947, but its thematic interests are firmly rooted in the decade or so following that date. More than any of his novels, *The Mansion* records the War's impact on the day-to-day life of North Mississippi. It's a kaleidoscopic record of Mississippi's full participation in the war and of the sweeping social changes brought about as soldiers, black and white, return home. In Faulkner's accounting, Mississippi is in all ways intimately implicated in the War's meanings.

The central story of *The Mansion* concerns Mink Snopes's revenge on his cousin Flem, and climaxes with Mink's murder of Flem as Flem sits alone in his new columned mansion in Jefferson. Subnarratives have to do with Flem's step-daughter, Linda Snopes Kohl, and her role in getting Mink out of Parchman so that in fact he can return and work his vengeance, and hers. But first, Linda leaves Jefferson, in the mid-thirties, to follow her dream in the bohemian quarters of New York's Greenwich Village. She finds part of that dream in the arms of Barton Kohl, a Jewish sculptor whose works are so modern, so abstract, that only V. K. Ratliff can understand them. Together they leave to fight on the side of the Communists in the Spanish Civil War. A bomb blast kills Barton and renders Linda completely deaf. She comes back to Jefferson as a highminded political radical, who would have carried her Communist party membership card if she had thought it were necessary to accomplish what she wanted to accomplish. She proceeds to associate herself with two other Communists in Jefferson, immigrants from Finland, one of whom speaks no English, and with such radical causes as Negro education, activities which rattle the cages of both black and white Jeffersonians. Her activities bring to Jefferson agents from the FBI, who, like later representatives of the House Un-American Activities Committee, want to trade her immunity for the names of other Communists she had known in Greenwich Village. When America enters the War, Linda betakes herself to Pascagoula to become Rosie the Riveter in the Ingalls Shipyard.

One of his main characters is shot down over Germany and incarcerated in a POW camp (an episode Faulkner borrowed from his future biographer, Joseph Blotner). Another episode involves a Colonel Devries, a decorated war hero who settles in Jefferson and eventually challenges Senator Clarence Snopes for his seat in Congress. But during the war, his opponent lets it be known, Devries commanded a batallion of black soldiers, and won his medals by saving the life of a wounded Negro soldier, and then he himself was rescued from danger by another Negro soldier. Snopes is on the verge of winning the election by using Devries's splendid war record against him, until V. K. Ratliff eliminates him—Snopes—from the race by borrowing a page or two from Rabelais.

As we have come to expect, Faulkner misses nothing of importance during the years of and after the War:

> now the troops could come home from all directions, back to the women they had begun to marry before the echo of the first Pearl Harbor bomb had died away, and had been marrying ever since whenever they could get two days' leave, coming back home now either to already going families or to marry the rest of the women they hadn't got around to yet, the blood money [federal subsidies] already in the hands of the government housing loan (as his Uncle Gavin put it: "The hero who a year ago was rushing hand grenades and Garand clips up to front-line foxholes, is now rushing baskets of soiled didies out of side- and back-street Veterans Administration tenements.") and. . . . when Charles reached home in September of '45, Jason [Compson]'s old lost patrimony was already being chopped up into a subdivision of standardised Veterans' Housing match-boxes. . . . By Christmas it was already dotted over with small brightly painted pristinely new hutches as identical (and about as permanent) as squares of gingerbread or teacakes, the ex-soldier or -sailor or -marine with his ruptured duck pushing the perambulator with one hand and carrying the second (or third) infant in the other arm, waiting to get inside almost before the last painter could gather up his dropcloth. (*Mansion* 332–333)[3]

In another passage, Charles meditates on economics. He

> thought how all the domestic American knights-errant liberal reformers would be out of work now, with even the little heretofore lost places like Yoknapatawpha County, Mississippi, fertilised to overflowing not only with ex-soldiers' blood money but with the two or three or four dollars per hour which had been forced on the other ex-riveters and -bricklayers and -machinists like . . . Linda Snopes Kohl, so fast that they hadn't had time to spend it. Even the two Finn Communists, even the one that still couldn't speak English, had got rich during the war and had had to become capitalists and bull-market investors simply because they had not yet acquired any private place large enough to put that much money down

while they turned their backs on it. And as for the Negroes, by now they had a newer and better high school building in Jefferson than the white folks had. Plus an installment-plan automobile and radio and refrigerator full of canned beer down-paid with the blood money which at least drew no color line in every unwired unscreened plumbingless cabin: double-plus the new social-revolution laws which had abolished not merely hunger and inequality and injustice, but work too by substituting for it a new self-compounding vocation or profession for which you would need no schooling at all: the simple production of children. *(Mansion* 350–51)

In one scene that takes place *before* the war, Gavin Stevens discusses the developments in Europe by way of comparing them with World War I, its aftermath, and with disturbing developments in this country:

Barely a decade since their fathers and uncles and brothers just finished the one which was to rid the phenomenon of government forever of the parasites—the hereditary proprietors, the farmers-general of the human dilemma who had just killed eight million human beings and ruined a forty-mile-wide strip down the middle of western Europe. Yet less than a dozen years later and the same old cynical manipulators not even bothering to change their names and faces but merely assuming a set of new titles out of the shibboleth of the democratic lexicon and its mythology, not even breaking stride to coalesce again to wreck the one doomed desperate hope. . . . That one already in Italy and one a damned sight more dangerous in Germany because all Mussolini has to work with are Italians while this other man has Germans. And the one in Spain that all he needs is to be let alone a little longer by the rest of us who still believe that if we just keep our eyes closed long enough it will all go away. Not to mention . . . the ones right here at home: the organizations with the fine names confederated in unison in the name of God against the impure in morals and politics and with the wrong skin color and ethnology and religion: K.K.K. and Silver Shirts; not to mention the indigenous local champions like Long in Louisiana and our own Bilbo in Mississippi, not to mention our very own Senator Clarence Egglestone Snopes right here in Yoknapatawpha County. . . . *(Mansion* 160–61).

But if *The Mansion* is a narrative of social and political change in Mississippi during and after the War, it is even more significantly a record of the evolution of Faulkner's political sensibilities. In one scene, for example, chilling in its structural ironies, Linda Snopes's two Finnish communist friends come to her sitting room in Flem Snopes's house, to have a meeting about their plans for revolution. Charles Mallison imagines the scene, in a comment that reflects Faulkner's own constant sense of the relationship between dream and reality, here applied to politics:

Gavin told me how over a year ago the two Finn communists had begun to call on her at night (at her invitation of course) and you can imagine this one. It would be the parlor. Uncle Gavin said she had fixed up a sitting room for herself upstairs, but this would be in the parlor diagonally across the hall from the room where old Snopes was supposed to spend all his life that didn't take place in the bank. The capitalist parlor and the three of them, the two Finnish immigrant laborers and the banker's daughter, one that couldn't speak English and another that couldn't hear any language, trying to communicate through the third one who hadn't yet learned to spell, talking of hope, millennium, dream: of the emancipation of man from his tragedy, the liberation at last and forever from pain and hunger and injustice, of the human condition. While two doors away in the room where he did everything but eat and keep the bank's cash money, with his feet propped on that little unpainted ledge nailed to his Adam fireplace and chewing steadily at what Ratliff called his little chunk of Frenchman's Bend air—the capitalist himself who owned the parlor and the house, the very circumambience they dreamed in, who had begun life as a nihilist and then softened into a mere anarchist and now was not only a conservative but a tory too: a pillar, rock-fixed, of things as they are. (*Mansion* 222)

In 1943 Faulkner conceived the work that would be his most extended commentary on the political and ideological muddle the War left us with. He began work on a new "thing," he called it: "It will be about 10–15 thousand words," he wrote a friend. "It is a fable, an indictment of war perhaps, and for that reason may not be acceptable now" (*Selected Letters* 178). In January 1944, he wrote to Bob Haas, his editor whose son had been killed in the Pacific, to describe the argument of the new work:

in the middle of that war, Christ (some movement in mankind which wished to stop war forever) reappeared and was crucified again. We are repeating, we are in the midst of war again. Suppose Christ gives us one more chance, will we crucify him again, perhaps for the last time.

That's crudely put; I am not trying to preach at all. But that is the argument: We did this in 1918; in 1944 it not only MUST NOT happen again, it SHALL NOT HAPPEN again. i.e. ARE WE GOING TO LET IT HAPPEN AGAIN? now that we are in another war, where the third and final chance might be offered to save him. (*Selected Letters* 180)

This novel became the consuming passion of his next decade. Published in 1954 as *A Fable*, it had become perhaps his longest and most difficult, and still most misunderstood, novel. Far from being the anti-war polemic that he envisioned it in 1943, *A Fable*, quite to the contrary, makes of war a trope for the ultimate extremes of ideological certitude, both cause and effect of nationalistic cohesion.

A Fable is set during May of 1918, during the so-called false armistice of that spring. In Faulkner's novel the reason for that armistice is the appearance of a

Christ-like corporal who brings the war to a screeching halt by convincing the soldiers on both sides to refuse to engage a battle, to mutiny. The novel focuses on the various responses to this mutiny of a variety of characters or groups. The moral dialectic of the narrative centers on the ideological relationship between the Powers that Be, the generals who run the war, and the teeming inarticulate masses of humanity who must fight it and suffer its immediate devastating effects of loss, displacement, and anxiety. Reacting to the mutiny, the generals on both sides of the conflict assemble to conspire against the mutineers to figure out how to get the war started again. This is simple and cynical enough, a hierarchy of class that knows no boundaries of politics or geography.

For their part, however, those teeming masses, who stand to benefit most from the Christ-corporal's passive resistance, actually despise and reject the corporal because by his action he offers them freedom from the politics and ideologies and nationalisms that keep them fighting for Fatherland and Motherland: You don't have to hate, you don't have to fight, he in effect assures them, though to be sure to refuse to fight is to risk near-certain execution for mutiny. The corporal thus offers them a way to break free of the bonds that keep them at the bottom of the political and economic hierarchy and, more, that keep them ready to do the bidding of whoever of those at the top of the hierarchy can keep them whipped up into an ideological frenzy with what the old general calls the "polysyllabic and verbless patriotic nonsense" (*A Fable* 994) of ideological rhetoric.

This would be a bleak enough reading of *A Fable*. But Faulkner's sense of Cold War realities pushes him toward the novel's climactic scene, which brings together the two chief protagonists, the corporal and the Allied Supreme Commander, a man born at the very topmost aerie of the West's social and financial and military hierarchies and so, as Faulkner called Flem Snopes, "a pillar, rock-fixed, of things as they are." The old general is in fact the corporal's father, from a long-ago liaison. He tries to convince his son to forsake the martyrdom, to take life; the corporal refuses. The point of the confrontation is its demonstration of the general's absolute power not just over the corporal's life, but over the *meaning* of his life, and the meaning he can grant to his death. By letting him go, the general can render his son's life meaningless. Only he, with his power, can make his son's life meaningful by depriving him of it; if he takes his son's life, he will inscribe his martyrdom across Western Europe not as freedom but as hope: in Faulkner's view two not just different but completely antithetical things. That is, under the circumstances, the only meaning the corporal's life and death can possibly have is that prescribed by the very power structure he has tried to subvert.

The really darker side of the picture—and here is Faulkner's own political conservatism at work, one suspects—is that the old general is a compassionate and wise man who understands that masses don't really want freedom, the responsibility of individual autonomy: they need the comfort and security of the hope that only ideological differentiation can give them. They must have the shibboleths of Fatherland and Motherland to cohere around: they would rather live in a world in which they are rigidly differentiated from others, an orderly world rigidly structured and definitively bounded, where all relationships are clear, and they would die to protect that differentiation rather than live fearfully in freedom from ideological illusion. They would rather die believing their own nation is divinely ordained and so will eventually reign supreme than to live in an undifferentiated, unstructured, disorderly world which they fear cannot guarantee that they will be, in all things, number one: the best, the strongest. Faulkner's bleakest final point is power's absolute bind: unillusioned itself, it must feed the illusions of the masses, not merely to conserve itself in power, but simply to invest the masses with direction, to keep them from trampling each other to death. It is indeed a bleak fictional portrait of the very humanity that Faulkner, from his Nobel Prize pulpit, had expressed such faith in.

By his engagement with the War, both hot and cold ones, Faulkner implicitly dissociated himself from other mainstream Southern writers even while the Southern literary establishment, for its own purposes, was pushing him forward as Southern and American literatures' champion. He dissociated himself both as artist and as citizen. For as much as he might have agreed with some of the Fugitives' and Agrarians' attitudes, he was too completely aware of the dynamic of historical change to agree with them about much of anything else. Indeed, for all of the emphasis on history in his fiction, he was no worshipper of the past; he built no shrines to The Way Things Were, or even to the Way Things Are—though to be sure many of his characters do, *always to their downfall in the contemporary world.* One of his most-often quoted phrases comes from *Requiem for a Nun*'s Gavin Stevens, who pontificates that "The past is never dead. It's not even past" (535). Because of Faulkner's manifest interest in the workings of history, the phrase has always been quoted as reflecting his own views, and has been taken by the Southern literary industry to align him with the Fugitives and Agrarians. But in fact his entire work rather specifically challenges that view. Another line from *Requiem* seems to me more nearly to define Faulkner's quite different view: history, he says, is "litter from the celestial experimental Work Bench" (540).

Faulkner never envisioned *any* historical moment as "golden," because if "golden" it would necessarily be static and so outside of history and therefore not possible. He and his works specifically disavow Sullivan's belief that the world before the Civil War was any more stable or ordered than the present moment: just ask Thomas Sutpen, Charles Bon, Isaac McCaslin, Joanna Burden. For Faulkner, history was a dynamic convergence—indeed, a collision—of various powerful forces, including chance and choice. World War II is thus a powerful trope for his sense of history. Like history, like life, it was a war on multiple simultaneous overlapping and interrelated fronts, a war of problematic and shifting allegiances among allies who even as they were shooting at one enemy were worried about and planning strategies against the enemy-to-be beyond the bullet and the bomb. It was, then, a war of shifting boundaries and conflicts, not like World War I, when the battle lines were clearly drawn in the ground, as though with a giant plow (an image which should have made the Agrarians happy), and when honorable enemies slugged it out with each other.

Faulkner knew what the Fugitives and Agrarians seemed not to have known, or been willing to learn, that boundaries are always moveable and shifting, that all political boundaries are ideological illusions created for political purposes, and he knew it was not just foolishness but a form of death to look to the past for a truth to hold the present to. History doesn't operate that way, and neither does Faulkner, whose fiction always tests his characters' capacity to cope with historical change. "I don't hold to the idea of a return," he told an interviewer in 1956:

> we mustn't go back to a condition, an idyllic condition, in which the dream [made us think] we were happy, we were free of trouble and sin. We must take the trouble and sin along with us, and we must cure that trouble and sin as we go. We can't go back to a condition in which there were no wars, in which there was no bomb. We got to accept that bomb and do something about it, eliminate that bomb, eliminate the war, not retrograde to a condition before it exists, because then if time is a [forward] and continuing thing which is a part of motion, then we have to run into that bomb again sooner or later and go through it again. (*Lion in the Garden* 131)

That is a lesson he alone among the Good Ole Boys seems to have learned from the most traumatic historical event of the twentieth century.

Works Cited

Blotner, Joseph. *Faulkner: A Biography.* Two volumes. New York: Random House, 1974. Revised, one-volume edition: New York: Random House, 1984.

Faulkner, William. *A Fable. William Faulkner: Novels 1942–1954.* New York: Library of America, 1994. 665–1072.

———. *Lion in the Garden. Interviews . . . 1926–1962.* Ed. Michael Millgate and James B. Meriwether. New York: Random House, 1968.

———. *The Mansion.* New York: Random House, 1959.

———. *The Portable Faulkner.* Ed. Malcolm Cowley. New York: Viking, 1946.

———. *Requiem for a Nun. William Faulkner: Novels 1942–1954.* New York: Library of America, 1994. 471–664.

———. *Selected Letters.* Ed. Joseph Blotner. New York: Random House, 1977.

McHaney, Thomas L. Review of Sullivan, *A Requiem for the Renaissance. Mississippi Quarterly* 30,1 (1976–77): 185–88.

Meriwether, James B. "Faulkner and the World War II Monument in Oxford." *A Faulkner Miscellany.* Ed. Meriwether. Jackson: University Press of Mississippi, 105–106.

Rubin, Louis D., Jr., and Robert D. Jacobs, eds. *Southern Renascence: The Literature of the Modern South.* Baltimore: Johns Hopkins Press, 1953.

Schwartz, Lawrence. *Creating Faulkner's Reputation.* Knoxville: University of Tennessee Press, 1988.

Sullivan, Walter. *A Requiem for the Renaissance: The State of Fiction in the Modern South.* Athens: University of Georgia Press, 1976.

Twelve Southerners. *I'll Take My Stand.* New York: Scribner's, 1930.

IX REMEMBERING HATTIESBURG
Growing Up Black in Wartime Mississippi

Arvarh E. Strickland

The heroic figure of the years of the Civil Rights Revolt in Mississippi who has been most inspiring to me is Mrs. Fannie Lou Hamer. Mrs. Hamer's lament that she was "sick and tired of being sick and tired" is often quoted, but another of her statements has meant more to me. She once said: "There are some things I feel strong about. . . . One is not to forget where I come from and the other is to praise the bridges that carried me over." " . . . [N]ot to forget where I come from and . . . to praise the bridges that carried me over."[1]

In 1978, those who planned the grand reunion of those of us who attended Hattiesburg's black high school between 1921 and 1971 did me the honor of inviting me to speak at the public meeting held in the old Saenger theater building.[2] That was one of the most difficult speeches that I have ever written for, in my own mind, I had to deal with the vexing question of why hundreds of black people from New York, Michigan, Ohio, Illinois, Connecticut, and as far away as California would return to Hattiesburg, Mississippi, for a celebration.

Black people from Hattiesburg were often thought of as a little peculiar. Even fellow Mississippians often wondered about us. Fellow students at Tougaloo College often asked how people from such a ragged, sandy, flood washed, backwater as Hattiesburg could think so highly of themselves. This question merited serious consideration. Life for African Americans in Hattiesburg was as oppressive as it was for those elsewhere in Mississippi. Those who joined members of the Student Nonviolent Coordinating Committee (SNCC) on Freedom Day in Hattiesburg, January 22, 1964, found that the basic right to protest still did not exist in the city. Policemen were still enforcing the rules of Jim Crow, and a double standard of justice was still being administered. A stone wall still separated black from white.[3]

I remember the rigid segregation that separated white and black Hattiesburg. I remember the "white" and "colored" drinking fountains in the S. K. Kress store, which was better than the no place for an African American to get a drink in the Woolworth or Scott's five-and-dime stores. I remember the lunch counters in Woolworth and Scott's where I dared not take a seat. I remember side or alley entrances to the Saenger, the Lomo, and the Buck theaters and the second balconies where I had to sit. I remember the side window to Gus's hamburger stand where my Grandfather—who refused to spend his money where African Americans were served through back doors or side windows— forbade me to buy a hamburger or hotdog. I remember the many many other places I could not go. I also remember the back of the buses and my uncle laying in waiting all night between his house and the house next door with my grandfather's shotgun after having a fight with a bus driver, who struck him because he did not have the exact fare. Fortunately, nothing happened.

If these memories and the general characterization of Hattiesburg had been the whole story, those of us who returned in the summer of 1978 probably should have been attended by psychiatrists. But our return and our celebration must be viewed within the context of the Black Experience.

On the black side of that racial wall that divided Hattiesburg was a community with institutions—families, churches, schools, and organizations. And, there were heroic figures. In that community we found faith and love. The history of black Hattiesburg, to borrow the conclusion Professor John Dittmer reached about blacks in Georgia, "is the struggle of men and women to develop their own institutions, improve their economic conditions, educate their children, gain political rights, and maintain a sense of dignity."[4]

This was the Hattiesburg I came from, and here existed the "bridges that carried me over." My Hattiesburg, however, had somewhat limited boundaries. The N. R. Burger Center, the city's black United Services Organization building during World War II, is the center of my Hattiesburg. My Hattiesburg included the downtown area running from a few blocks south of Main street to the rivers on the north, from Buschman street on the east to north Main street on the west. Of course, I ventured beyond these boundaries from time-to-time, but essentially, this is where I lived. Also, during the years just before, during, and immediately after World War II, this was the vibrant heart of black Hattiesburg. I was born about six blocks from the USO building at 909 Atlanta Street. There is where I lived the first seventeen years of my life and where I lived when I came home to teach for a year after graduating from college.

The years when the impact of World War II were felt in Hattiesburg, 1940–1945, were the tenth through the fifteenth years of my life. In school years, these were the years of the fifth through the tenth grades. In these years, the most important institution in my life was, of course, my family. The house on Atlanta street housed an extended family. My mother and I lived there with my grandparents. Mama was Clotiel Marshall Strickland. She married at eighteen, had a son at nineteen, and was a single parent soon thereafter. She attended what was then called normal school, received a license to teach, and worked in a four-month school in Perry County for about twenty dollars a month. Each year after her short school term ended, she sought work as a domestic. During World War II, she cooked full time in local restaurants. I was always proud that I had a beautiful mother, and, in my eyes, years of hard work never diminished that beauty.

The person to be reckoned with in the house on Atlanta Street, however, was my grandmother, Big Mama, Mamie Waldrip Calloway. She was the towering influence in all of our lives. But, the head of the house at 909 Atlanta Street was granddaddy, John W. Calloway, and not even Big Mama questioned that.

Then, there was my father, Eunice Strickland. He attended Piney Wood School and Tuskegee Institute, where he learned the plastering and brick mason trades. He also learned to play the violin. Somewhere along the line, he became addicted to alcohol. I was a man and a father before I fully understood my father. Then I came to know well the stress and frustrations that sensitive, intelligent black men faced daily in a racist society. I must say that neither my mother nor anyone else in my community ever said anything derogatory to me about my father. Periodically, older members of my church recalled how they loved to listen to him play the violin during church services. Others pointed to the beautiful job he did in plastering the inside of St. Paul church.

Next in importance to my family as an institutional bridge that carried me over was St. Paul Methodist Episcopal Church (now United Methodist Church) located just about two blocks from the Burger Center, "on the hill." St. Paul was not only where I went to worship: There I found others to share my joys and sorrows, there I found comfort in the face of frustration, bewilderment, and defeat, there I found hope, when it seemed that "hope unborn had died," there I found faith that within the community and within each of us was the power to remake our world. At St. Paul, I found sympathetic audiences to listen to my first attempts at public speaking. There I was given my first opportunities to lead. My family's support, supplemented by quarters and half-dollars from members of St. Paul sent me to meetings at Gulfside—the Methodist conference center and camp ground at Waveland, Mississippi—to conferences throughout the state, and, in 1945, to my first meeting of the National Conference of Methodist Youth in far away Michigan. Above all, at St. Paul, I was somebody, as were we all.

Eureka school, which housed both elementary and high school grades, was an important institution in this community. In spite of the overcrowded facilities, in spite of the unequal pay of the teachers, in spite of the lack of supplies and equipment, in spite of all of these things and many more, we were taught and we learned to value excellence. We were taught and we learned respect for ourselves, that respect which manifests itself in respect for others. We developed pride, we acquired ambition, and above all, we learned to dream and to appreciate the dreams others had for us.

Black Hattiesburg consisted of several neighborhoods, but the area centered around Mobile Street was where the action was. It was here that the majority of African American business and professional people had their businesses and offices and where they lived. In those days, Mobile Street began at Pine Street. In the blocks between Pine Street and Second streets, along with such white-owned businesses as the Coca Cola Bottling Plant, Blue Ribbon Bakery, and the A. & P. Store, were several black-owned businesses. Mr. Dove operated a hotel and restaurant, and there was another restaurant and at least two barber shops. In the area set back from the street known as London's Hitch Yard, my grandfather and Mr. L. A. Flowers operated their blacksmith shops.

The major cluster of black-owned businesses was located north of Second Street. The Dixie Theater, owned and operated by Mr. Garnett Jones, was in that area, and Mr. Jones's store and filling station was on the corner of Mobile and Fifth. He lived first in that building and later he moved to a house a block away on Fifth Street. In the next block, Mr. Paul Weston, who distributed the *Hattiesburg American* in African American neighborhoods, had his office. On down Mobile Street were several dry cleaners. Mr. Garfield Warren's neatly painted window proclaimed beneath the name of his establishment: "Come Clean with Us and We will Dye for You." Two funeral homes, several grocery stores, including Mr. Gaither Hardaway's store at Mobile and Seventh and Mrs. S. K. Triggs's store on Seventh were there among other businesses. Mr. Hammond Smith operated his drug store in the 600 block, and Dr. Charles Smith had offices above the drug store. Dr. J. S. Love owned the building at Seventh and Mobile. There he had his office upstairs over a white-run grocery store. He also rented a hall next to his office for dances and other such affairs. Two to three dentists had offices in the area. Those entering Reverend Henry Clark's shoe repair shop were greeted with a sign reading: "We mend the rips and patch the holes, raise the heels and save the soles." Mr. Clark, a member of St. James C. M. E. Church and a part-time minister, said that his business and his church had the same objectives, one for shoes and the other for people. The real action was in Mr. Bill Carmichael's beer garden. It was a rare weekend when a few rips and holes were not put in someone's anatomy in Bill's place. That was one of the places that was strictly off-limits to me.

Standing as seemingly unheeded sentinels watching over Mobile Street were the Church of God in Christ, housed in a two-story frame structure at Fifth and Mobile, and Mt. Carmel Missionary Baptist Church, a modest but imposing white frame building at Mobile and Seventh streets. Nearby were St. James C. M. E. Church on Seventh and Zion Chapel A. M. E. Church on New Orleans. Further out were True Light Missionary Baptist Church, with its crusading and militant pastor, the Reverend James H. Ratliff, and across the street from my family home on Atlanta Street, was the Church of God, whose pastor and my grandfather were great friends. They fished together, but they never discussed religion.

These examples of people and institutions do not begin to cover the many and diverse components of my Hattiesburg. We were blessed with a grand array of mentors and role models.

World War II brought sudden and radical changes in my life and to the life of this community. In 1940, the winds of change began to stir Hattiesburg from its depression-induced lethargy. Some changes, however, had nothing to do with the war. When we returned to school in September 1940, for example, we received free textbooks. This was a first. Before that year, the opening of school meant a trip downtown to Geiger's Book Store to buy the books on the list the teacher had provided. These free textbooks were new and shiny. I remember that Big Mama retrieved several pieces of cloth from the bag holding the quilt scraps. These remains of dresses or other garments became book covers. Those flimsy paper covers furnished by the Coca Cola Company were not good enough for these beautiful books. At the end of the year, thanks to our parents, most of our books were as clean as they were the day they were issued, at least the covers were.

Also, in 1940, New Deal measures and actions related to preparedness began to bring change. We were accustomed to such small WPA projects as the laying of concrete sidewalks, even in our neighborhoods, and the building of fancy red outhouses. But beginning in April, a project of a different magnitude was underway. Robertson Place, a federal housing project, was under construction across town in Arledge Quarters, and it was for the exclusive use of black residents. According to newspaper accounts, between April and August, this project provided work for 150 men and pumped nearly $50,000 into the Hattiesburg economy.[5]

Discussion in the community focused less on the economic impact of Robertson Place than on the nature of the housing it would provide. At the time, few Hattiesburg blacks enjoyed the luxury of living in brick dwellings. Also, neither indoor plumbing nor electricity was enjoyed by large segments of the community. Robertson Place was to have all of these and much more. In fact, these homes were to be so far above the average that wild rumors began to circulate concerning the restrictions that would be placed on residents.

When tenant selection began in March 1941, the Housing Authority had to deal with these rumors. The Authority announced that:

> During the construction period of the housing projects in Hattiesburg many false rumors have brought questions to the minds of the prospective tenants of these units and it is the desire of the authority to clear up as many of these rumors as possible. Such rumors are to the effect that: No children will be allowed in the project; the lights will be turned off at a specified time; the doors will be locked at a set hour; no phonographs or radios will be allowed; friends and relatives will not be permitted to visit the homes of tenants, without permission. . . .
>
> The Authority wished to make it clear that there are no complicated rules or regulations any more than in renting a house elsewhere. However, the management must be sure that each family can and will pay their rent and that they will be good neighbors.[6]

It was a matter of some satisfaction to black Hattiesburg residents to learn that plans for the white project lagged far behind those for Robertson Place. Construction of Robertson Place was well underway when land acquisition began for the white project. Land acquisition, however, caused the displacement of several black families who owned property north of Second Street between Mobile and Bowie streets.

The building of Camp Shelby had the greatest economic impact on both white and black Hattiesburg. In September 1940, the federal government allocated $11,000,000 for the construction of the camp, and the War Department allocated $3,300,000 for the training of two army divisions. Banner headlines in the *Hattiesburg American* announced the need for 5,000 workers, both skilled and common labor. The wage scale was set by the federal government, and common laborers could earn the unheard of wage among black workers of forty cents an hour for a ten-hour shift.[7] By January 1941, the paper could exclaim that "Hattiesburg hit the jackpot." During the last months of 1940 the Camp Shelby payrolls contained some 17,000 workers and the first 10,000 soldiers had arrived. Businesses of all types boomed. A dry goods store had increased sales five and a half times over the previous year; sawmills were operating twenty-four hours a day; rents had increased; and bank deposits were at an all time high. An estimated 100 new businesses had opened in Forrest County.[8]

Amid the excitement of business expansion and population growth in 1941 came the added thrill of the latest technological advance on the railroad reaching Hattiesburg. In March, The Southerner, the Southern Railroad System's new deluxe, diesel powered, streamline train came through town for the first time. I remember dreaming of one day riding this beautiful silver machine, with its distinctive sounding whistle, to some place far away from Hattiesburg.

The migration of men seeking jobs at Camp Shelby brought radical change to life at 909 Atlanta Street. Men from Neshoba, Kemper, Winston, and other counties in that area who knew my grandparents, began inquiring about living with us if they obtained jobs in Hattiesburg. Some of these men claimed kinship, and others were from families that had long-standing friendship with my grandparents or their relatives. So, my grandmother decided to go into the boarding house business, at least temporarily. The three unoccupied bedrooms were fitted out with several beds that would sleep from two to five men in each room. A long table was improvised by my grandfather and placed in the hallway that ran the length of the house. From Monday through Friday, and sometimes until Saturday evening, ten to twelve men shared our home. They all tried to get home to their families for the weekend and would return late Sunday night or early Monday morning in time to go to work.

My grandmother presided over this enlarged household as if the men were her sons. She served them two meals and prepared lunches for them to take to work. Of course, there was a great deal of washing and ironing of bed linen and cleaning to be done. Looking back on it, I don't know how my grandmother was able to do so much without help. One of my daily chores was to ride my bicycle to the Colonial Baking Company's outlet on Market Street and bring back the oversized basket I used for delivering newspapers filled with day-old bread. Loaves which sold for ten cents in the stores were five cents day old. When the construction of the camp was completed, life returned to a semblance of normal in the Calloway household.

In the rest of the community, however, life was far from normal. By the end of 1940, African American soldiers were stationed at Camp Shelby, and they came to Mobile Street seeking the things that soldiers look for when they are off duty. Often what they found was violence and encounters with Hattiesburg and military policemen. Many of these men seemed to show little awe of white policemen. Constable C. J. Cargill learned this when he and another constable, along with two military policemen, entered Bill Carmichael's beer garden. During a melee, a black soldier knocked Cargill to the floor, and the constable was only able to gain control of the situation by pulling his revolver while on the floor and firing into crowd of black soldiers and civilians in the restaurant. The local newspaper did not report whether or not Cargill wounded or killed any of the bystanders.[9]

Some white residents became concerned that caste lines were not being respected. One such person complained that while riding a crowded city bus with "both white ladies and men" standing in the aisle, the whites had to move to the rear of the bus, which caused them to stand among black riders. This man pointed out that "this action is not only against [the] sentiment of the Southern people but is against the laws of our State." He believed that an earlier incident in which a black rider refused to use the rear exit and attacked and beat the white bus driver when he insisted that the black man do so would not have occurred had the races been properly separated.[10]

Obviously, this seeming relaxation of Jim Crow practices had become a matter of more than passing concern. In February 1941, the chief of police, M. M. Little, announced that the bus line had been notified that partitions had to be placed between the sections in all buses to be occupied by white and black riders. This was required by both state law and city ordinance. "When such partitions are placed in the buses and properly marked so as to designate the white and colored sections of the vehicles," the chief stated, "passengers who refuse to occupy the sections designed for them may be put off the bus by the driver and will be subject to a fine for failure to obey the law." "Likewise," he continued, "drivers of buses who fail to keep the white and colored passengers in the section designated for them, will be subject to a fine." Chief Little also warned taxi companies that the hauling of white and black passengers in the same vehicle would not be tolerated.[11]

White Hattiesburg made it clear that although both white and black men wore the uniform of the United States Army, their roles were different. The white soldiers were learning how to fire rifles and machine guns and other necessary skills of combat; the black soldiers were performing the peaceful "house-keeping" duties needed on the post. We could not help but notice that the black military policemen patrolling Mobile Street were only armed with night sticks. White military policemen downtown and those who occasionally rode into the Mobile Street area were also armed with .45 caliber pistols.

The Hattiesburg policemen did not find the black soldiers particularly easy to deal with. In June 1941, the police chief warned black servicemen that when they visited Hattiesburg, they were "expected to conduct themselves in the same manner as [N]egro civilians residing in the city." This included not walking the streets in white neighborhoods at night, "except when going to or from work." Black soldiers, like black civilians were expected to stay in the black sections of town. As an afterthought, he added that the black sections were off-limits to white soldiers.[12]

The black soldiers were welcomed into the homes and hearts of the people of this community. A number of them found wives while stationed here. Even before the USO was built, the community sponsored activities for the entertainment of these men. In late 1941, work began on recreation centers for white and black soldiers. Of course, these were separate-but-equal centers. The USO building for white soldiers was a brick structure on Front Street, built at a cost of nearly $116,000. The building for black soldiers on Sixth Street was a frame structure costing about $42,000. Both buildings were opened in March 1942.[13]

The USO became a center for community activities. Five black business leaders served as the club advisory committee and groups of African American women, most of them teachers, served as the Volunteer Service Organization. Along with the business leaders, ministers, teachers, students, and other community residents worked with the six-member club staff to make the USO an exciting place.

In fact, defense preparations and the war brought a general air of excitement to the community. In July 1941, Lionel Hampton and his orchestra gave both a concert at Eureka school and played for a dance at Love Hall, on the corner of Mobile and Seventh streets. In July 1942, Mrs. Mary McLeod Bethune came to town briefly and spoke at the USO. Added to the parade of quartets from nearby towns that visited the city on a regular basis now came singing groups with national reputations. The Golden Gate Quartet of New York City appeared at Mt. Carmel Baptist Church in 1942, and the Southernaires Quartet performed at Eureka school in 1943.[14]

Black Hattiesburg was deeply involved in about all defense and war related activities. Under the leadership of N. R. Burger, the community organized for civilian defense. If the Germans or the Japanese had decided to bomb Hattiesburg, our air raid wardens were ready to spring into action. Black residents participated in all Red Cross drives, raised money to support the USO, and subscribed liberally to all of the war loan drives. In September 1942, I joined my fellow *Hattiesburg American* newspaper boys in collecting scrap metal from the people on our paper routes.

The presence of soldiers brought increased attention to health issues, especially the menace of venereal diseases. Such things were not openly discussed before the opening of Camp Shelby. Boys whispered about infection and remedies, and some boasted that infection was a sign of manhood. But this was not something you talked about with adults. We were fortunate at Eureka to have periodic unofficial sessions on sex education when Mr. and Mrs. H. C. Harper, the state Y.M.C.A. staff persons who worked with the Hi-Y and Tri Hi-Y clubs, came to town.

This all changed when large numbers of soldiers became infected while visiting Hattiesburg. Health became a major concern. Syphilis was especially virulent. In 1941, an estimated 275,000 black Mississippians were afflicted with this disease.[15] Prostitutes, or suspected women, as they were euphemistically referred to in the press, were required to register and undergo tests. They were provided cards indicating whether or not they were infected and giving the date of their last examination. Oscar R. Jackson, a black man with a masters degree in public health, was employed and given the title of health educator, largely to keep track of the black women in this group. Mr. Jackson also served as a health educator for us at Eureka. Moreover, when I arrived at Tougaloo College in 1947, he was Dean of Men and a familiar face to those of us from Hattiesburg.

Other measures were also taken to combat venereal disease. The military established what were called prophylactic stations and required soldiers to visit them when they arrived in town and before they left. One such station was in an alley a block from Mobile Street. Forrest County even provided us our own health centers. The one in my area was a house on Short Eighth Street. Another was opened across town on Fredna Avenue. In spite of the undistinguished appearance of the facilities, we were proud that the clinics were staffed by a black doctor and other black medical professionals. The war years also brought special emphasis on National Negro Health Week. In 1942, for example, Dr. A. W. Dent, president of Dillard University, was the featured speaker, and the week closed with a mass meeting at the USO.[16]

In 1943, the war brought another greatly perplexing problem to white Hattiesburg. On January 8, the 100th Infantry Battalion arrived at Camp Shelby. This unit was composed of Japanese American troops from the Hawaiian National Guard. In February, the 442nd Infantry Regiment was organized. This regiment was composed of Americans of Japanese ancestry from both Hawaii and the mainland. The officers, however, were mainly white. In April 1943, the men of the 442nd Regiment joined those of the 100th Infantry Battalion at Camp Shelby.[17]

Now white Hattiesburg had to deal with a third element in a society built for two. City officials sought to solve this problem by classifying Japanese Americans as "white." This meant that they could patronize white establishments, were not to enter black sections of the city, and were discouraged from having friendly relationships with African Americans. Hattiesburg blacks seemed to have found this situation more ludicrous than a cause for resentment. Moreover, the black community enjoyed the white community's predicament when the Nisei soldiers became a troublesome presence in the city.

By 1943, Mama had left her twenty-dollar a month teaching job and was earning about that much a week cooking at the Ritz cafe, a white restaurant at 211 South Main Street. For a time, I worked as a bus boy there on Saturdays before running my paper route. A major part of my duties was to keep the many coolers filled with the popular brands of beer. Men from the 442nd frequented the Ritz on Saturdays, and I observed groups of them largely keeping to themselves and quietly consuming rather large amounts of beer.

Of course, black Hattiesburg was rife with rumors about the Japanese American soldiers. Some of these men did not readily accept their classification as "white." Some of them defied authority and used Jim Crow facilities. My community especially enjoyed the reports of conflicts between men of the 442nd Regiment and white bus drivers and policemen. White Hattiesburg, we were sure, breathed a sigh of relief when the "Go for Broke" Regiment was shipped to Europe.

The ending of the war in 1945 was overshadowed for me by other events of that year. In May, Big Mama fell while attending to her beloved baby chicks and died of tetanus infection. In large measure, she was a victim of our Jim Crow system of health delivery.

Later in the year, we learned that the war had not changed the working of the Mississippi system of justice as it was applied to African Americans. On Saturday, November 3, Willie McGee of Laurel was arrested in Hattiesburg and charged with raping a white woman in Laurel that day. His trial in early December lasted one day, and it took the all-white jury only two and one-half minutes to find him guilty. The judge sentenced him to die in the electric chair on January 7, 1946. He did not die on that day, however.

We had to live with the trauma of the Willie McGee case for several years. It was not until the eve of my graduation from college that, on May 7, 1951, Willie McGee paid the supreme price for his indiscretion. His death was adjudged by black people in Laurel and in Hattiesburg as a legal lynching, as few if any thought him guilty of rape.[18]

Nevertheless, to a greater extent than I realized at the time, World War II brought changes in the relations between black and white Hattiesburg. There were changes both in attitude and in behavior. Of course, some of these changes were too subtle for young people my age to appreciate, and we were unaware of much that was going on.

In August 1941, for example, black business, civic, and fraternal leaders organized the Negro Civic Welfare Association to "promote civic pride and better co-operation" among members of the community and to "bring about better relations between whites and [N]egroes in the city." The businessmen who organized this association were well-known leaders of our community. They selected Paul J. Weston as president, Alfonso Clark as secretary, and Garfield Warren as treasurer. In October, the association called upon city officials to clean community streets, provide better police protection, and take measures to protect school children crossing busy streets.[19] I do not recall whether or not any stop signs were installed at that time.

Mr. Burger recalled that members of the black community lodged strong protests with the War Department on at least two occasions. At one point, there was a danger that the War Department might take over the Robertson Place housing project and use it to house whites. According to Mr. Burger, black protest forestalled this. It was, Mr. Burger believed, "the first successful civil rights action taken by the Hattiesburg Negro community."[20] Black protest also led to the arming of black military policemen and the eventual assigning of white and black MPs to ride in the same vehicles.[21]

The struggle for the ballot was one of the most difficult battles waged by black Hattiesburg. Even before the war ended, Richard Boyd and others were confronting the circuit clerk and demanding to be registered to vote. Mr. Boyd—an employee of Hercules, Inc., a Mason, and an officer in the Forrest County branch of the NAACP—the Reverend Ratliff, and a few others were permitted to register, but they were the token exceptions. Mr. Smith and fifteen other men brought suit in the 1950s for the same purpose. After taking their case to the United States Supreme Court, in 1963, they were finally registered by court order. Their efforts underscored how deeply the seeds of change had been planted during the war years.[22]

My personal awakening to this fact came in the 1960s when my mother used one of her indirect methods to tell me that she had been down to register. Somewhat matter-of-factly she told me that she had an enjoyable visit with some of the young movement people working on voter registration in Hattiesburg. She said after talking with her for a time, they finally, somewhat timidly, asked if she was brave enough to go down to the courthouse and try to register, if they went with her. At this point in the telling of her story, she laughed and looked at me to judge my reaction so far. Then, continuing, she said: "I told them, honey, I don't need you to go with me to no courthouse. I have been down there, and I registered. Here is my card."

These were my generation's role models and mentors. They were the bridges that carried us over. We have a goodly heritage from our mothers and fathers and from the other residents of this community. This was my Hattiesburg, and, like Mrs. Hamer, I want never to forget where I came from, and I want to be ever thankful for the bridges that carried me over.

Notes

Introduction

1. James C. Cobb, *The Selling of the South: The Southern Crusade for Industrial Development* (Baton Rouge, 1982) and *Industrialization and Southern Society* (Lexington, Ky., 1984); Pete Daniel, *Breaking the Land: The Transformation of Cotton, Tobacco and Rice Cultures since 1880* (Urbana, 1985); David R. Goldfield, *Cotton Fields and Skyscrapers: Southern City and Region, 1607–1980* (Baton Rouge, 1982); Jack Temple Kirby, *Rural Worlds Lost: The American South 1920–1960* (Baton Rouge, 1987); Bruce J. Schulman, *From Cotton Belt to Sunbelt: Federal Policy, Economic Development, and the Transformation of the South, 1938–1980* (New York, 1991); Gavin Wright, *Old South, New South: Revolutions in the Southern Cotton Economy Since the Civil War* (New York, 1986).

2. Bernard L. Weinstein and Robert E. Firestone, *Regional Growth and Decline in the United States: The Rise of the Sunbelt and the Decline of the Northeast* (New York, 1978), 49; William H. Miernyk, *The Changing Structure of the Southern Economy* (Research Triangle Park, N.C., 1977), 8; Harold G. Vatter, *The U.S. Economy in World War II* (New York, 1986), 128; Wright, *Old South, New South*, 256; Nicholas Lemann, *The Promised Land: The Great Black Migration and How It Changed America* (New York, 1991), 6.

3. Carl Carmer, *The Stars Fell on Alabama* (New York, 1934), xiv.

4. The implications of this discrepancy have been most notably analyzed by C. Vann Woodward in his seminal essay "The Search for Southern Identity," in Woodward, *The Burden of Southern History* (Baton Rouge, 1960), 3–25.

5. Vatter, *The U.S. Economy in World War II*, 127–29; Kirby, *Rural Worlds Lost: The American South 1920–1960* (Baton Rouge, 1987), 304–06; "Labor in the South," *Monthly Labor Review*, 63 (October 1946), 497.

6. Gunnar Myrdal, *An American Dilemma: The Negro Problem and Modern Democracy* (New York, 1944) quickly became the definitive analysis of American race relations. Interestingly, Myrdal included an appendix comparing "the race question" to "the woman question." Although he saw similarities between the two, Myrdal did not by any means regard them as analogous. See Myrdal, 1073–78.

1 ## World War II and the Mind of the Modern South

1. Wilbur J. Cash, *The Mind of the South* (New York: Vintage Books, 1991), 96, 429; see also James C. Cobb, "Does 'Mind' No Longer Matter? The South, the Nation, and the Mind of the South, 1941–1991," *Journal of Southern History* (November 1991), 681–718.

2. Bruce Clayton, *W. J. Cash: A Life* (Baton Rouge: Louisiana State University Press, 1991), 3, 187.

3. Morton Sosna, "More Important than the Civil War? The Impact of World War II on the South," in James C. Cobb and Charles R. Wilson, eds., *Perspectives on the American South: An Annual Review of Society, Politics, and Culture* 4 (New York and London: Gordon and Breach Science Publishers, 1987), 145–161.

4. John Ray Skates, Jr., "World War II as a Watershed in Mississippi History," *Journal of Mississippi History* (May 1975), 135.

5. William R. Parker, "The South in the National Economy, 1865–1970," *Southern Economic Journal* 46 (April 1980), 1045–46.

6. Numan V. Bartley, "The Era of the New Deal as a Turning Point in Southern History," in James C. Cobb and Michael V. Namorato, eds., *The New Deal and the South* (Jackson, Miss.: University Press of Mississippi, 1984), 138. See also George B. Tindall, *The Emergence of the New South, 1913–1945* (Baton Rouge: Louisiana State University Press, 1967). For recent examples of the emerging historiographical focus on World War II, see Bartley, *The New South, 1945–1980: The Story of the South's Transformation* (Baton Rouge: Louisiana State University Press, 1995). See also Allen Cronenberg, *Forth to the Mighty Conflict: Alabama and World War Two* (Tuscaloosa: University of Alabama Press, 1995) and C. Calvin Smith, *War and Wartime Change: The Transformation of Arkansas, 1940–1945* (Fayetteville: University of Arkansas Press, 1986).

7. Dewey W. Grantham, *The South in Modern America: A Region at Odds* (New York: Harper Collins Publishers, 1994), 175; James C. Cobb, *The Selling of the South: The Southern Crusade for Industrial Development, 1936–1990* (Urbana, Ill.: University of Illinois Press, 1993), 13–28.

8. Frank E. Smith, *Congressman from Mississippi* (New York: Pantheon Books, 1964), 64; Cobb, *The Most Southern Place on Earth: The Mississippi Delta and the Roots of Regional Identity* (New York and Oxford: Oxford University Press, 1992), 210.

9. Jennifer E. Brooks, "From Fighting Nazism to Fighting Bossism: Southern World War II Veterans and the Assault on Southern Political Traditions" and Craig S. Pascoe, "The Monroe Rifle Club: Finding Justice in an Ungodly and Social Jungle Called 'Dixie,' " both unpublished papers presented at the 1996 Southern Historical Association meeting in New Orleans, La.

10. John Egerton, *Speak Now Against the Day: The Generation before the Civil Rights Movement in the South* (New York: Alfred A. Knopf, 1994), 326.

11. Ibid., 327.

12. Smith, *Congressman*, 101.

13. Ibid., 55; Adam Nossiter, *Of Long Memory: Mississippi and the Murder of Medgar Evers* (Reading, Mass.: Addison-Wesley, 1994), 117.

14. Editorial, *Montgomery (Ala.) Advertiser*, May 21, 1946, cited in Brooks, "Fighting Nazism."

15. Pete Daniel, "Going Among Strangers: Southern Reactions to World War II," *Journal of American History 77* (December 1990), 893–94; Egerton, *Speak Now*, 366–69.

16. John Egerton, Interview with Sid McMath, September 8, 1990, A–302, Southern Oral History Program, Southern Historical Collection, University of North Carolina, Chapel Hill, North Carolina; James C. Cobb, "Colonel Effingham Crushes the Crackers: Political Reform in Postwar Augusta," *South Atlantic Quarterly* 89 (Autumn, 1979), 507–19; Cobb, *The Selling of the South*, 156.

17. Brooks, "Fighting Nazism."

18. Ibid.

19. The three governors controversy is outlined in detail in James C. Cobb's "Georgia Odyssey," in *The New Georgia Guide* (Athens, Ga.: University of Georgia Press, 1996). See also, Numan V. Bartley, *The Creation of Modern Georgia* (Athens, Ga.: University of Georgia Press, 1983), 187–91. Herman E. Talmadge, interview with Harold Henderson, July 17, 1987, cited in Brooks, "Fighting Nazism."

20. Katharine DuPre Lumpkin, *The Making of a Southerner* (Athens, Ga.: University of Georgia Press, 1991), 233–34; Bartley, *Modern Georgia*, 187.

21. See James C. Cobb, "Introduction," in Cobb and Namorato, eds., *The New Deal and the South*, 3–15.

22. Bruce J. Schulman, *From Cotton Belt to Sunbelt: Federal Policy, Economic Development, and the Transformation of the South, 1938–1980* (New York: Oxford University Press, 1991), 72–87.

23. Ibid., 72; Sosna, "More Important than the Civil War," 149–50.

24. Jacqueline Jones, *The Dispossessed: America's Underclass from the Civil War to the Present* (New York: Basic Books, 1992), 226, 228; Harry L. Wright to George Mitchell, February 23, 1946, cited in Brooks, "Fighting Nazism."

25. Jones, *The Dispossessed*, 226–27; *U.S. Bureau of the Census, Census of Population, 1950*, Volume II, *Characteristics of the Population*, Pt. 24, Mississippi, 188.

26. *Atlanta Constitution*, August 13, 1995; Schulman, *From Cotton Belt to Sun Belt*, 81–82.

27. Bill C. Malone, *Southern Music, American Music* (Lexington, Ky.: University of Kentucky Press, 1979), 88–93; Tony Scherman, "Country," *American Heritage* 45 (November, 1994), 40–50.

28. Curtis W. Ellison, *Country Music Culture: From Hard Times to Heaven* (Jackson, Miss.: University Press of Mississippi, 1995), 33; Bill C. Malone, *Country Music U.S.A.: A Fifty-Year History* (Austin, Tex.: University of Texas Press, 1974), 128, 313–16, 323–24; Cobb, *The Most Southern Place*, 284, 299, 302.

29. Samuel C. Adams, Jr., "The Acculturation of the Delta Negro," *Social Forces* 26 (December 1947), 202–205; Peter Guralnick, *Sweet Soul Music: Rhythm and Blues and the Southern Dream of Freedom* (New York: Harper and Row, 1986), 32–37.

30. Pete Daniel, "Rhythm of the Land"; *Agricultural History* 68 (Fall, 1994), 22; see also George Lipsitz, *Class and Culture in Cold War America: A Rainbow at Midnight* (New York: Praeger, 1981), 205.

31. David L. Cohn, *Where I Was Born and Raised* (Cambridge, Mass.: Harvard University Press, 1948), 41, x.

32. Sosna, "More Important than the Civil War," 154. Faulkner is quoted in David Minter, *William Faulkner: His Life and Work* (Baltimore: Johns Hopkins University Press, 1980), 199–200; see also Frederick R. Karl, *William Faulkner: American Writer* (New York: Weidenfeld and Nicholson, 1989), 711.

33. Morton Sosna, "The G.I.'s South and the North-South Dialogue during World War II," in Winfred B. Moore, Jr., Joseph F. Tripp, and Lyon G. Tyler, Jr., *Developing Dixie: Modernization in a Traditional Society* (Westport, Conn.: Greenwood Press, 1988), 813, 322; William Faulkner, *Intruder in the Dust* (New York: Random House, 1948), 153.

34. C. Vann Woodward, *Thinking Back: The Perils of Writing History* (Baton Rouge: Louisiana State University Press, 1986), 88; ———, *The Origins of the New South, 1877–1913* (Baton Rouge: Louisiana State University Press, 1951); ———, *The Strange Career of Jim Crow* (New York: Oxford University Press, 1955).

35. John Hope Franklin, "John Hope Franklin: A Life of Learning," in *Race and Southern History: Selected Essays, 1938–1988* (Baton Rouge: Louisiana State University Press, 1989), 287–90.

36. Arnold Rampersad, *The Life of Langston Hughes*, Vol. II: *I Dream a World* (New York: Oxford University Press, 1988), 36, 46, 50.

37. Michel Fabre, *The Unfinished Quest of Richard Wright*, 2nd ed. (Urbana and Chicago: University of Illinois Press, 1993), 223, 227.

38. Robert E. Hemenway, *Zora Neale Hurston: A Literary Biography* (Urbana, Ill.: University of Illinois Press, 1977), 287, 288, 294, 295.

39. Lillian Smith, *Strange Fruit: A Novel by Lillian Smith* (New York: Reynal and Hitchcock, 1944); Morton Sosna, *In Search of the Silent South: Southern Liberals and the Race Issue* (New York: Columbia University Press, 1977), 186, 191.

40. *Smith v. Allwright*, 321 U.S. 664; Sosna, *In Search of the Silent South*, 198–211; Bartley, *The New South*, 71.

41. Hollinger F. Barnard, ed., *Outside the Magic Circle: The Autobiography of Virginia Foster Durr* (Tuscaloosa, Ala.: University of Alabama Press, 1985), 171–72, 191.

42. Walker Percy, Interview with Jan Nordby Gretlund, January 2, 1981, *South Carolina Review* (Spring, 1981), 12. See also, James C. Cobb, "Southern Writers and the Challenge of Regional Convergence," *Georgia Historical Quarterly* 73 (Spring, 1989), 3–9; Faulkner, *Intruder in the Dust*, 119–20; Cohn, *Where I Was Born and Raised*, 299–300; Adams, "The Acculturation of the Delta Negro," 203.

43. Flannery O'Connor, "The Displaced Person," in *Flannery O'Connor: The Complete Stories* (New York: Farrar, Straus, and Giroux, 1971), 405–20.

44. Terry Kay, *The Year the Lights Came On* (Athens, Ga., and London: University of Georgia Press, 1989), 11, 12.

45. Flannery O'Connor, "The Fiction Writer and His Country," in Granville Hicks, ed., *The Living Novel: A Symposium* (New York: Macmillan, 1957), 159; Walker Percy, "The Southern Moderate" and "A Southern View," in Patrick Samway, ed., *Signposts in a Strange Land* (New York: Farrar, Straus, and Giroux, 1991), 101 (first quotation), 91 (second quotation); ———, "Southern Comfort," *Harper's* 258 (January 1979), 83. On Percy's influence, see Fred Hobson, *The Southern Writer in the Post-Modern World* (Athens, Ga.: University of Georgia Press, 1991), 57–72. See also Richard Ford, *The Sportswriter* (New York: Vintage Books, 1986) and Josephine Humphreys, *Dreams of Sleep* (New York: Penguin, 1984).

46. John Egerton, *The Americanization of Dixie: The Southernization of America* (New York: Harper's Magazine Press, 1974); ———, *Speak Now Against the Day*, 327–28.

47. Bertram Wyatt-Brown, "The Mind of W. J. Cash," introduction to 1991 Vintage Press edition of W. J. Cash, *The Mind of the South* (New York: Vintage Books, 1991), vii-viii.

48. James C. Cobb, "Oh, Lord, Won't You Buy Me a Mercedes Plant?" *Reckon* 1 (Fall, 1995), 20–21.

49. Charlayne Hunter-Gault, *In My Place* (New York: Farrar, Straus, and Giroux, 1992), 253. See the *Atlanta Journal-Constitution* Poll, *Atlanta-Journal Constitution*, February 16, 1992.

50. Sosna, "The G.I.'s South," 322.

II   The South and Congressional Politics

An earlier version of this paper was presented at a conference sponsored by the University of Richmond in March 1993. In revising the paper, the author has made use of material contained in his book, *The South in Modern America: A Region at Odds* (New York: HarperCollins, 1994), ch. 7.

1. V. O. Key, Jr., with the assistance of Alexander Heard, *Southern Politics in State and Nation* (New York, 1949), p. 315.

2. Thomas L. Stokes, "The Congress," in Jack Goodman, ed., *While You Were Gone: A Report on Wartime Life in the United States* (New York, 1946), pp. 135–36.

3. In 1942 the Republicans gained forty-four seats in the House of Representatives and nine seats in the Senate. The Democrats were left with majorities of 57 to 38 in the upper house and 222 to 209 in the lower house.

4. For southern congressional leaders' dominance of key committees during the war, see *Official Congressional Directory,* 77 Cong., 1 Sess., 2nd ed. (Washington, D.C., 1941), pp. 177–83, 197–209; *Official Congressional Directory,* 78 Cong., 1 Sess., 2nd ed. (Washington, D.C., 1943), pp. 177–83, 197–209; *Official Congressional Directory,* 79 Cong., 1 Sess., 1st ed. (Washington, D.C., 1945), pp. 179–85, 199–211.

5. Richard L. Watson, Jr., "A Testing Time for Southern Congressional Leadership: The War Crisis of 1917–1918," *Journal of Southern History* 44 (February 1978): 3–40.

6. James MacGregor Burns, *Roosevelt: The Soldier of Freedom* (New York, 1970), pp. 37–40.

7. Tennant S. McWilliams, *The New South Faces the World: Foreign Affairs and the Southern Sense of Self, 1877–1950* (Baton Rouge, 1988), p. 138. See also Wayne S. Cole, "America First and the South, 1940–1941," *Journal of Southern History* 22 (February 1956): 36–47, and Alexander DeConde, "The South and Isolationism," *ibid.* 24 (August 1958): 332–46.

8. Gilbert C. Fite, *Cotton Fields No More: Southern Agriculture, 1865–1980* (Lexington, Ky., 1984), pp. 164, 172–73; Roland Young, *Congressional Politics in the Second World War* (New York, 1956), pp. 73–76, 103, 107–108; Walter W. Wilcox, *The Farmer in the Second World War* (Ames, Iowa, 1947), pp. 120, 131, 217–18, 243; George Brown Tindall, *The Emergence of the New South, 1913–1945* (Baton Rouge, 1967), pp. 705–707.

9. Stokes, "The Congress," pp. 154–55; Young, *Congressional Politics in the Second World War*, pp. 109–10.

10. Robert Dallek, *Lone Star Rising: Lyndon Johnson and His Times, 1908–1960* (New York, 1991), p. 228.

11. Gavin Wright, *Old South, New South: Revolutions in the Southern Economy Since the Civil War* (New York, 1986), pp. 240, 259; Gilbert C. Fite, *Richard B. Russell, Jr., Senator From Georgia* (Chapel Hill, 1991), pp. 433–34.

12. Bruce J. Schulman, *From Cotton Belt to Sunbelt: Federal Policy, Economic Development, and the Transformation of the South, 1938–1980* (New York, 1991), pp. 72–111.

13. Quoted in *ibid.,* p. 100.

14. Party-votes were those in which a majority of one party was opposed by a majority of the second party.

15. Young, *Congressional Politics in the Second World War*, pp. 239–65; James T. Patterson, *Mr. Republican: A Biography of Robert A. Taft* (Boston, 1972), p. 260. For the conservative tendencies of southern politicians during the war, see Numan V. Bartley, *The New South, 1945–1980* (Baton Rouge, 1995), pp. 1–37.

16. J. Donald Kingsley, "Congress and the New Deal," *Current History* 4 (March 1943): 28.

17. Richard Polenberg, *War and Society: The United States, 1941–1945* (Philadelphia, 1972), pp. 73–98; Tindall, *The Emergence of the New South*, pp. 707–10; John Morton Blum, *V Was for Victory: Politics and American Culture During World War II* (New York, 1976), pp. 234–41.

18. Burns, *Roosevelt: The Soldier of Freedom*, p. 426 (first quotation); Polenberg, *War and Society*, p. 199 (second quotation). See also Blum, *V Was for Victory*, pp. 221–22, 231; Key, *Southern Politics*, pp. 346, 349, 357–58, 361–62, 366, 374–75; and John Robert Moore, "The Conservative Coalition in the United States Senate, 1942–1945," *Journal of Southern History* 33 (August 1967): 368–76.

19. Robert A. Garson, *The Democratic Party and the Politics of Sectionalism, 1941–1948* (Baton Rouge, 1974), pp. 38–41, 58; Bruce J. Dierenfield, *Keeper of the Rules: Congressman Howard W. Smith of Virginia* (Charlottesville, 1987), pp. 84, 93–100, 105; Nelson Lichtenstein, *Labor's War at Home: The CIO in World War II* (Cambridge, Eng., 1982), pp. 48, 82, 207, 210–11.

20. David Brinkley, *Washington Goes to War* (New York, 1988), p. 203.

21. Burns, *Roosevelt: The Soldier of Freedom*, pp. 429–32; Garson, *The Democratic Party and the Politics of Sectionalism*, pp. 46, 52, 90–93; Young, *Congressional Politics in the Second World War*, pp. 82–89; Darlene Clark Hine, "The Elusive Ballot: The Black Struggle Against the Texas Democratic White Primary, 1932–1945," *Southwestern Historical Quarterly* 81 (April 1978): 371–92.

22. The quotation is from Polenberg, *War and Society*, p. 119. For the role of the FEPC, see Merl E. Reed, *Seedtime for the Modern Civil Rights Movement: The President's Committee on Fair Employment Practice, 1941–1946* (Baton Rouge, 1991); James A Nuechterlein, "The Politics of Civil Rights: The FEPC, 1941–1946," *Prologue* 10 (Fall 1978): 171–91; Charles W. Eagles, *Jonathan Daniels and Race Relations: The Evolution of a Southern Liberal* (Knoxville, Tenn., 1982), pp. 117–18; and Robert J. Bailey, "Theodore G. Bilbo and the Fair Employment Practices Controversy: A Southern Senator's Reaction to a Changing World," *Journal of Mississippi History* 42 (February 1980): 27–42.

23. Eagles, *Jonathan Daniels and Race Relations*, p. 117.

24. Fite, *Richard B. Russell, Jr.*, p. 185. For the ideas of a liberal minority of southerners during the war, see John Egerton, *Speak Now Against the Day: The Generation Before the Civil Rights Movement in the South* (New York, 1994), pp. 201–330.

25. Garson, *The Democratic Party and the Politics of Sectionalism*, pp. 53–54, 96, 100–105, 113–15, 122, 124–25, 128, 130; Polenberg, *War and Society*, pp. 184–214; Carroll Kilpatrick, "Will the South Secede?" *Harper's Magazine* 186 (March 1943): 415–21; Leon C. Phillips, "A Southern Democrat Renounces the New Deal Party," *Manufacturers' Record* 112 (August 1943): 32–33, 60.

26. Seth Shepard McKay, *Texas Politics, 1906–1944, With Special Reference to the German Counties* (Lubbock, Texas, 1952), pp. 391–466.

27. Garson, *The Democratic Party and the Politics of Sectionalism*, p. 96.

28. Allen Drury, *A Senate Journal, 1943–1945* (New York, 1963), p. 141.

29. Quoted in Garson, *The Democratic Party and the Politics of Sectionalism*, pp. 30 (quotation), 42, 59, 72–75.

30. *Ibid.*, p. xi.

31. Morton Sosna, "The GIs' South and the North-South Dialogue During World War II," in Winfred B. Moore, Jr., Joseph F. Tripp, and Lyon G. Tyler, Jr., eds., *Developing Dixie: Modernization in a Traditional Society* (Westport, Conn., 1988), pp. 311–26. See also Sosna, "War and Region: The South and World War II" (unpublished manuscript), p. 185; Howard W. Odum, *Race and Rumors of Race: Challenge to American Crisis* (Chapel Hill, 1943), p. 6; and Larry J. Griffin and Don H. Doyle, eds., *The South as an American Problem* (Athens, Ga., 1995).

32. Quoted in Tindall, *The Emergence of the New South*, p. 727.

33. Dallek, *Lone Star Rising*, pp. 276–78. See also "The South's Bitterness Centers on Wallace," *Christian Century* 61 (July 19, 1944): 844, and Garson, *The Democratic Party and the Politics of Sectionalism*, pp. 52, 99, 127.

34. Earlier Williams had publicly condemned the "Republican-Southern Tory coalition." See John Salmond, *A Southern Rebel: The Life and Times of Aubrey*

Willis Williams, 1890–1965 (Chapel Hill, 1983), pp. 179–97, and Leonard Din-nerstein, "The Senate Rejection of Aubrey Williams as Rural Electrification Administrator," *Alabama Review* 21 (April 1968): 133–43.

35. Key, *Southern Politics,* p. 317.
36. Tindall, *The Emergence of the New South,* p. 731.
37. This theme is explored in Sosna, "War and Region," pp. 15–18.

III   *World War II and the Transformation of Southern Higher Education*

1. One of the few historians to explore the subject in the 1960s was Wayne Flynt, whose excellent essay "Southern Higher Education and the Civil War," *Civil War History,* 14 (September, 1968): 211–225 appeared after the conclusion of the Civil War centennial.

2. Franz Samelson, "World War I Intelligence Testing and the Development of Psychology," *Journal of the History of the Behavioral Sciences,* 13 (July, 1977): 271–282.

3. Carol S. Gruber, *Mars and Minerva, World War I and the Uses of Higher Learning in America* (Baton Rouge: Louisiana State University Press, 1975), pp. 223–232.

4. I. L. Kandel, *The Impact of the War Upon American Education* (Chapel Hill: University of North Carolina Press, 1949), pp. 136–140; Robert F. Durden, *The Launching of Duke University, 1924–1949* (Durham: Duke University Press, 1993), p. 455.

5. Joe Gray Taylor, *McNeese State University, 1939–1987* (n. p., n. d.), pp. 16–18; V. R. Cardozier, *Colleges and Universities in World War II* (Westport, CT: Praeger Publishers, 1993), p. 16.

6. Cardozier, *Colleges and Universities in World War II,* pp. 11–14.

7. Cardozier, *Colleges and Universities in World War II,* pp. 22–30, 53.

8. Cardozier, *Colleges and Universities in World War II,* pp. 23, 85, 142; Allen Cronenberg, *Forth to the Mighty Conflict, Alabama and World War II* (Tuscaloosa AL: University of Alabama Press, 1995), pp. 77–78; Robert J. Norrell, *A Promising Field, Engineering at Alabama, 1837–1987* (Tuscaloosa AL: University of Alabama Press, 1990), pp. 116–117.

9. Paul Conkin, *Gone With the Ivy, A Biography of Vanderbilt University* (Knoxville: University of Tennessee Press, 1985), p. 418; Francis P. Gaines to Rufus C. Harris, March 17, 1944, Box 10, Rufus C. Harris Papers, Tulane University (Hereinafter abbreviated RCHP).

10. Cardozier, *Colleges and Universities in World War II,* pp. 38–41.

11. Leon C. Standifer, *Not in Vain, A Rifleman Remembers World War II* (Baton Rouge: Louisiana State University Press, 192), Chapters 1–3.

12. James G. Schneider, *The Navy V-12 Program: Leadership for a Lifetime* (Boston: Houghton Mifflin Company, 1987), pp. 10–19; Cardozier, *Colleges and Universities in World War II,* pp. 55–58; Cronenberg, *Forth to the Mighty Conflict,* pp. 77–78; Spright Dowell, *A History of Mercer University, 1833–1953* (Macon GA: Mercer University, 1958), pp. 340–341; Elizabeth S. Peck, *Berea's First 125 Years, 1855–1980* (Lexington: University Press of Kentucky, 1982), pp. 191–192.

13. Schneider, *The Navy V-12 Program*, pp. 209–218; Cardozier, *Colleges and Universities in World War II*, pp. 55–58; Durden, *The Launching of Duke University*, p. 459 (quotation).

14. Schneider, *The Navy V-12 Program*, pp. 57–61; Cardozier, *Colleges and Universities in World War II*, pp. 55–58, 67–68.

15. Cardozier, *Colleges and Universities in World War II*, pp. 83–90, 97, 147; James Riley Montgomery, Stanley J. Folmsbee, and Lee Seifert Greene, *To Foster Knowledge, A History of The University of Tennessee, 1794–1970* (Knoxville, 1984), p. 202; John K. Bettersworth, *People's College: A History of Mississippi State* (University AL: University of Alabama Press, 1953), p. 329; James W. Covington and C. Herbert Laub, *The Story of the University of Tampa, A Quarter Century of Progress from 1930 to 1955* (Tampa: University of Tampa Press, 1955), pp. 42–45; Cronenberg, *Forth to the Mighty Conflict*, pp. 77–78; Charles E. Diehl to Rufus C. Harris, December 17, 1943, Box 10, RCHP.

16. Henry C. Dethloff, *A Centennial History of Texas A & M University, 1876–1976*. 2 vols. (College Station: Texas A & M University Press, 1975), II, p. 456.

17. Viola Carruth, *Shreveport 1000, A History of Shreveport* (Shreveport: Shreveport Magazine, 1970), p. 182; Thomas Ray Shurbutt, *Georgia Southern: Seventy-Five Years of Progress and Service* ([Statesboro]: Georgia Southern College Foundation, 1982), p. 76.

18. Cardozier, *Colleges and Universities in World War II*, pp. 163–164; Chester M. Morgan, *Dearly Bought, Deeply Treasured [:] The University of Southern Mississippi, 1912–1987* (Jackson MS: University Press of Mississippi, 1987), p. 73.

19. Joe M. Richardson, *A History of Fisk University, 1865–1946* (University AL: University of Alabama Press, 1980), pp. 132–133; Maxine D. Jones and Joe M. Richardson, *Talladega College, The First Century* (Tuscaloosa AL: University of Alabama Press, 1990), pp. 140–141.

20. B. Carlyle Ramsey, "The Public Black College in Georgia: A History of Albany State College, 1903–1965," (Ph. D. dissertation: Florida State University, 1973), pp. 174–177; Helen E. Cheslik, "The Effect of World War II Military Educational Training on Black Colleges," (Ed. D. dissertation: Wayne State University, 1980), Appendix D; Clarence A. Bacote, *The Story of Atlanta University, A Century of Service, 1865–1965* (Atlanta: Atlanta University, 1969), pp. 340–341; Cardozier, *Colleges and Universities in World War II*, pp. 163, 176.

21. Thomas G. Dyer, *The University of Georgia, A Bicentennial History* (Athens: University of Georgia Press, 1985), pp. 242–243.

22. William D. Snider, *Light on the Hill, A History of the University of North Carolina at Chapel Hill* (Chapel Hill: University of North Carolina Press, 1992), pp. 228–229; Daniel Walker Hollis, *University of South Carolina, College to University*. 2 vols. (Columbia SC: University of South Carolina Press, 1956), II, p. 339; Cardozier, *Colleges and Universities in World War II*, p. 147.

23. Robert J. Jakeman, *The Divided Skies: Establishing Segregated Flight Training at Tuskegee, Alabama, 1934–1942* (Tuscaloosa AL: University of Alabama Press, 1992), passim.

24. Marietta M. LeBreton, *Northwestern State University of Louisiana 1884–1984: A History* (Natchitoches LA: Northwestern State University Press, 1985), pp. 203–205.

25. Richard B. Davis to Joe Farrar, January 2, 1946, quoted in LeBreton, *Northwestern State University*, p. 207.

26. Schneider, *The Navy V-12 Program*, pp. 236–237, 428, 433.

27. Clarice F. Pollard, "WAACs in Texas During the Second World War," *Southwestern Historical Quarterly*, 93 (July, 1989): 60–74, p. 64 (first quotation), p. 65 (second quotation), p. 63 (all subsequent quotations).

28. Thomas A. Rumer, *The American Legion: An Official History, 1919–1989* (New York: M. Evans & Company, Inc., 1990), pp. 241–248 asserts that the idea of a comprehensive approach to veteran's benefits had been "rattling around National [Legion] Headquarters" (p. 241) but fails to analyze why and how the Legion came to support the approach to postwar college benefits that was eventually adopted.

29. *Preliminary Report of the Armed Forces Committee on Post-War Educational Opportunities for Service Personnel, October 27, 1943*. [House of Representatives Document No. 344, 78th Congress, 1st Session] esp. pp. 6, 9. On fears of "cheap education" by Harris and other Southern educators, see Minutes of the Board of Administrators of the Tulane Educational Fund, October 8, 1952; H. Claude Horack to Rufus C. Harris, November 12, 1943, Rufus C. Harris to H. Claude Horak, November 18, 1943, Goodrich C. White to Francis J. Brown, July 22, 1943, all in RCHP, Box 64; Keith W. Olson, *The G.I. Bill, The Veterans, and the Colleges* (Lexington: University Press of Kentucky, 1974), Chapter 1.

30. Minutes of the Executive Committee of the Southern University Conference, December 15, 1943, Box 10, RCHP; Charles E. Diehl to Rufus C. Harris, December 18, 1943, Box 10, RCHP.

31. Covington and Laub, *The Story of the University of Tampa*, p. 45; James L. Rogers, *The Story of North Texas, From Texas Normal College, 1890, to North Texas State University, 1965* (Denton, Texas: North Texas State University, 1965), pp. 312–313.

32. Eoline Wallace Moore, "Women Faculty Members in Alabama Colleges in War Time," *AAUW Journal*, 39 (Spring, 1946): 150–151, p. 150 (quotation).

33. Barbara M. Solomon, *In the Company of Educated Women, A History of Women and Higher Education in America* (New Haven, 1985), pp. 189–198; *Trends in Liberal Arts Education for Women* (New Orleans: Newcomb College of Tulane University, 1954); Dorothy C. Holland and Margaret C. Eisenhart, *Educated in Romance: Women, Achievement and College Culture* (Chicago, 1990); Amy Thompson McCandless, "Maintaining the Spirit and Tone of Robust Manliness: The Battle Against Coeducation at Southern Colleges and Universities, 1890–1940," *NWSA Journal* 2 (Spring, 1990): 199–216; Jean E. Friedman, *The Enclosed Garden, Women and Community in the Evangelical South, 1830–1900* (Chapel Hill, 1985); Lynn D. Gordon, *Gender and Higher Education in the Progressive Era* (New Haven, 1990), chapter 5; Anne Firor Scott, *The Southern Lady, From Pedestal to Politics* (Chicago, 1970).

34. At the peak of veteran enrollments men outnumbered women by as much as five or six to one at Auburn University. Ratios of 3:1 were common at other

public and private white universities in the South during the late 1940s and the 1950s. At the South's well established coeducational white liberal arts colleges (e.g. Millsaps, Birmingham Southern, Hendrix) and church related universities (Mercer, Loyola, Trinity) women typically comprised between one third and 40 percent of the 1950s student body. Several land grant schools excluded women (e.g. Clemson, Texas A&M) or admitted them only in minuscule numbers (e.g. Mississippi State, North Carolina State, Virginia Polytechnic Institute). These patterns went hand-in-hand with the continued emphasis upon public and private women's colleges throughout the region. Women usually outnumbered men in the smaller public and private black colleges of the postwar South and a majority of the aggregate black student population was female throughout the 1950s. At leading black schools like Howard University, Tuskegee Institute, and Hampton Institute men were in the majority. Federal Security Agency, Office of Education, *Summary of Statistics on Higher Education 1945–46*, Circular No. 256, table 2 (all subsequent Office of Education reports are abbreviated "O. E."); *Statistics of Land-Grant Colleges and Universities . . . June 30, 1947* O. E. Bulletin 1948, No. 8, tables 9, 10; *ibid. . . . June 30, 1948*, O. E. bulletin 1949, No. 8, tables 9–11; *ibid. . . . June 30, 1949*, O. E. Bulletin 1950, No. 11, tables 9–11; *ibid. . . . June 30, 1959*, O. E. Circular No. 639, table 13; *1949 Fall Enrollment in Higher Education Institutions November 10, 1949*; *ibid., November 15, 1950*, O. E. Circular No. 281; *ibid., November 25, 1951*, O. E. Circular No. 328; *ibid. November 24, 1952*, O. E. Circular No. 359; *ibid. December, 1955*, O. E. Circular No. 460; *ibid. 1960; Institutional Data*, O. E. Circular No. 637; *ibid., 1960, Analytic Report*, O. E. Circular No. 652, pp. 13–15, 25–26; *ibid., 1966* (O. E. 54003–66); Nancy B. Dearman and Valena White Plisko, *The Condition of Education*, 1979 Edition [Statistical Report, National Center for Education Statistics] (Washington, D.C., 1979), Chart 3.9.

35. Leila Amal Zahlan, "From Caroline Coed to the Carolina Woman: Women at the University of North Carolina Since 1945," (B.A. Honors Thesis, University of North Carolina, 1992), pp. 8–9, 40, 47.

36. Conkin, *Gone With the Ivy*, pp. 470, 516–17, 719.

37. Fredericka Meiners, *A History of Rice University, The Institute Years, 1907–1963* (Houston: Rice University Studies, 1982) pp. 206 (first quotation), 163 (second quotation).

38. Diane Ravitch, *The Troubled Crusade, American Education 1945–1980* (New York, 1983) p. 15 repeats a previous writer's description of the GI Bill as "the most important educational and social transformation in American history." Ravitch concludes that after the law's passage, "The doors [of college] were opened for all who wished to come . . . ." But her subsequent description of the more ambitious proposals of the President's Commission on Higher Education during 1947 and 1948 (*ibid.*, pp. 16 ff.) provides a convenient yardstick for measuring the GI Bill's inherent limitations.

39. Mary F. Berry and John W. Blassingame, *Long Memory, The Black Experience in America* (New York, 1982), p. 286. In 1947, when college enrollment peaked among black veterans, some 61,000 blacks attended white colleges outside the South where they comprised roughly 3 percent of the total enrollment of those schools, and 47 percent of all black enrollment. By 1952, however,

the veterans were gone and approximately 70 percent of black college students attended segregated colleges in the South. Susan T. Hill, *The Traditionally Black Institutions of Higher Education 1860–1982* (Washington, D.C., 1985), Table 1.7; James R. Mingle, "The Opening of White Colleges and Universities to Black Students," in *Black Students in Higher Education*, edited by Gail E. Thomas (Westport, 1981), pp. 20–21. On the overall state of black higher education in the South prior to World War II see James D. Anderson, *The Education of Blacks in the South, 1860–1935* (Chapel Hill: University of North Carolina Press, 1988), Chapter 7; Neil R. McMillen, *Dark Journey: Black Mississippians in the Age of Jim Crow* (Urbana: University of Illinois Press, 1989), pp. 98–108.

40. Henry G. Badger, *Statistics of Negro Colleges and Universities: Students, Staff, and Finances, 1900–1950* [Office of Education Circular No. 293, April, 1951]; Olson, *GI Bill,* p. 74. ; Cheslik, "The Effect of World War II Military Educational Training on Black Colleges," Appendix G, H, I (pp. 178–204).

41. G. N. Redd, "Resources for Graduate Work for Negroes in the States of Alabama, Kentucky, and Tennessee," *Journal of Negro Education* 15 (Spring, 1946): 161–171; Richard Kluger, *Simple Justice* (New York, 1975), p. 257. The entire Summer, 1948 issue of the *Journal of Negro Education* examines black higher and professional education in the United States. See esp. Part 2.

42. Jeanie Thompson, *The Widening Circle: Extension and Continuing Education at the University of Alabama, 1904–1992* (Tuscaloosa AL: University of Alabama Press, 1992), pp. 53–54; Tennant S. McWilliams, "The Birth of UAB," Chapter One, pp. 46–51 (manuscript in author's possession).

43. Stephan Lesher, *George Wallace, American Populist* (Reading MA: Addison-Wesley Publishing Company, 1994), pp. 70–72.

44. Hugh Davis Graham, "Structure and Governance in American Higher Education: Historical and Comparative Analysis in State Policy," *Journal of Policy History* 1 (November 1, 1989): 80–107, pp. 89–90; Norrell, *A Promising Field,* pp. 167–168; Lesher, *George Wallace,* p. 448 (quotation).

45. Steven Brint and Jerome Karabel, *The Diverted Dream, Community Colleges and the Promise of Educational Opportunity in America, 1900–1985* (New York, 1987), pp. 71–73, 81–86 esp. Table 3–3; James L. Wattenberger, "Community Colleges: A Friendly Critique" in *Effective Use of Resources in State Higher Education* (Atlanta: Southern Regional Education Board, 1970) pp. 19–28, esp. Table I.

46. President's Commission on Higher Education, *Higher Education for American Democracy* 5 vols. (Washington, D.C., 1947), I, pp. 37, 39.

47. The best account of Wallace's impact upon the University of Alabama is E. Culpepper Clark, *The Schoolhouse Door: Segregation's Last Stand at the University of Alabama* (New York, 1993), chapters 8–12.

48. *Opening (Fall) Enrollment in Higher Education, 1960: Analytic Report,* O. E. Circular No. 652, pp. 27–29, esp. Table 15; Charles P. Roland, *The Improbable Era, The South Since World War II* (Lexington, 1976), pp. 99, 107–108; *Statistical Abstract of the United States 1960* (Washington, D.C., 1960) Table 162; *Digest of Educational Statistics, 1990* Table 174.

49. Adam Yarmolinsky, *The Military Establishment, Its Impacts on American Society* (New York, 1971), pp. 289–290; John T. Bethell, "Harvard and the Arts of War," *Harvard Magazine*, 98 (September–October, 1995): 32–48; Barton J. Bernstein, "The Birth of the U.S. Biological-Warfare Program," *Scientific American* 256 (June, 1987): 116–121 documents the participation of approximately twenty-eight American universities in secret biological warfare research during World War II.

50. Roger L. Geiger, *To Advance Knowledge: The Growth of American Research Universities 1900–1940* (New York, 1986), Chapters 5 and 6; Cardozier, *Colleges and Universities in World War II*, pp. 200–201.

51. E. C. Andrus et. al., *Advances in Military Medicine Made by American Investigators Working Under the Sponsorship of the Committee on Medical Research*. 2 vols. (Boston: Little, Brown and Company, 1948), II, pp. 832–879; Robert C. McMath et. al., *Engineering the New South, Georgia Tech 1885–1985* (Athens: University of Georgia Press, 1985), pp. 214–216; Ronnie Dugger, *Our Invaded Universities* (New York, 1974), pp. 261–263.

52. Southern University Conference, Report of the Committee on Graduate Instruction, December 15, 1943, Box 10, RCHP; "Report of the Dean of the Graduate School . . . 1943–1944," *Tulane Bulletin* Series 46, Number 2 (February, 1945), pp. 39–40 (first quotation); Roger P. McCutcheon to Howard Munford Jones, August 3, 1943, Box 39, RCHP (second quotation).

53. Yarmolinsky, *The Military Establishment*, pp. 291 (first quotation) - 293; Harold Orlans, *The Nonprofit Research Institute* (New York, 1972), pp. 13–14.

54. Charles P. Roland, *The Improbable Era, The South Since World War II* (Lexington: University Press of Kentucky, 1976), p. 108; Allan M. Carter, "Qualitative Aspects of Southern University Education," *Southern Economic Journal* 32 (July, 1965) [Supplement]: 39–69, esp. Table II.

55. Carter, "Qualitative Aspects of Southern University Education," pp. 47–53, esp. Table V; John A. Crowl, "Facing the Yankees Across the Education Gap" in *Dixie Dateline* edited by John B. Boles [Rice University Studies, New Series, No. 1] (Houston, 1983) p. 57; Kenneth D. Roose and Charles J. Andersen, *A Rating of Graduate Programs* (Washington, D.C.: American Council on Education, 1970), pp. 11–13, *passim*.

56. Cardozier, *Colleges and Universities in World War II*, pp. 101–102, 130–131, 154–155; *Wartime Intercollegiate Athletics at Tulane, A Statement of Policy From the President of the University*, [separate leaflet reprinted from *Tulanian* (April-May, 1943)], Box 10, RCHP; Rufus C. Harris to Lowell P. Dawson, November 12, 1943, Box 10, RCHP; Dowell, *A History of Mercer University*, pp. 380–81.

57. *New York Times*, January 10, 1942, p. 22, December 10, 1942, p. 10, January 12, 1943, p. 28, June 2, 1943, p. 30, June 5, 1943, p. 20, June 16, 1943, p. 25, July 3, 1943, p. 9, July 4, 1943 Section III, p. 4, August 22, 1943, Section III, p. 3, August 26, 1943, p. 25, August 27, 1943, p. 13; Charles Gano Talbert, *The University of Kentucky, The Maturing Years* (Lexington: University of Kentucky Press, 1965), p. 150; Conkin, *Gone With the Ivy*, p. 430; Morgan, *Dearly Bought, Deeply Treasured*, p. 92; Dowell, *A History of Mercer University*, p. 380; Duncan

Lyle Kinnear, *The First 100 Years: A History of Virginia Polytechnic Institute and State University* (Blacksburg, Va.: Virginia Polytechnic Institute Educational Foundation, Inc., 1972), p. 328.

58. Donald W. Rominger, "From Playing Field to Battleground: The United States Navy V-5 Preflight Program in World War II," *Journal of Sport History*, 12 (Winter, 1985): 252–264, p. 256 (all quotations).

59. Rufus Carrollton Harris, "Post-War Intercollegiate Athletics," *Southern Coach and Athlete* (April, 1944), offprint in RCHP (all quotations).

60. Paul R. Lawrence, *Unsportsmanlike Conduct: The National Collegiate Athletic Association and the Business of College Football* (New York, 1987), pp. 41–42 and Appendix C (pp. 158–59).

61. Ibid., pp. 43–47, 48 (first quotation), 49 (second and third quotations).

62. Ibid., pp. 52 (first quotation), 49 (second quotation). For a more detailed account of the episode see Charles Rosen, *Scandals of '51: How Gamblers Almost Killed College Basketball* (New York, 1978). Cf. Bert Nelli, *The Winning Tradition: A History of Kentucky Wildcat Basketball* (Lexington, KY, 1984).

63. Conkin, *Gone With the Ivy*, p. 526 (quotation).

64. *Special Committee on Athletic Policy of the American Council on Education* (Washington, D.C., 1951); Conkin, *Gone With the Ivy*, p. 527; Minutes of the Board of Administrators of the Tulane Education Fund, May 12, 1952, items #12 and 13 of President's monthly report, Tulane University Archives; Rufus Carrollton Harris, "Intercollegiate Athletic Policies at Tulane," *Tulanian* (March, 1952), p. 1; "An eight point plan for the restraint of intercollegiate athletics . . . presented to the presidents of the Southeastern Conference . . . by President Rufus Harris of Tulane University" [undated typescript, November–December, 1951], Box 19, RCHP; Forrest U. Lake to J. G. Stipe, February 21, 1952, ibid.; Harvie Branscomb, "Intercollegiate Athletics in the Southern Association of Colleges and Secondary Schools," Southern Association of Colleges and Secondary Schools *Proceedings* (December, 1952), offprint in ibid.

65. Conkin, *Gone With the Ivy*, pp. 527–528; "Self-Survey Tulane University Athletic Program, Preliminary Report on Intercollegiate Athletics, December 10, 1957," p. 9, Box 20, RCHP; "Annual Report of the [Tulane] University Senate Committee on Athletics, 1957–58, ibid., 1958–59, ibid., 1959–60, Box 19, RCHP; Minutes of the Board of Administrators of the Tulane Education Fund, December 10, 1958, item #12 of President's monthly report, Tulane University Archives. All of the preceding documents contain tables of SEC athletic scholarships based upon data furnished by the Conference Commissioner.

66. John Duffy, *The Tulane University Medical Center: One Hundred and Fifty Years of Medical Education* (Baton Rouge: Louisiana State University Press, 1984), pp. 167–169. See also the 1943–44 annual reports of the President, Dean of Arts and Sciences, and Dean of Engineering in *Tulane Bulletin* Series 46, Number 2, (February, 1945), pp. 6–13, 20–25.

67. Norrell, *A Promising Field,* Chapters 5 and 6.

68. Hutchins address to University of Chicago Trustee-Faculty Dinner, January 13, 1943 as quoted in Harry S. Ashmore, *Unseasonable Truths, The Life of Robert Maynard Hutchins* (Boston: Little, Brown and Company, 1989), p. 236.

69. George Keller, *Academic Strategy, The Management Revolution in American*

Higher Education (Baltimore MD: Johns Hopkins University Press, 1983). On the response of Georgia Tech and other entrepreneurial universities to the financial challenges of the 1970s and 1980s see Roger L. Geiger, *Research and Relevant Knowledge: American Research Universities Since World War II* (New York, 1993), pp. 283–296; McMath et. al., *Engineering the New South*, pp. 415–422, 436–449.

IV Southern Women in a World at War

1. Lucy Somerville Howorth, "Women's Responsibility in World Affairs," *Journal of the American Association of University Women* 37 (Summer 1944): 195.
2. The papers of Lucy Somerville Howorth are located in the Somerville-Howorth Papers, Schlesinger Library on the History of Women in America (SL), Radcliffe College, Cambridge, Massachusetts. Martha H. Swain and Dorothy Shawhan are preparing a biography of Howorth. On the women's "network" of the New Deal, see Susan Ware, *Beyond Suffrage: Women in the New Deal* (Cambridge: Harvard University Press, 1981) and *Partner and I: Molly Dewson, Feminism, and New Deal Politics* (New Haven: Yale University Press 1987).
3. "Biographical Note," Charl Ormond Williams Papers, Manuscript Division, Library of Congress (LC), Washington, D.C.; cited hereafter as Williams Papers; Eleanor Roosevelt, "Women at the Peace Conference," *Reader's Digest* 44 (April 1944): 48-49.
4. Report of the Conference, "How Women May Share in Post-War Policy Making," Williams Papers, Box 8.
5. Charl Ormond Williams to Mrs. Franklin D. Roosevelt, January 29, April 10, April 18, May 5, June 11, 1944, Williams Papers, Box 7.
6. For this paper, I have used the "census South" (Alabama, Arkansas, Delaware, the District of Columbia, Florida, Georgia, Kentucky, Louisiana, Maryland, Mississippi, North Carolina, Oklahoma, South Carolina, Tennessee, Texas, Virginia, and West Virginia) plus Missouri as my geographical definition of the South.
7. For a list of the women who attended the conference, see "Conference on How Women May Share in Post-War Policy Making." The statement from "every section of the country" appears in Charl Ormond Williams to Dear Member of the White House Conference, June 7, 1944, Williams Papers, Boxes 7, 8. A wealth of information on the World War II work of Mary McLeod Bethune and the National Council of Negro Women is contained in the Records of the National Council of Negro Women, Bethune Museum and Archives (BMA), Washington, D.C.
8. See Martha H. Swain, *Ellen S. Woodward: New Deal Advocate for Women* (Jackson: University Press of Mississippi, 1995), especially pages 169–176 which deal specifically with UNRRA. Ellen S. Woodward, "My Experience at the UNRRA Conference," addresses delivered at the White House Conference, June 14, 1944, Williams Papers, Box 8.
9. Howorth, "Women's Responsibility in World Affairs," 197; "Resolution on Continuation Committee," "Background and Facts on Roster of Qualified Women, January 22, 1945," Charl Ormond Williams to Edward R. Stettinius,

Jr., January 17, 1945, "Roster of Qualified Women, January 3, 1945," Williams Papers, Box 8.

10. Roosevelt, "My Day," June 15, 16, 1944; "Women and the Peace," *New York Times*, June 16, 1944; Woodward to Williams, June 22, 1944, Williams Papers, Box 8. See also numerous clippings of press notices, including *New York Times*, June 14, 15, 1944, *Washington Evening Star*, June 14, 1944, *Christian Science Monitor*, June 14, 1944, *New York Herald Tribune*, June 15, 1944, *Oregon Journal*, June 15, 1944, *Washington Post*, June 15, 1944, *Union Signal*, July 1, 1944, *Independent Woman*, 23 (July 1944): 225, in Williams Papers, Box 8.

11. On the history of Dumbarton Oaks, see Ruth B. Russell, *A History of the United Nations Charter: The Role of the United States 1940-1945* (Washington, D.C.: Brookings Institute, 1958), pp. 205-477.

12. Department of State, *Postwar Foreign Policy Preparation, 1939-1945*, Publication 3580 (Washington, D.C.: Government Printing Office, 1950), p. 416; Bess Furman, "Hails Honor Given Dean Gildersleeve," *New York Times*, February 15, 1945. Agnes E. Meyer, "Dean Gildersleeve—Popular Choice," *Journal of the American Association of University Women* (Spring 1945): 151-153; Virginia C. Gildersleeve, "Women Must Help Stop Wars," *Woman's Home Companion* 72 (May 1945): 32; Edith Efron, "Portrait of a Dean and Delegate," *New York Times Magazine*, April 1, 1945, 13, 43; Charl Ormond Williams to Dear Mrs. Roosevelt, February 23, 1945, March 1, 1945, Williams Papers, Box 8; Lucy Somerville Howorth to My dear Gladys, February 18, 1945, Somerville-Howorth Papers, Series III, Box 5, Folder 114, SL.

13. Quoted in Swain, *Ellen S. Woodward*, p. 172.

14. Margaret Culkin Banning, *Women for Defense* (New York, 1942), p. ix.

15. Stephen E. Ambrose, *D-Day June 6, 1944: The Climatic Battle of World War II* (New York: Simon & Schuster, 1994).

16. On the important relationship between mail and morale during World War II, see Judy Barrett Litoff and David C. Smith, " 'Will He Get My Letter?': Popular Portrayals of Mail and Morale during World War II," *Journal of Popular Culture* 23 (Spring 1990): 21-45.

17. Since the early 1980s, David C. Smith and I have collected some 30,000 letters written by more than 1,500 United States women representing diverse social, economic, ethnic, and geographical circumstances. See Judy Barrett Litoff and David C. Smith, *We're In This War, Too: World War II Letters From American Women In Uniform* (New York: Oxford University Press, 1994); idem, " 'Writing Is Fighting, Too': The World War II Correspondence of Southern Women," *The Georgia Historical Quarterly* 76 (Summer 1992): 436-457; idem, *Miss You: The World War II Letters of Barbara Wooddall Taylor and Charles E. Taylor* (Athens: University of Georgia Press, 1990); idem, *Dear Boys: World War II Letters from a Woman Back Home* (Jackson: University Press of Mississippi, 1991); idem, *Since You Went Away: World War II Letters from American Women on the Home Front* (New York: Oxford University Press, 1991). Another good collection of letters written by a southern couple during World War II is Jane Weaver Poulton, ed., *A Better Legend: From the World War II Letters of Jack and Jane Poulton* (Charlottesville: University Press of Virginia, 1993).

18. On the public role of wartime women, see Susan M. Hartmann, *The Home Front and Beyond: American Women in the 1940s* (Boston: Twayne Publishers, 1982); D'Ann Campbell, *Women at War with America: Private Lives in a Patriotic Era* (Cambridge: Harvard University Press, 1984); Maureen Honey, *Creating Rosie the Riveter: Class, Gander, and Propaganda during World War II* (Amherst: University of Massachusetts Press, 1984).

19. Conter to My Dearest Daddy and Mother, December 22, 1941, United States Army, Medical Department Museum, Fort Sam Houston, Texas; Conter to Flikke [December 1941], reprinted in the *American Journal of Nursing* 2 (April 1942): 425-426.

20. Harris to Hastie, December 11, 1941, Civilian Aide to the Secretary, Records of the Secretary of War, Box 225, Record Group 107, Entry 91, NARA.

21. The letters are located at Record Group 107, Entry 91, Secretary of War, Office, Assistant Secretary of War, Civilian Aide to the Secretary, Boxes 225 and 228, NARA. A selection of these letters is reprinted in Litoff and Smith, *We're In This War, Too*, pp. 65-77. In particular, see Major Harriet M. West to Truman K. Gibson, 22 February 1944 and Constance E. Nelson to Dear People [May 1944], pp. 73-75. See also Martha S. Putney, *When the Nation Was in Need: Blacks in the Women's Army Corps During World War II* (Metuchen, New Jersey: Scarecrow Press, 1992); Charity Adams Earley, *One Woman's Army: A Black Officer Remembers the WAC* (College Station: Texas A & M University Press, 1989).

22. See Mary Martha Thomas, *Riveting and Rationing in Dixie: Alabama Women and the Second World War* (Tuscaloosa: University of Alabama Press, 1987), pp. 43-45, 114-115; Karen Tucker Anderson, "Last Hired, First Fired: Black Women Workers during World War II," *Journal of American History* 69 (June 1982): 82-97.

23. Nannie Helen Burroughs Papers, General Correspondence, Box 2, Manuscript Division, LC.

24. *Bolivar Commercial*, April 23, 1943, July 3, 1942.

25. The letter of Mabel Opal Miller is reprinted in Litoff and Smith, *Since You Went Away*, pp. 210-211.

26. *1943 South Carolina Annual Report*, pp. 1-2, Narrative Reports, Box 8 and *1943 Virginia Annual Report*, p. 17, Narrative Reports, Box 10, Record Group 33, NARA. On the history of the WLA, see Judy Barrett Litoff and David C. Smith, " 'To The Rescue of the Crops': The Women's Land Army during World War II," *Prologue* 25 (Winter 1993): 347-361.

27. [name withheld] to John H. Sengstacke, January 8, 1944, reprinted in Litoff and Smith, *We're In This War, Too*, p. 76; "The Annual Workshop," *Aframerican Woman's Journal* 4 (Fall 1944): 3; "Human Relations in Transition to Peace. For National Congress of Negro Women. Oct. 13, 1944," Box 31, Mary Church Terrell Papers, Manuscript Division, LC.

28. "The Annual Workshop," *Aframerican Woman's Journal* 4 (Fall 1944): 3; Burroughs to Mrs. Belle Pinn Taylor, March 5, 1943. Nannie Helen Burroughs Papers, General Correspondence, Box 43, Manuscript Division, LC. On wartime efforts at interracial cooperation among women, see "From the National

Planning Conference on Building Better Race Relationships," *Aframerican Woman's Journal* 3 (Spring 1944): 4-7; "Roundtable Discusses Race Relations," *Aframerican Woman's Journal* 4 (Fall 1944): 16-17; "Statement of Conference—February 11, 1944"; "Roundtable Conference on 'Building Better Race Relations,' November 18, 1944"; "Agenda—Coordinating Committee for Building Better Race Relations, November 24, 1945," Records of the National Council of Negro Women, Series 5, Box 9 Folders 161, 162, 164; BMA, Washington, D.C. For conflicting assessments of the longterm impact of these interracial encounters in wartime, see Susan Lynn, "Gender and Progressive Politics: A Bridge to Social Activism of the 1960s," in *Not June Cleaver: Women and Gender in Postwar America, 1945-1960*, Joanne Meyerowitz, ed. (Philadelphia: Temple University Press, 1994), pp. 103-127; Lillian E. Smith to Dear Mrs. Terrell, September 4, 1943, Box 13, Mary Church Terrell Papers, Manuscript Division, LC; and Margaret Rose Gladney, ed., *How Am I To Be Heard?: Letters of Lillian Smith* (Chapel Hill: University of North Carolina Press, 1993), pp. 74-78.

29. For additional information on the letter writing efforts of Keith Frazier Somerville, see Litoff and Smith, *Dear Boys.* "Dear Boys" was one of two letter columns undertaken in Bolivar County. Florence Sillers Ogden of Rosedale wrote a similar column, "My Dear Boys," for the *Bolivar County Democrat.* In Trenton Tennessee, "Miss Bobbie" Dodds wrote a column, "A Letter to the Boys in Service," for the *Herald-Register.*

30. "Dear Boys," *Bolivar Commercial,* April 23, 1943, September 8, 1944.

31. The classic statement on the "southern lady" is Anne Firor Scott, *The Southern Lady: From Pedestal to Politics, 1830-1930* (Chicago: University of Chicago Press, 1970).

32. Keith Frazier Somerville, 1943 Wartime Journal, January 10, December 17; 1944 Wartime Journal, January 1, 1945, in the possession of Keith Somerville McLean, Cleveland, Mississippi.

33. Frances Zulauf to Robert Zulauf, January 4, 1945, the World War II Letters of U.S. Women Archive, Bryant College Smithfield, Rhode Island. For additional information on the wartime correspondence of the Zulaufs, see Litoff and Smith, *Since You Went Away,* pp. 24-31, and Judy Barrett Litoff and David C. Smith, "'I Wish That I Could Hide Inside This Letter': World War II Correspondence," *Prologue* 24 (Summer 1992): 102-114.

34. Barbara Wooddall Taylor to Charles E. Taylor, October 25, 1944, reprinted in Litoff and Smith, *Miss You,* 146. On the wartime experiences of Barbara Wooddall Taylor, see Judy Barrett Litoff and David C. Smith, "Since You Went Away: The World War II Correspondence of Barbara Wooddall Taylor," *Women's Studies* 17 (1990): 249-276.

35. Good discussions on women and war work are included in Hartmann, *The Home Front and Beyond,* pp. 77-100 and Campbell, *Women at War with America,* pp. 101-138.

36. Polly Crow to William Crow, June 8, 12, 17, November 6, 9, and December 5, 1944, reprinted in Litoff and Smith, *Since You Went Away,* 146-152.

37. Christine Cockerham to George Cockerham, October 1, 1945, reprinted in Litoff and Smith, *Since You Went Away,* pp. 257-258.

38. Maud Tuner Cofer to her parents, November 5, 1944, Maud Turner Cofer Papers, Georgia Department of Archives and History, Atlanta, Georgia.
39. Helen K. McKee to My Dear Ones, June 25, 1944, reprinted in Litoff and Smith, *We're In This War, Too*, pp. 133-134.
40. Ruth Hess to Dear Miss Losby and the rest of you at Louisville General Hospital, August 8, 1944, University Archives and Records Center, Ekstrom Library, University of Louisville, Louisville, Kentucky.
41. Marian Stegeman to Mrs. H. J. Stegeman, April 24, 1943, reprinted in Litoff and Smith, *We're In This War, Too*, p. 115.
42. Rita Pilkey to her parents, March 8, 1944, July 4, 1945, November 13, 1944, and March 1945, Rita Pilkey Collection, Blagg-Huey Library, Texas Woman's University, Denton, Texas.
43. "Dear Boys," *Bolivar Commercial*, May 11, 1945; Helen K. McKee to her parents, May, 25, 1945, reprinted in Litoff and Smith, *We're In This War, Too*, pp. 135-136.
44. "Dear Boys," *Bolivar Commercial*, August 31, 1945.
45. Constance Hope Jones to Donald C. Swartzbaugh, August 18, 1945, reprinted in Litoff and Smith, *Since You Went Away*, pp. 279-280.
46. Barbara Wooddall Taylor to Charles E. Taylor, August 16, 1945, reprinted in Litoff and Smith, *Miss You*, pp. 284-285.

V *African American Militancy in the World War II South*

1. Especially important in promulgating this viewpoint are Richard M. Dalfiume, "The 'Forgotten Years' of the Negro Revolution," *Journal of American History*, 55 (June 1968), 90–106 and *Desegregation of the U.S. Armed Forces* (Columbia, Missouri, 1969), esp. 105–113, 122–23; Peter Kellogg, "Civil Rights Consciousness in the 1940s," *The Historian*, 42 (Nov. 1979), 18–41; Richard Polenberg, *War and Society: The United States, 1941–1945* (New York, 1972), 99–130; Harvard Sitkoff, "The Detroit Race Riot of 1943," *Michigan History*, 53 (fall 1969), 183–206, and "Racial Militancy and Interracial Violence in the Second World War," *Journal of American History*, 58 (Dec. 1971), 661–81; and Neil A. Wynn, *The Afro American and the Second World War* (New York, 1975), esp. 99–121. Their views of a wartime racial crisis owe much to Charles S. Johnson and Associates, *To Stem This Tide: A Survey of Racial Tension Areas in the United States* (Boston, 1943).
2. Lee Finkle, *Forum for Protest, The Black Press During World War II* (Rutherford, N.J., 1975), 222; P. L. Prattis, "The Role of the Negro Press in Race Relations," *Phylon*, 7 (Third Quarter, 1946), 274; Thomas Sancton, "The Negro Press," *New Republic*, April 26, 1943, 560; and Sterling A. Brown, "Out of Their Mouths," *Survey Graphic*, 31 (Nov. 1942), 480–83.
3. Saunders Redding, "A Negro Looks at War," *American Mercury*, Nov. 1942, 585–92; Edgar T. Rouzeau to Franklin Roosevelt, Feb. 24, 1942, OF 93, Roosevelt Papers, Franklin D. Roosevelt Library; Finkle, *Forum for Protest*, 113–114, 205; Robin D. G. Kelley, *Hammer and Hoe, Alabama Communists During the Great Depression* (Chapel Hill, 1990), 218; *New York Times*, Dec. 8, 10, 14, 1941; *Opportunity*, 20 (Oct. 1942), 296, and 21 (Oct. 1943), 147; Byron R. Skinner,

"The 'Double V': The Impact of World War II on Black America" (Ph.D. Diss. University of California, Berkeley, 1978), 30–31; Leroi Jones, *Blues People: Negro Music in White America* (New York, 1963), 178, and Paul Oliver, *The Meaning of the Blues* (New York, 1960), 278–85; New York *Age*, May 16, 1942; William Pickens, "The Democracy of War Savings," *Crisis*, 49 (July 1942), 221; Richard Wright to Archibald MacLeish, Dec. 21, 1941, Office of Facts and Figures, RG 208, National Archives; and *Daily Worker*, Dec. 13, 1941.

4. Baltimore *Afro-American* and Savannah *Tribune*, Dec. 13. 1941; Norfolk *Journal and Guide* and Chicago *Defender*, Dec. 20, 1941, and *California Eagle*, Dec. 13, 1941; Ernest Johnson, "The Negro Press Reacts to War," *Interracial Review*, 15 (March 1942), 39–41; Ralph N. Davis, "The Negro Newspapers and the War," *Sociology and Social Research*, 27 (March–April 1943), 373–78; *Crisis*, 48 (March 1941), 71; Revels Cayton, "The Yanks Are Not Coming," Chicago *Defender*, Nov. 25, 1939; Max Yergan and Joseph Bibb columns in Chicago *Defender*, Dec. 27, 1941; Adam Clayton Powell, Jr., "Is This a White Man's War?" *Common Sense*, 2 (April 1942), 111; and "Publishers Pledge Support to President During Crisis," Pittsburgh *Courier*, June 13, 1942.

5. Walter White, *A Man Called White* (New York, 1948), 207–08; Florence Murray, "The Negro and Civil Liberties During World War II," *Social Forces*, 24 (Dec. 1945), 211; Patrick S. Washburn, *A Question of Sedition: The Federal Government's Investigation of the Black Press During World War II* (New York, 1986); and Herbert Garfinkel, *When Negroes March, The March on Washington Movement in the Organizational Politics for FEPC* (Glencoe, Illinois, 1959), 109.

6. Chicago *Defender*, Jan. 11, 18, 1941; George Q. Flynn, "Selective Service and American Blacks during World War II," *Journal of Negro History*, 69 (Winter 1984), 14–25; A. Philp Randolph, "Pro-Japanese Activities Among Negroes," *The Black Worker*, Sept. 1942, 4; Chicago *Defender*, Jan. 16, 1943; Roi Ottley, *New World A'Coming* (New York, 1943), 327–43; *U.S. Selective Service System, Special Groups* (Washington D.C., 1953), vol. I, 51; and Granger in *Opportunity*, 21 (April 1943), 2.

7. Pittsburgh *Courier*, Aug. 18, 1942; George Martin, "Why Ask 'Are Negro Americans Loyal?'" *Southern Frontier*, 2 (Feb. 1942), 2–3; Louis Martin, "Fifth Column Among Negroes," *Opportunity*, 20 (Dec. 1942), 358–59; Finkle, *Forum for Protest*, 150–54; J. Saunders Redding, "A Negro Looks at War," *op. cit.*; J. A. Rogers column, Pittsburgh *Courier*, July 4, 1942; and *Militant*, June 19, 1943.

8. Joseph D. Bibb, "We Gain By War," Pittsburgh *Courier*, Oct. 10, 1942; New York *Amsterdam News*, March 20, 1943; New York *Age*, Nov. 7, 1942; Baltimore *Afro-American*, Nov. 7, 1942; Earl Brown column in New York *Amsterdam News*, Jan. 8, 1944; George Schuyler, "A Long War Will Aid the Negro," *Crisis*, 50 (Nov. 1943), 328–29; and *Crisis*, 49 (Aug. 1942), 264–65, and 50 (Sept. 1943), 268. Also see Bureau of Intelligence, Office of Facts and Figures, "Survey of Intelligence Materials No. 14," March 16, 1942, and "Special Intelligence Report No. 38," May 22, 1942, RG 44, National Archives.

9. Pittsburgh *Courier*, Jan. 31, Aug. 8, 1942, Feb. 27, 1943, and June 10, 1944; Rogers column and column by George Rouzeau in Pittsburgh *Courier*, July 4, 1942, Jan. 1, 1944; Finkle, *Forum for Protest*, 9–10, 60; Charles S. Johnson, *To Stem This Tide* (Chicago, 1943), 105; V. V. Oak, "What of the Negro Press?"

Saturday Review of Literature, 26 (March 6, 1943), 45–46; Alain Locke, "The Unfinished Business of Democracy" and Edwin R. Embree, "Negroes and the Commonweal," *Survey Graphic*, 31 (Nov. 1942), 455–59, 491–94; St. Clair Drake and Horace Cayton, *Black Metropolis: A Study of Negro Life in a Northern City*, 2nd ed. (New York, 1962), 748; Albert Parker column, *Militant*, April 4, 1942; "Negro Morale," *Crisis*, 49 (April 1942), 111; Washburn, *A Question of Sedition*, 98, 131–132; and "Publishers at the White House," Michigan *Chronicle*, Feb. 19, 1944.

10. Office of Facts and Figures, "The Negro Looks at the War," 1942, RG 44, National Archives; Morris Milgram to Walter White, Dec. 1, 1942, NAACP Papers, Library of Congress; Pittsburgh *Courier*, Oct. 17, 1942, Jan. 2, 23, April 24, July 10, 1943; California *Eagle*, July 15, 1943; Chicago *Defender*, July 3, 1943; Garfinkel, *When Negroes March*, 134–138; and Paula F. Pfeffer, *A. Philip Randolph, Pioneer of the Civil Rights Movement* (Baton Rouge, 1990), 80–83.

11. Ellen Tarry, *The Third Door: The Autobiography of an American Negro Woman* (New York, 1955), 193; Rayford Logan, ed., *What the Negro Wants* (Chapel Hill, 1944), esp. 148; Eight Point Program of March-on-Washington Movement and Relationship of NAACP to March-on-Washington Movement, in Board of Directors' Minutes, Sept. 14, 1942, and A. Philip Randolph and Rev. Dr. Allan Knight Chalmers to Roy Wilkins, Feb. 29, 1944, NAACP Papers; Adam Clayton Powell, Jr., *Marching Blacks* (New York, 1945), 159. Louis Kesselman, *The Social Politics of FEPC: A Study in Reform Pressure Movements* (Chapel Hill, 1948), 222, describes Randolph during the war as a "political butterfly," flitting from one cause to another but never staying long enough to accomplish his goals.

12. George M. Hauser, *Erasing the Color Line* (New York, 1945); Bayard Rustin, "The Negro and Non-Violence," in *Down the Line: The Collected Writings of Bayard Rustin* (Chicago, 1971), 8–12; Helen Buckler, "The CORE Way," *Survey Graphic*, 35 (Feb. 1946), 2; August Meier and Elliot Rudwick, *CORE: A Study in the Civil Rights Movement, 1942–1968* (New York, 1973), 20–39, and "The Origins of Nonviolent Direct Action in Afro-American Protest," in their *Along the Color Line: Explorations in the Black Experience* (Urbana, 1976), 347–350.

13. Marjorie McKenzie column, Pittsburgh *Courier*, July 25, 1942; Dorothy Autrey, "The National Association for the Advancement of Colored People in Alabama, 1913–1952" (Ph.D. Diss. University of Notre Dame, 1985), chap. X; Charles M. Payne, *I've Got the Light of Freedom: The Organizing Tradition and the Mississippi Freedom Struggle* (Berkeley, 1995), 90; David R. Colburn, *Racial Change and Community Crisis: St. Augustine, Florida, 1877–1980* (New York, 1985), 8, 22; Earl Lewis, *In Their Own Interests: Race, Class, and Power in Twentieth-Century Norfolk, Virginia* (Berkeley, 1991), 188; Thurgood Marshall to Roy Wilkins, Oct. 28, 1947, Marshall File, NAACP Papers; Mark V. Tushnet, *The NAACP's Legal Strategy against Segregated Education, 1925–1950* (Chapel Hill, 1987), esp. 107–09, George B. Tindall, *The Emergence of the New South, 1913–1945* (Baton Rouge, 1967), 565; "NAACP Not Backing Rent Hike Protests," Baltimore *Afro-American*, Oct. 17, 1942; and I. A. Newby, *Black Carolinians: A History of Blacks in South Carolina from 1865 to 1968* (Columbia, S.C., 1973), 277–78.

14. Forrester Washington, "A Functional Analysis of the National Urban League and Its Affiliates," November 1943, National Urban League Papers, Library of

Congress; Jesse Thomas Moore, Jr., *A Search for Equality: The National Urban League, 1910–1961* (University Park, Pa., 1981), 153–54; Michael K. Honey, *Southern Labor and Black Civil Rights: Organizing Memphis Workers* (Urbana, 1993), 205; and "Report on Memphis," Nov. 18, 1943, National Urban League Papers.

15. David M. Tucker, *Lieutenant Lee of Beale Street* (Nashville, 1971), 127–33; Finkle, *Forum for Protest*, 65; Norfolk *Journal and Guide*, July 4, 1942, and Feb. 12, 1944; Gunnar Myrdal, *An American Dilemma: The Negro Problem and Modern Democracy* (New York, 1944), 729–32, 768–74, 917–21; Sheldon B. Avery, "Up From Washington: William Pickens and the Negro Struggle for Equality, 1900–1954" (Ph.D. Diss. University of Oregon, 1970), 243–46; and Julius E. Thompson, *The Black Press in Mississippi, 1865–1985* (Gainesville, 1993), 23–39, quote at 38.

16. Newby, *Black Carolinians*, 277–80; Stephen O'Neill, "From the Shadow of Slavery: The Civil Rights Years in Charleston" (Ph.D. Diss. University of Virginia, 1994), 74; and "The Negroes' Role in the War," Surveys Division, Bureau of Special Services, Office of War Information, July 18, 1943, RG 44, National Archives.

17. Kenneth Williams, "Mississippi and Civil Rights, 1945–1954" (Ph.D. Diss. Mississippi State University, 1985), 18, 34–36; Chester Himes, "All God's Chillun Got Pride," *Crisis*, 51 (June 1944), 188; Haskell Cohen, "Mello like a Cello," *Negro Digest*, I (Aug. 1943), 7; Lewis, *In Their Own Interests*, 192; Joseph Burran, "Racial Violence in the South During World War II" (Ph.D. Diss. University of Tennessee, 1977), 2, 11–13, 200; O'Neill, "From the Shadow of Slavery," 71–72, 82, 125; Resolution, July 1950, Board of Directors, NAACP Papers. The best analysis of the inhibiting consequences of white domination on black thought and behavior at this time remains Richard Wright, *Black Boy* (New York, 1937), esp. 65–71, 150–57, 160–61. Also see Hortense Powdermaker, "The Channeling of Negro Aggression by the Cultural Process," *American Journal of Sociology*, 48 (May 1943), 750–58.

18. Jessie Daniel Ames to Gordon Hancock, April 7, July 24, 1942, and Virginius Dabney to Alfred Dasheill, Aug. 4, 1942, Virginius Dabney Papers, University of Virginia; Jacquelyn Dowd Hall, *Revolt Against Chivalry: Jessie Daniel Ames and the Women's Campaign Against Lynching* (New York, 1979), 256–60; *Southern Frontier*, 4 (Aug. 1943), 3; Raymond Gavins, *The Perils and Prospects of Southern Black Leadership: Gordon Blaine Hancock, 1884–1970* (Durham, N.C., 1977), 117–19; and Benjamin Mays, *Born to Rebel* (New York, 1971), 218.

19. Morton Sosna, *In Search of the Silent South: Southern Liberals and the Race Issue* (New York, 1977), 7–9, 105–20, 166; Myrdal, *An American Dilemma*, 466–73; Virginius Dabney, "Nearer and Nearer the Precipice," *Atlantic Monthly*, 171 (Jan. 1943), 94–100, and "The South Marches On," *Survey Graphic*, 32 (Nov. 1943), 441–43; John Temple Graves, *The Fighting South* (New York, 1943), 120; and Johnson, *To Stem This Tide*, 140–42. Also see Walter White, "Decline of Southern Liberals," *Negro Digest*, I (Jan. 1943), 43; and Lillian E. Smith, "Buying a New World With Old Confederate Bills," *South Today*, 7 (Autumn–Winter, 1942–43), 7–30.

20. *Southern Frontier*, 4 (Aug. 1943), 3; "Southern Regional Council," *Monthly*

Summary of Events and Trends in Race Relations, 1 (Aug. 1943), 38–39; Charles S. Johnson, et al., *Into the Mainstream* (Chapel Hill, 1947), 5–11; Virginius Dabney to Guy B. Johnson, April 28, 1945, and Guy B. Johnson to Virginius Dabney, May 8, 1945, Southern Regional Council Papers, Atlanta University; Lillian Smith, "Southern Defensive-II," *Common Ground*, 4 (Spring 1944), 43–45; and Guy B. Johnson, "Southern Offensive," *ibid.* (Summer 1944), 87–93.

21. Randall L. Patton, "The Popular Front Alternative: Clark H. Foreman and the Southern Conference for Human Welfare, 1938–1948," in John C. Inscoe, ed., *Georgia in Black and White: Explorations in the Race Relations of a Southern State, 1865–1950* (Athens, Ga., 1994), 230–35; Lillian Smith to James Dombrowski, May 19, 1942, and Tarleton Collier to Clark Foreman, June 12, 1942, Southern Conference for Human Welfare Papers, Atlanta University; Sosna, *In Search of the Silent South*, 93, 103.

22. Lucy Randolph Mason to Frank Dorsey, July 16, 1943, Lucy Randolph Mason to Philip Murray, Oct. 30, 1944, and E. L. Sandefur to Lucy Randolph Mason, May 29, 1945, CIO Organizing Committee Papers (New York, 1981), Series 5–1; Clark Foreman to Philip Murray, Nov. 16, 1944, and James Dombrowski to Durward McDaniel, March 21, 1945, SCHW Papers; Clark Foreman Oral History, Southern Historical Collection, University of North Carolina, Chapel Hill, 55; Honey, *Southern Labor and Black Civil Rights*, 212, 219; Michael Honey, "Black Workers Remember, Industrial Unionism in the Era of Jim Crow," in Gary M. Fink and Merl E. Reed, eds., *Race, Class, and Community in Southern Labor History* (Tuscaloosa, 1994), 134; Michael Honey, "Industrial Unionism and Racial Justice in Memphis," Rick Halpern, "Interracial Unionism in the Southwest: Fort Worth's Packinghouse Workers, 1937–1954," and Judith Stein, "Southern Workers in National Unions: Birmingham Steelworkers, 1936–1951," in Robert H. Zieger, ed., *Organized Labor in the Twentieth-Century South* (Knoxville, 1991), 144–52, 168–69, 198–99, 208; Jack Stieber, *Governing the UAW* (New York, 1962), 124–25; Robert J. Norrell, "Caste in Steel: Jim Crow Careers in Birmingham, Alabama," *Journal of American History*, 73 (Dec. 1986), 669–94; Stetson Kennedy, "Total Equality and How to Get It," *Common Ground*, VI (Winter 1946), 63; John Glen, *Highlander: No Ordinary School, 1932–1962* (Lexington, 1988); Robert F. Martin, *Howard Kester and the Struggle for Social Justice in the South, 104–77* (Charlottesville, 1991), 124–28. The extent to which the CIO fought for racial equality during the war is now a matter of significant historical dispute, and for the more positive view see Bruce Nelson, *Workers on the Waterfront* (Urbana, 1988), esp. 259, and "Organized Labor and the Struggle for Black Equality in Mobile during World War II," *Journal of American History*, 80 (Dec. 1993), 952–88; Robert R. Korstad, "Daybreak of Freedom, Tobacco Workers and the CIO, Winston-Salem, North Carolina, 1943–1950" (Ph.D. Diss. University of North Carolina—Chapel Hill, 1987); and Robert Korstad and Nelson Lichtenstein, "Opportunities Found and Lost: Labor, Radicals, and the Early Civil Rights Movement," *Journal of American History*, 75 (Dec. 1988), 786–811.

23. Columns by J. A. Rogers and Horace Cayton, Pittsburgh *Courier*, April 11, 25, 1942; Daily *Worker*, June 8, 14, 16, 18, 1942, April 12, May 22, July 18, 1943, June

27, 1944; Ben Davis, *The Negro People and the Communist Party* (New York, 1943); Ben Davis, "The Army Tackles Jim Crow," *New Masses*, 55 (April 1945), 15–16; Gerald Horne, *Black Liberation/Red Scare: Ben Davis and the Communist Party* (Newark, Del., 1994), 143; Mark Naison, *Communists in Harlem during the Depression* (Urbana, 1983), 313–14; and John Williamson, *Dangerous Scot, The Life and Work of an American "Undesirable"* (New York, 1969), 147.

24. *Negro Quarterly, A Review of Negro Life and Culture*, I (Spring 1942), 21–32 (Fall 1942), 197–206 (Winter 1943), 295–302; Earl Browder in *Sunday Worker*, March 4, 1945; James W. Ford, *The War and the Negro People* (New York, 1942); Pettis Perry, *The Negro Stake in This War* (San Francisco, 1942); Maurice Isserman, *Which Side Were You On? The American Communist Party During the Second World War* (Middleton, 1982), 141–43; Kelley, *Hammer and Hoe*, 220–22; Art Preis column, *Militant*, Oct. 3, 1942; *Daily Worker*, June 22, 1943; "Have the Communists quit fighting for Negro rights?" *Negro Digest*, 2 (Dec. 1944); and *People's Voice*, March 17, 1945.

25. Rumors and/or incidents of racial violence are reported in "Racial Tension Files," Fair Employment Practices Committee, RG 228 and "Reports on Recent Factors Increasing Negro-White Tension," Special Services Division, Bureau of Intelligence, Office of War Information, RG 44, National Archives; Howard Odum, *Race and Rumors of Race* (Chapel Hill, 1943), esp. 96–101, 113–28; "Cities, North and South: A Reconnaissance Survey of Race Relations," *Monthly Summary of Events and Trends in Race Relations*, I (Oct. 1943), 11–12; Gloria Brown-Melton, "Blacks in Memphis, Tennessee, 1920–1955: A Historical Study" (Ph.D. Diss. Washington State University, 1982), 201–217; Dolores Janiewski, *Sisterhood Denied: Race, Gender, and Class in a New South Community* (Philadelphia, 1985), 141; and Clifford M. Kuhn, Harlon B. Joye, and E. Bernard West, *Living Atlanta: An Oral History of the City, 1914–1948* (Athens, Ga., 1990), 77–82. The most sophisticated argument interpreting black violence or anti-social behavior as direct black challenges to racist practices is Robin D. G. Kelley, *Race Rebels: Culture, Politics, and the Black Working Class* (New York, 1994), 35–75.

26. Burran, "Racial Violence in the South During World War II," 129–160; Ulysses Lee, *The Employment of Negro Troops* (Washington, D.C., 1966), 348–79; "Negroes in the Armed Forces," *New Republic*, 109 (Oct. 18, 1943), 542–44; "The Pattern of Race Riots Involving Negro Soldiers," *Monthly Summary of Events and Trends in Race Relations*, I (Aug. 1943), 8–9, II (Aug.–Sept. 1944), 1–2; Florence Murray, *Negro Handbook, 1946–1947* (New York, 1947), 347–56; "Violence Against Negro Military Personnel" and "Reports—Racial Tension," Civilian Aide to the Secretary of War, Records of the Office of the Secretary of War, RG 107, National Archives; "What the Soldier Thinks," No. 2, August 1943, 14–15, 58–59, War Department, Special Services Division, Research Branch, RG 330, National Archives; and Samuel A. Stouffer, et al., *The American Soldier, I, Adjustment During Army Life* (Princeton, 1949), 502–506, 525–26, 587–89. The range of responses to discrimination in the military, and their causes, is portrayed in Charles Fuller, *A Soldier's Play* (New York, 1982), later made into the film *A Soldier's Story*.

27. *Monthly Summary of Events and Trends in Race Relations*, 1 (Nov. 1943), 22, and

(Jan. 1944), 22; Adam Clayton Powell, Jr., "A Big Stride Forward," *Spotlight*, 2 (April 1944), 3; William Hastie, "Negro Officers in Two World Wars," *Journal of Negro Education*, 12 (Summer 1943), 316–22; Chicago *Defender*, Dec. 2, 1944; Norfolk *Journal and Guide*, Oct. 21, 1944; Pittsburgh *Courier*, March 10, 1945; Baltimore *Afro-American*, March 31, 1945; column by P. L. Prattis in Pittsburgh *Courier*, March 31, 1945; and *People's Voice*, March 31, 1945.

28. Meier and Rudwick, *Along the Color Line*, 224–37; "Summary of a Report on the Race Riots in the Alabama Dry Dock Shipbuilding Company Yards in Mobile, Alabama," June 25, 1943, National Urban League Papers; Chicago *Defender* and Pittsburgh *Courier*, June, 5, 26, July 17, Aug. 14, 21, 1943; and *Crisis*, 50 (July 1943), 199.

29. Dominic J. Capeci, Jr., *The Harlem Riot of 1943* (Philadelphia, 1977); New York *Age* and New York *Amsterdam News*, Aug. 7, 1943; Pittsburgh *Courier*, Aug. 14, 1943; Adam Clayton Powell, Sr., *Riots and Ruins* (New York, 1945), 45–46; Charles V. Hamilton, *Adam Clayton Powell, Jr.: The Political Biography of an American Dilemma* (New York, 1991), 105, 148, 153; *People's Voice*, Aug. 7, 14, 1943; Powell, *Marching Blacks*, 171–72; New York *PM*, Aug. 3, 1943.

30. Stuart Cosgrove, "The Zoot-Suit and Style Warfare," *History Workshop Journal*, 18 (Autumn 1984), 78–80; Bruce Tyler, "Black Jive and White Repression," *Journal of Ethnic Studies*, 16 (no. 4, 1989), 32–38; Langston Hughes and S. I. Hayakawa columns and editorial, Chicago *Defender*, June 19, 1943; Powell, *Riots and Ruins*, 36, 87; Albert Libby, "The Vanguarders," *Common Ground*, VI (Summer 1946), 83–87.

31. William J. Norton, "The Detroit Riots—and After," *Survey Graphic*, 32 (Aug. 1943), 317–18; Pittsburgh *Courier*, Oct. 9, 1943; "Federal, State, and City Action" and "Programs of Action on the Democratic Front," *Monthly Summary of Events and Trends in Race Relations*, 1 (Aug. 1943), 15, 34, and 2 (Aug. 1944), 1–2; and Robert C. Weaver, "Whither Northern Race Relations Committees?" *Phylon*, V (Third Quarter, 1944), 205–18.

32. Alfred B. Lewis, "Reducing Racial Tensions," *Opportunity*, 21 (Oct. 1943), 157; Edwin R. Embree, "Balance Sheet in Race Relations," *Atlantic Monthly*, 175 (May 1945), 87–91; "To Minimize Racial Conflicts: Committees to Work on Human Relationships," *American Century*, LX (Jan. 1945), 80; and Winifred Raushenbush, "How to Prevent Race Riots," *American Mercury*, 57 (Sept. 1943), 302–09.

33. James Boyd, "Strategy for Negroes," *Nation*, 156 (June 26, 1943), 884–87; Harvard Sitkoff, *A New Deal for Blacks, The Emergence of Civil Rights as a National Issue: The Depression Decade* (New York, 1978), *passim*; and Meier and Rudwick, *Along the Color Line*, 307–404, esp. 313–362.

34. Minutes of the NAACP Board of Directors, Dec. 14, 1943, Dec. 9, 1944, Roy Wilkins to Rev. E. S. Hardge, Dec. 19, 1944, and Wilkins to Walter White, Dec. 29, 1944, NAACP Papers; Baltimore *Afro-American*, Nov. 17, 1944. From 1948 to 1953 the AJC and NAACP collaborated on a joint annual report, *Civil Rights in the United States: A Balance Sheet of Group Relations*.

35. Myrdal, *An American Dilemma*, esp. 520, 625–27, 771, 834–53.

36. Jones, *Blues People*, 180; Baltimore *Afro-American*, Jan. 22, 1944, Chicago *Defender* and Pittsburgh *Courier*, Jan. 29, 1944; David W. Southern, *Gunnar*

Myrdal and Black-White Relations: The Use and Abuse of An American Dilemma, 1944–1969 (Baton Rouge, 1987), esp. chapters III–IV and IX; and Walter A. Jackson, *Gunnar Myrdal and America's Conscience, Social Engineering and Racial Liberalism, 1938–1987* (Chapel Hill, 1990), 245–52, 272–94.

37. Logan, ed., *What the Negro Wants*, 330, 65, 92, 193, 116, 129, 124, 28, 11, 336–38, 341–42, 151, 242–43, 274.

38. *Ibid.*, 197, 210, 77, 340, 9, 249, 151–52, 187, 15–17, 129, 162, 148, 210–11, 61–62, 106, 344, 304–05, 256, 185–87.

39. *Ibid.*, 233–37, 242, 273–74, 280, 76–77, 334, 305. Although even the Logan and Myrdal books proved too much for southern whites like W. T. Couch, a founder of the SCHW, this does not in and of themselves make them examples of racial militancy.

VI *Fighting for What We Didn't Have*

1. I have audiotaped more than 120 hours of conversation with nearly fifty black Mississippians of the World War II generation. In all but two cases they were veterans, although the spouses of some veterans did participate in some phases of the interviews. Most of these subjects were men. The sample was not scientifically selected. Most sections of the state were represented, either through the interviewees' places of current residence or places of upbringing. Although postwar employment histories ranged from custodian and garbage collector to educator to health professional—and education levels varied from the barely literate to the highly trained—the sample probably included somewhat more white collar workers and professional people than the state's black population in general. Despite the sample's technical limitations, I believe that the views expressed are reasonably representative. The transcriptions rendered here are literal in every sense, save one: in the interest of more readable narratives I have not littered these pages with elipsis points to indicate the omission of habitual filler words, frequent false rhetorical starts, or even material extraneous to a particular line of thought or story. Because unrehearsed speech is rarely seamless, and interviewees often revisit a single topic repeatedly over the course of an interview, I have in some cases merged these related and recurrent strands of conversation into a single, coherent discourse. These few liberties can be identified by the page numbers cited in the endnotes. Otherwise, of course, the respondents' words, syntax, and meaning are reproduced exactly as given. Although the narratives are temporarily closed pending completion of transcription and binding, interested scholars will soon have unrestricted access through the Mississippi Oral History Program, University of Southern Mississippi, Hattiesburg (hereinafter cited as MOHP).

2. See Harvard Sitkoff, "Black Militancy in the World War II South?", above, note 1.

3. Luella Newsome, interviewed by the author, December 14, 1993, v. 486, p. 57, MOHP. (Except where otherwise indicated, all citations are to MOHP interviews and all interviews are by the author. The absence of numbers for volume and page indicates an interview not yet fully processed.)

4. Wilson Asford, December 3, 1993, v. 477, pp. 13, 25. See also Sears Ward, April 19, 1994.

5. Ulysses Lee, *The Employment of Negro Troops*, United States Army in World War II, Special Studies (Washington, D.C., 1966); Richard Dalfiume, *Desegregation of the United States Armed Forces: Fighting on Two Fronts, 1939–1953* (Columbia, Missouri, 1969); Neil A. Wynn, *The Afro-American and the Second World War*, rev. ed. (New York, 1993), 21–38.

6. Luella Newsome, December 14, 1993, v. 486, p. 57.

7. Nathan Harris, December 2, 1994, v. 598, p. 8. In another example, an infantry sergeant remembered the happiness of his soldiers while on assignment in Western Europe: "their only question was, 'Why can't it be this nice in America?'" (Dabney Hamner, December 2, 1994, v. 606, p. 22).

8. Dabney Hamner, December 2, 1994, v. 606, p. 56.

9. Charles H. Jones, Sr., December 2, 1994. But see also John C. Berry, November 16, 1993, v. 471, p. 6; Roscoe Simmons Pickett, November 5, 1993, v. 468, p. 12; Nathan Harris, December 2, 1994, v. 598, p. 12; Napoleon Coney, November 28, 1994; James B. Jones, December 14, 1993, v. 499, p. 25; Claude Montgomery, Jr., December 2, 1994, v. 597, p. 9.

10. Henry Murphy, October 24, 1994, v. 595, p. 20.

11. Brunetta Garner, interviewed by James Nix [December, 1993], v. 495, p. 10.

12. Eugene Russell, Sr., March 3, 1994, v. 498, p. 37. See also Clell Qualls, March 2, 1994, v. 609, p. 36; Sears Ward, April 19, 1994; Charles H. Jones, Sr., December 2, 1994; Haywood Stephney, December 2, 1994; James Boykins, November 23, 1993.

13. Clemon F. Jones, September 21, 1994. Similar experiences are described in Nathan Harris, December 2, 1994, v. 598, p. 16; Ollie Jackson, February 3, 1994, v. 529, pp. 18–20; Douglas Conner, December 2, 1993, v. 479, p. 11–13; Alva Temple, December 3, 1993, v. 481, p. 18; Edward L. Thompkins, April 16, 1994, v. 592, p. 22.

14. Vertie Bell to Elliott Freeman, September 14, 1943, S. D. Redmond to Truman Gibson, September 27 and December 12, 1943, Leslie Perry to Henry Stimson, November 23, 1943, T. Hughes to Gibson, December 12, 1943, Box 198, Records of the Office of the Secretary of War (Hastie Files), RG 107, National Archives, Washington, D.C.; miscellaneous Rieves Bell materials, Soldier Troubles, Legal File, 1940–1955, Box B156, Papers of the National Association for the Advancement of Colored People, Library of Congress, Washington, D.C.; Washington *Tribune*, December 11, 1943; Wilson Ashford, December 3, 1993, v. 477, pp. 30–31.

15. Henry Murphy, October 24, 1994, v. 595, p. 25.

16. See, for example, letters from soldiers, spouses, and parents in Soldiers Complaints, Legal Files, 1940–1955, Boxes B148-B151, NAACP Papers.

17. Henry Murphy, October 24, 1994, v. 595, 21. Although military records document many interracial conflicts, some veterans believed that the War Department was engaged in a continuing cover-up. See, for example, Edward L. Thompkins, April 16, 1994, v. 592, pp. 12, 17, 19.

18. Napoleon B. Evans, interviewed by James Nix, November 27, 1993, v. 489, p. 14. See also Edward L. Thompkins, April 16, 1994, v. 592, pp. 77–83.

19. Wilson Ashford, December 3, 1993, v. 477, p. 2.

20. Lamar Lenoir, December 21, 1993, v. 496, p. 16. Other expressions of this point of view include, Henry Kirksey, March 4, 1994; William A. McDougal, December 3, 1994.

21. Ben Fielder, January 27, 1994, field notes only. Similar stories are told by Ollie Jackson, February 3, 1994, v. 529, pp. 21–22; Matthew Burks, interviewed by Arvarh Strickland, July 12, 1994 (in author's possession).

22. Dabney Hamner, December 2, 1994; Napoleon Coney, November 28, 1994. See also, Charles H. Jones, Sr., December 2, 1994.

23. Henry Murphy, October 24, 1994, v. 595, pp. 26–30.

24. Wilson Evans, II, interviewed by Orley Caudill, n.d.

25. Sam Jackson, November 20, 1993, v. 473, p. 8.

26. Dabney Hamner, December 2, 1994. In the 1950s, Hamner became the first black deputy sheriff in Coahoma County since Reconstruction.

27. William Nicholson, interviewed by Roscoe Pickett, November 29, 1993.

28. Nathan Harris, December 2, 1994, v. 598, pp. 11, 16. Representative POW stories include: Emmett J. Stringer, December 3, 1993, v. 480, pp. 38–39; Alva Temple, December 3, 1993, v. 481; James B. Jones, December 14, 1993, v. 499, p. 18.

29. In a typical example, a WAC veteran said of her wartime experiences in the North: "It [racism] was still there, but not in abundance like it was here. In New York, it was just more subtle. They didn't just do you like the people down here [in Mississippi] did you. But I think it was just the same, but you didn't feel it as much" (Brunetta Garner, interviewed by James Nix [December, 1993], v. 495, p. 16). See also Lillian McLaurin, February 17, 1994; Douglas Conner, December 2, 1993, v. 479, p. 12.

30. Haywood Stephney, December 12, 1994. A retired Scott County garbage collector remembered: "They'd treat you better anywhere than in Mississippi. In Europe and all them places, you was just the same as a white man" (Clell Qualls, March 2, 1994, v. 609, pp. 14, 22).

31. Eugene Russell, Sr., March 3, 1994, v. 498, pp. 2–3, 9–11, 9–11, 31, 56–57.

32. Dabney Hamner, December 2, 1994, v. 606, pp. 16–17, 23. This interviewee reported that he then knocked down his white antagonist! The police, he said, advised him to "overlook those things" in the future, but took no other action. The white man actually later apologized. Aware that this series of events had few parallels in the history of contemporary Deep South race relations, the veteran expressed the belief that he could perhaps respond to white insult with such impunity because he was then a letter carrier on leave from military duty and whites were "afraid to fool with a federal employee." The annals of wartime racial conflict in Mississippi suggest that such immunity was rarely enjoyed by other black federal employees, military or civilian.

33. "The first experience I had reminding me that I was back home," one veteran remembered, came on a bus from Jackson to Hermanville, when he moved the Jim Crow curtain forward so that an overflow of black passengers could sit

in seats not used by whites: "The driver reminded me that I'd better not do that again: 'Don't you ever do that on a bus I'm driving. You're back home'" (William J. Heath, Sr., September 8, 1994, v. 596, pp. 14–15). See also Napoleon Harris, December 2, 1994; Sam Jackson, November 20, 1993, v. 473, pp. 27–29.

34. Roscoe Simmons Pickett, November 5, 1993, v. 468, p. 7; John C. Berry, November 16, 1993, p. 471, p. 9; William Nicholson, interviewed by Roscoe S. Pickett, November 29, 1993; Sears Ward, April 19, 1993; Claude Montgomery, Jr., December 2, 1994, v. 597, p. 5.

35. Brunetta Garner, interviewed by James Nix [December, 1993], v. 495, p. 2; Douglas Conner, December 2, 1993, v. 479, pp. 4, 7–8.

36. Clemon F. Jones, September 21, 1994.

37. David W. White, September 30, 1994, v. 610, p. 11.

38. Wilson Evans II, interviewed by Orley Caudill, n.d.

39. James B. Jones, December 14, 1993, v. 499, p. 8.

40. Alva Temple, December 3, 1993, v. 481, p. 13–14; Benjamin O. Davis, Jr., *Benjamin O. Davis: American* (Washington and London: Smithsonian Institution Press, 1991), p. 132.

41. However, one former infantryman, a technical sergeant who had been wounded in Italy, did remember the shock and deep humiliation of discovering in 1946 that neither a Purple Heart medal nor an honorable discharge carried any weight at the Forrest County court house. Encouraged by his commanding officer, a northern white, to exercise as a civilian the voting rights he had earned as a soldier, he presented himself upon returning home to a very angry registrar of voters: "He told me, 'If you don't get out of here, I'll take my foot, kick you plumb out there in the middle of that street,' just like that. Yes sir" (Ollie Jackson, February 3, 1994, v. 529, p. 15).

42. David W. White, September 30, 1994, v. 610, p. 12.

43. German Levy, December 21, 1993. v. 487, pp. 21, 35.

44. William A. McDougal, December 3, 1994. See also Clell Qualls, March 2, 1994, v. 609, p. 37.

45. Matthew Burks, interviewed by Arvarh Strickland, July 12, 1994, p. 4, and Strickland to McMillen, October 2, 1994, author's possession.

46. Ben Fielder, January 29, 1994, v. 483, pp. 51, 84; Henry Murphy, October 24, 1994, v. 595, p. 40.

47. John C. Berry, November 16, 1993, v. 471, pp. 9, 21. But cf. Claude Montgomery, Jr., December 2, 1994, v. 597, p. 18.

48. Charles H. Jones, Sr., December 2, 1994. See also William A. McDougal, December 3, 1994; Dabney Hamner, December 2, 1994; Edward L. Thompkins, April 16, 1994, v. 592, pp. 24–27; William J. Heath, Sr., September 8, 1994, v. 596, p. 15.

49. Henry Kirksey, March 4, 1994.

50. Alva Temple, December 2, 1994, v. 481, p. 29.

51. Henry Murphy, October 24, 1994, v. 595, p. 33. Other representative examples include: Sam Jackson, November 20, 1993, v. 473, 20; Brunetta Garner, interviewed by James Nix [December 1993], v. 495, 4.

52. Douglas Conner, December 2, 1993, v. 479, pp. 9, 22, 30; Douglas L. Conner, with John F. Marszalek, *A Black Physician's Story: Bringing Hope in Mississippi* (Jackson: University Press of Mississippi, 1985), p. 51.
53. Nathan Harris, December 2, 1994, v. 598, p. 22.

VIII   Faulkner and World War II

1. I make no claims that the novels of Mailer, Shaw, Cozzens or Hersey are great literature, but merely note the extent to which other American writers engaged the War in ways that Southerners seem not to have. A more extended essay on this topic might well broaden the discussion to compare the American fiction of the post-1945 generation to that of their post-1918 predecessors, though to be sure many American literary careers spanned both wars. What such an extended essay would confront, of course, is the fact that very few American "war" novels deal directly with War itself, the actual fighting; none comes even close to the achievement of Remarque's WWI masterpiece *All Quiet on the Western Front*, and of the works that deal with war's social and psychological aftereffects, only three seem to me unqualifiedly masterpieces of American fiction: Hemingway's *The Sun Also Rises* and Fitzgerald's *The Great Gatsby* and *Tender Is the Night*. And they all fall way short, of course, of the defining masterpiece of the genre, *War and Peace*.

   It would seem, then, that one of the characteristics of the American "war" novel is its avoidance of the conflict itself in favor of those more social and psychological aftereffects. Perhaps the proper question to be asking here, then, is not why did Southerners not engage the War directly, but rather why have writers in the Great Western tradition generally avoided war?—or, more pointedly, why did Faulkner engage it so directly? Were two World Wars so incomprehensibly terrifying that a post-Freudian world could not face the trauma directly, but had to deal with it indirectly? Faulkner even in *A Fable*, as we will see, preferred to cast his fictional analysis of the Cold War in the terms of a World War I setting, and, to be fair, it of course may well be that other Southerners also used other wars as tropes for the massive bloodletting of 1939-1945.

2. I say intellectually, because of course many of these folks, like so many of the contributors to *I'll Take My Stand* had, by this time, long since abandoned their stands and headed for the city.

3. And here I must note Germany's Peter Nicolaisen, whose recent work has suggested how disturbingly similar the Fugitive and Agrarian's regionalism and anti-industrialism were to intellectual movements in Europe in the thirties which the National Socialists embraced.

IX   Remembering Hattiesburg

1. Julius Lester and Mary Varela, *To Praise Our Bridges, An Autobiography, Mrs. Fannie Lou Hamer* (Jackson, Mississippi: KIPCO, 1967) 3.
2. Between 1921 and 1971, the city of Hattiesburg operated a segregated high school for African American students. The school's first name was Eureka.

When a new building was built and the high school moved to Royal Street, the name was changed first to Royal Street High School and later to Rowan High School. In 1977, a group of former students of this school met and decided to call a reunion of all of those who attended the school under any of its three names. They called the reunion EURO. They set as its purpose to celebrate the achievements of those who attended the school and to preserve the history of this institution that played such a significant role in Hattiesburg's black community.

3. See, for example, Howard Zinn, *SNCC: The New Abolitionists* (Boston: Beacon Press, 1964, 1965) 102–122.

4. John Dittmer, *Black Georgia in the Progressive Era, 1900–1920* (Urbana, Illinois: University of Illinois Press, 1977) xi.

5. *Hattiesburg American,* September 5, 1940.

6. *Hattiesburg American,* March 15, 1941.

7. *Hattiesburg American,* September 12, 13, and 14, 1940

8. *Hattiesburg American,* January 1, 1941.

9. *Hattiesburg American,* December 10, 1940.

10. See *Hattiesburg American,* January 10 and 29, 1941.

11. *Hattiesburg American,* February 22, 1941.

12. *Hattiesburg American,* June 9, 1941.

13. *Hattiesburg American,* September 18, October 4 and 18, and November 18, 1941; March 11 and 23, 1942.

14. See *Hattiesburg American*, July 14, 1941; September 6, 1942; and November 23, 1943.

15. *Hattiesburg American,* April 10, 1941.

16. *Hattiesburg American,* April 4, 1942.

17. For an account of the establishment of the Japanese-American units and the experience of the Nisei soldiers see, Thomas James, *Exile Within: The Schooling of Japanese Americans, 1942–1945* (Cambridge: Harvard University Press, 1987); Masayo Umezawa Duus, *Unlikely Liberators: The Men of the 100th and 442nd,* trans. Peter Duus (Honolulu: University of Hawaii Press, 1987); Bill Hosokawa, *Nisei: The Quiet Americans* (New York: William Morrow & Company, Inc., 1969).

18. *Hattiesburg American,* November 5, December 4 and 7, 1945; John Dittmer, *Local People: The Struggle for Civil Rights in Mississippi* (Urbana and Chicago: University of Illinois Press, 1994) 21–22.

19. *Hattiesburg American,* October 8, 1941.

20. William Y. Schmidt, "The Impact of the Camp Shelby Mobilization on Hattiesburg, Mississippi, 1945–1946" (Ph.D. dissertation, University of Southern Mississippi, 1972), 103.

21. "An Oral History with Professor N. R. Burger," The Mississippi Oral History Program of the University of Southern Mississippi, 356 (1982): 32–36.

22. See "An Oral History with Mr. Richard Boyd and Mrs. Earline Boyd," The Mississippi Oral History Program of the University of Southern Mississippi, 383 (1992); "An Oral History with Mr. E. Hammond Smith," The Mississippi Oral History Program of the University of Southern Mississippi, 369 (1982).

Contributors

James C. Cobb, University of Tennessee—Knoxville. Publications include *The Selling of the South: The Southern Crusade for Industrial Development* (1982) and *The Most Southern Place on Earth: The Mississippi Delta and the Roots of Regional Identity* (1992).

Dewey W. Grantham, Vanderbilt University. Books include *Hoke Smith and the Politics of the New South* (1958), winner of the Sydnor Award, and *The South in Modern America: A Region at Odds* (1994).

Anne Goodwyn Jones, University of Florida. Author of *Tomorrow Is Another Day: The Woman Writer in the South* (1982).

Judy Barrett Litoff, Bryant College. Published works include *Dear Boys: World War II Letters from a Woman Back Home* (1991) and *We're in This War Too: World War II Letters from American Women in Uniform* (1994), both with David C. Smith.

Neil R. McMillen, University of Southern Mississippi. Author of *The Citizens' Councils: Organized Resistance to the Second Reconstruction* (1971) and *Dark Journey: Black Mississippians in the Age of Jim Crow* (1989), winner of the Bancroft Prize.

Clarence L. Mohr, Tulane University. Author of *On the Threshold of Freedom: Masters and Slaves in Civil War Georgia* (1986) and editor of two volumes of *The Frederick Douglass Papers* (1979, 1982).

Noel Polk, University of Southern Mississippi. Publications include the Library of America editions of William Faulkner's novels; co-editor of a 44 volume set of Faulkner manuscripts (1987); *Eudora Welty: A Bibliography of Her Work* (1994); and *Children of the Dark House* (1996).

Harvard Sitkoff, University of New Hampshire. Author of *A New Deal for Blacks:*

The Emergence of Civil Rights as a National Issue (1978) and *The Struggle for Black Equality* (1981).

Morton Sosna, Cornell University. Author of *In Search of the Silent South: Southern Liberals and the Race Issue* (1977) and a forthcoming history of the South during World War II.

Arvarh E. Strickland, University of Missouri—Columbia. Publications include *History of the Chicago Urban League* (1966) and an edition of the diary of Lorenzo J. Greene (1989).

INDEX